Civilising rural Ireland

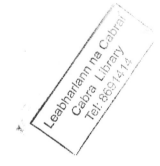

MANCHESTER
1824

Manchester University Press

Civilising rural Ireland

*The co-operative movement, development
and the nation-state, 1889–1939*

Patrick Doyle

Manchester University Press

Published by Manchester University Press
Altrincham Street, Manchester M1 7JA, UK
www.manchesteruniversitypress.co.uk

British Library Cataloguing-in-Publication Data is available

ISBN 978 1 5261 2456 2 hardback
ISBN 978 1 5261 5056 1 paperback

First published by Manchester University Press in hardback 2019

This edition published 2020

Typeset by Toppan Best-set Premedia Limited

Contents

Figures and tables

Figures

Tables

Acknowledgements

The origins of this book project have deep roots. Both sets of my grandparents who lived and worked in rural Ireland were members of the local co-op creamery. Family stories and memories frequently coalesced around the site of the co-op and therefore this project was gestating for a long time. In particular I remember the strong attachment that my grandfather John Durkin had to the co-op and the stories he told me as a child awoke my interest in history. Growing up in Manchester meant that I was aware of the co-operative movement from the consumer's side of the equation as well as that city's role in shaping the modern co-operative movement. A desire to link my Irish upbringing to my Mancunian surroundings led to my initial interest and eventual fascination with co-operative ideas and institutions, and the ways in which they connected people.

This book has been shaped by the intellectual co-operation of many other people. I am indebted to Pedro Ramos-Pinto, Till Geiger and Natalie Zacek for their guidance during the initial research. In particular, Pedro provided an invaluable source of wisdom and encouragement throughout the writing of the book. For that, and his friendship, I am very grateful. I'd like to thank Peter Gatrell and Cormac Ó Gráda whose feedback and advice on early drafts shaped the project. I wish to thank Sarah Roddy with whom I have enjoyed talking and working in recent years, and from whom I have learned so much. Christopher Godden provided me with his support and wisdom, frequently dispensed in a chat over coffee, but which was always profoundly affecting. I have also benefited from meeting other co-operative historians with whom I have been lucky enough to discuss my work. In particular, I would like to thank Tony Webster, Mary Hilson, Rachael Vorburg-Rugh and Peter Gurney who provided stimulating insights into the wider history of the movement alongside their collegiality and warm support and welcome to those who work in the field of co-operative research.

Any historical research would be a failure before it began if not for the assistance of dedicated archivists. The staff at the National Library of Ireland, the National Archives of Ireland and the Public Record Office of Northern Ireland always provided the assistance and advice on sources that I needed to undertake this work. I have benefited from the deep knowledge and insight that particular individuals have over their respective collections. To that extent I would like to thank Gillian Lonergan and Sophie Stewart at the National Co-operative Archive, Noelle Dowling at the Dublin Diocesan Archive, David Bracken at the Limerick Diocesan Archive and Michael Lynch at Kerry's Local History Archive, all of whose assistance and wisdom was greatly appreciated by this researcher.

I'd also like to thank everyone at Manchester University Press who has made the production of book itself a relatively painless experience. In particular I'd like to thank Tony Mason for his encouraging words along the way and for making the process more fun.

James Greenhalgh, Kat Fennelly, Barry Hazley, Tom Sharp, Muzna Rahman, Michael Durrant and Michael Kelly were fine companions at the University of Manchester, sources of intellectual inspiration, and more importantly, friends. Quintin Morgan, James Cregg and Daniel Comerford offered plenty of perspective to the project. Although we share wildly divergent and incompatible views on all matters football related, I am grateful for their patience and good humour. Andy Seddon, Alex Mitchell, Catherine Bolsover and Mark Crosher in Manchester continue to exert great efforts to watch out for me for which I am truly thankful. In London, I am deeply indebted to Richard Cooke and Amy Cox (thanks for the room!), Tom Green, Laura Teece, Fay Benson, Chris Flavin and Martina Booth. All made my time in the 'big smoke' a less traumatic experience. Kim Walker deserves a special mention for convincing me to finally submit a book proposal which I sat on for too long. She was, and remains, an excellent purveyor of sage advice. I have also been blessed with wonderful friendships with people in Ireland. Dorothy Ingoldsby and Áine O'Shea provided me with necessary friendship and support, all of which was offered with characteristic openheartedness for which I am eternally grateful. Thanks also to Brian and Sheila Ingoldsby who took this stranger into their home and ensured I never wanted for anything. Meanwhile, my cosmic twin, Sarah Hunt, has always had my back in Dublin.

My family have always supported me in a way that made me feel valued. I'd especially like to thank my aunt, Margaret Doyle, for her hospitality and homemade bread; my uncle and aunt, Anthony and Catherine Doyle, for their generosity and willingness to shepherd me back and forth for research trips to Tralee at the height of the Rose of Tralee madness; my uncle Gerard who put up with my unrequested, but unstintingly endured, history lectures; my aunt and uncle, Helen and Alan Breakey, who provided sanctuary in Monaghan; and my godfather, John Doyle, who has always taken that vow seriously and looked out for me. My sister Ann has always kept my feet firmly on the ground whenever I threatened to lose the run of myself, but has always ensured I had the help I needed without my ever asking for it.

Finally, I wish to thank my parents, Michael and Mary. None of this work would have been possible without their encouragement, and they continue to provide me with a source of inspiration. The love and faith in me they have shown down all the years have eased anxieties, doubts and difficulties that I have encountered and given me the belief to continue. I dedicate this book to them.

Abbreviations

ACC	Agricultural Credit Corporation
CDB	Congested Districts Board
CMC	Condensed Milk Company of Ireland
CWS	Co-operative Wholesale Society
DATI	Department of Agriculture and Technical Instruction for Ireland
DDC	Dairy Disposal Company
HCPP	House of Commons Parliamentary Parties
IAC	Irish Associated Creameries
IAOS	Irish Agricultural Organisation Society
IAWS	Irish Agricultural Wholesale Society
ICMA	Irish Creamery Managers Association
IPP	Irish Parliamentary Party
ITGWU	Irish Transport and General Workers Union
NAI	National Archive of Ireland
NLI	National Library of Ireland
PRONI	Public Records Office of Northern Ireland
UAOS	Ulster Agricultural Organisation Society
UI	United Irishwomen

Introduction

Wherever the problem of rural life, as it is now commonly called, is under discussion, the Irish three-fold scheme – better farming, better business, better living – is regarded as the final solution, and the [Irish Agricultural Organisation] Society is hailed as the parent of a new agency of social service which was needed before any conceivable governmental action could avail to right what was wrong with the rural economy of nations absorbed in the interests of city life. (Horace Plunkett, Irish Agricultural Organisation Society's Annual General Meeting, 1915).[1]

Co-operation is a complex thing. Whether between individuals, organisations or nation-states an ability to co-operate is a crucial part of any successful relationship. An inability to co-operate often leads to a downturn in relationships with potential drastic consequences. Today, the promotion of co-operatives is one of the most effective tools used by international policymakers to stimulate economic development.[2] Yet, despite the apparent commitment to co-operatives that exists at the highest levels of global politics there remains a popular misunderstanding that these are just another type of business in a crowded marketplace. Yet the contribution made by co-operative experts, practitioners and administrators must surely represent one of the most singular and major contributions to the emergence of modern economic behaviour. Getting at the historical dimensions of the practice of co-operation can be a daunting task as it takes in such a broad sweep of human experience. Co-operation defines people's relationships at all levels of social interaction; from the intimate level between partners within the home, or at the highest level of geopolitics in an organisation like the United Nations. From the nineteenth century onwards, a wide range of efforts to formalise the co-operative impulse in the arrangement of social, economic and political relations came to the fore in a response to ameliorate the worst effects released by industrialisation. This book is an attempt to outline a history of one of these formalised efforts attempted in Ireland at the end of the nineteenth century.

The history of the co-operative movement in Ireland is one that spans an important period in the formation of the modern nation-state. This book charts the movement's progress from the establishment of the first co-operative creamery in 1889 through to the creation of a network of creameries, credit societies and agricultural stores under the umbrella of the Irish Agricultural Organisation Society (IAOS). This organisation defined the direction of economic development in the independent Irish Free State. The essence of what constitutes co-operation can be difficult to reach and its parameters often shift, depending on the historical situation. However, at its most general, co-operative movements share the objective that members aim to derive a mutually shared benefit from a transaction. Richard Sennett defined co-operation as 'an exchange in which the participants benefit from the encounter ... [and] co-operate to do what they can't do alone'.[3] In Ireland, the form of co-operation analysed in this book occurred in the context of an agrarian economy that contemporaries viewed as losing ground to international competition. A multitude of economic experiments and movements emerged across the globe in this period. Irish co-operators were influenced by, and in turn influenced, co-operative experimenters elsewhere. Co-operative movements sprang up around Europe in the late nineteenth century populated by people who saw advantages in mutual partnership with others to achieve a shared objective. These societies allowed individuals to combine their resources, talents and ideas to effect an economy of scale that granted them advantageous access to the marketplace. The co-operative principle made its greatest inroads within the retail, credit and agricultural sectors during the age of industrialisation with highly influential long-term consequences for societal development in those countries where practised.

Horace Plunkett, the founder of the IAOS, coined the slogan 'better farming, better business, better living' to summarise the co-operative movement's objectives. He believed that an improvement in farming and business methods flowed into the third part of the aphorism, and maintained that the impulse to create a better quality of life in rural Ireland formed the true priority of the IAOS. A member of the Anglo-Irish elite, Plunkett came from the paternalist tradition of his class and performed many public roles during his lifetime: Member of Parliament, a Unionist who became a supporter of Home Rule, author and controversialist, and most importantly an agricultural reformer who led the co-operative movement in Ireland in its first decades. The local co-operative society possessed the potential to overhaul farming methods and make agriculture a viable, even desirable, lifestyle. The reform of rural society proposed by Plunkett addressed contentious questions that included how to stem emigration from the countryside; how to create sustainable employment for the rural population; and how to keep Irish agriculture sustainable and competitive within an international marketplace. Plunkett saw the IAOS as an agency that encouraged farmers to reorganise the agrarian economy along mutualist lines, while instilling characteristics of dignity and self-reliance in the rural population.[4] From the establishment of the first co-operative creamery in Drumcollogher, County Limerick in 1889, the movement peaked at over 1,000 societies and 150,000 members by 1920.[5]

Under Plunkett's leadership, the IAOS promoted a distinct and radical form of democratic economics. The co-operative structure of creamery societies meant farmer-members collectively owned this latest technology, but IAOS activists also believed the particular business structure presented a solution to problems of rural life and addressed social anxieties and uncertainties prevalent in the countryside.[6] The result of the IAOS's interventions in the rural economy held far-reaching consequences for Irish society. The farmer sat at the centre of the IAOS's radical economic blueprint that advocated their control of all agricultural business. The formation of a co-operative society then would equip agricultural workers with the skills, tools and means to take command of their own economic destiny. Their major success came when they married together the contemporary innovation of the creamery separator to the principle of co-operation and transformed the Irish dairying industry. Co-operative societies worked along the one member, one vote principle. This granted all members an equal say in shaping the direction of the business regardless of the amount of start-up capital contributed or produce they supplied to the creamery. In a context of ongoing land redistribution from landlords to tenants, the promotion of agricultural businesses placed under the joint and equal ownership of its members further empowered farmers.[7]

Wherever formal attempts to organise economic activity around co-operative principles have been attempted then its outward appearance and effects have taken on a particular character. Historical circumstances and the socio-economic contexts in which co-operatives were promoted produced locally distinctive characteristics. To take the case of Burma/Myanmar, the attempts to establish a successful co-operative movement occurred in a top–down fashion, but failed to embed itself as the state did not provide the necessary structures, resources or legal environment within which these efforts might prosper. The necessary cadre of national experts in co-operation never emerged and the movement never really managed to make a profound impact on the form of development in Burma/Myanmar.[8] Another factor that influenced the impact of co-operation upon national development related to the fact that co-operators organised to compete with other types of co-operators. Nowhere was this divergence in co-operative forms starker than the competing versions that originated in Ireland and Britain. The IAOS's concern with organising rural producers marked out the Irish understanding of the co-operative principle from the British co-operative movement that concentrated upon the consumer – with important consequences for the two movements. The Irish and British co-operative movements aggressively competed with one another in a race to control the Irish dairying industry.

But the rivalry between the two movements represented a clash between co-operative ideologies as much as a race to gain dominance over the Irish butter market. While Britain can claim the title of home of the modern co-operative movement, the type of co-operatives promoted as a tool for international development bear a more striking resemblance to the form that emerged in Ireland. Irish co-operatives arose to address common problems that faced farmers such as the need to access new agricultural technologies and to expand the availability of credit. These new co-operatives had an immediate effect upon the people's working lives in rural districts. Moreover, a co-operative society also played an important part in framing how the rural economy functioned, created new gender norms, and made decisive contributions to the political culture of the time.

Co-operation and the Irish question

The late nineteenth and early twentieth centuries saw a great deal of economic and technical experimentation take place across Ireland. The IAOS led the way in this regard, as it outlined and promoted its vision as a new way to structure Ireland's economy and society. The idea that economic modernisation resulted from improvements to agriculture formed an intellectual orthodoxy in Ireland throughout the nineteenth century. On the eve of the Great Famine, the Irish chemist and economist Robert Kane of Queen's College in Cork had argued that 'it is by improvements in agriculture … that the most rapid and most extensive amelioration in the condition of the people must be effected'.[9] The efforts by Plunkett and others to spread economic co-operation and attempt to develop the economy built upon aspirations expressed by Kane. However, the novelty of their intervention prioritised the active participation of the peasantry. Co-operators quickly seized upon the co-operative creamery as a practical and effective institution through which a New Ireland would emerge.

The history of the IAOS highlights the complex ways in which Ireland modernised during the nineteenth century and onwards. In putting forward an economic plan rooted in a political economy of communalism, co-operators worked along a paradigm of modernisation that stressed the importance of social value and sustainable communities as well as that of increased productivity. The historical understanding of modernisation applied to Ireland is a complicated one. However, the historiography stresses how the increased social and economic liberalism that became apparent throughout the twentieth century represents Ireland's embrace of modernity. R.F. Foster argues that 'a good deal of what characterized the country in the mid-twentieth century was obdurately pre-modern', and not until 1972, with Ireland's entry into the European Economic Community, were 'old moulds … broken with apparent decisiveness'.[10] This arrival into the modern era strikes one as rather late and sudden. Joseph Lee views modernisation as a cumulative process that emerged out of nineteenth-century peasant-based society due to slow improvements to farming, combined with concurrent processes of depopulation and infrastructural reform. Lee gauged Irish modernity throughout the twentieth century in terms of the state's economic performance.[11]

Oliver MacDonagh offers a more ambivalent impression of Ireland's social and political progress. He argues how opposing views on time and place held by Irish and English people led to misunderstandings and conflict. The way in which opposing *mentalités* found expression in the countryside created a situation wherein social conflict over land ownership persisted throughout the nineteenth century. However, the rural Irish economy remained one operated by family units and communalism as demonstrated by the practice of cooring, or informal co-operation at the level of the neighbourhood.[12] Co-operative organisers aimed to build its network of democratic businesses within this *Gemeinschaft* – an attempt to both preserve communal aspects of rural life while simultaneously integrating Irish farmers into a global marketplace.

With its concentration upon agriculture as the engine-house of economic progress and modernity, the Irish co-operative movement anticipated a wider process of development that grew in prominence on the global stage throughout the twentieth century. The IAOS framed an influential ideal of how development should take place through co-operation. The creation of a vibrant network of co-operative creameries, credit societies and other businesses meant that Irish farmers actively participated in directing how their communities were structured. Interventions made by co-operative organisers to the daily lives of rural people formed a central part of efforts to instigate a programme of modernisation that gained international prominence. The ideas and arguments used to promote such a modernisation project found their way into the later developmental agendas of international agencies such as the League of Nations and the United Nations.[13] At present the United Nations views co-operatives as an important part of their global sustainability agenda, estimate that co-operatives comprise a global member-ship of 1 billion, and employs 12.6 million.[14] Akhil Gupta's work has demonstrated that the concept of 'development' emerged as the *raison d'état* in postcolonial states in which agriculture forms a critical link in the forging of the modern nation.[15] Ireland, then, provided international observers with a case study where dynamic attempts to solve the crisis of rural existence worked themselves out. Other agrarian nations looked to the example set by Plunkett and the IAOS as they applied a social blueprint across the Irish countryside.[16]

The co-operator's focus on spreading a form of modernity defined by values such as community ownership and economic democracy meant co-operative businesses viewed development as a wider project than simply one of increased productivity. The co-operative society aimed to promote local democracy in industry, foster an engaged and participatory membership, and educate farmers through practical instruction from co-operative employees. The leadership of the movement demonstrated a large degree of paternalism in the way they viewed farmers as subjects of improvement. The establishment of a co-operative society provided a means by which a modern farmer well versed in scientific business practices might be cultivated. However, Plunkett viewed the co-operative move-ment's establishment as occurring at a crucial juncture. The unfolding process whereby land ownership changed from landlord to tenant farmer in the late nineteenth century empowered the latter group. At the same time, farmers also faced greater responsibilities over the stewardship of Ireland's most important resource – land. The envisioned educational role to be played by co-operatives prepared farmers to maximise the resources under their control and therefore that they generated wealth to ensure that sustainable, rural communities proliferated across Ireland. In this way, the spread of the co-operative movement anticipated the idea of development as a means to secure freedom from poverty, as articulated by Amartya Sen.[17] The fact that this experience of economic freedom coincided with a demand for political freedom in the early twentieth century is also not mere coincidence.

The co-operative movement played a crucial role in conceptualising the Irish nation-state by imagining this entity through its project of agricultural development and early chapters trace how this process unfolded. Yet within the narrative of Ireland's own economic development, the example of the co-operative movement is seldom more than a footnote. The dominant historical narrative suggests that the valorisation of technical and economic expertise only became wedded to national identity in the mid- to late twentieth century.[18] The idea that economic nation-building in Ireland was due to a policy shift towards a more liberal, open economy in the late 1950s is now a standard trope of Irish political and historical discourse. However, this narrative downplays other developmental paradigms that existed before that date and instead signalled a story about Irish modernity that policymakers found useful to justify a particular consensus that prioritised economic liberalisation and an opening up of the Irish economy along the lines of foreign direct investment-led growth.[19] The flexible developmental state that existed in Ireland by the end of the twentieth century was defined by an 'uneasy structure of multiple alliances' across society and between transnational corporations. A growth in socio-economic inequality characterised this type of Irish state arrangement, which continued to spiral after the economic crash of 2007–8 and the implementation of a swathe of austerity policies.[20] Although the specific problems that faced the Irish state in recent years were different, there was little new in the scale and nature of these challenges. Irish co-operators at the end of the nineteenth century looked to empower and improve the quality of life for a population integrated within a globalised economy. Irish society back then was porous, responsive to change, and despite having a reputation for being economically backwards until the 1950s, proved an innovative one.

Chapter 1 looks at why Ireland's uneven integration into the nineteenth-century's global economy provided cause for concern and how co-operation provided possible solutions. The country's largest sector, agriculture, faced new challenges from a glut of overseas butter producers, but primarily from the rapid rise of Denmark's well organised dairy industry during the 1880s. However, a globally integrated marketplace also provided a source of inspiration as well as challenges and the introduction of co-operatives illustrate how this situation led to a new path for development; that is, the application of a principle with international antecedents to mitigate the effects of global sources of competition. The role of the flexible developmental state was not to instigate developmental activities per se, but rather provide the correct environment through which corporations and local networks might stimulate their own forms of economic momentum. Economic historians who have utilised a comparative approach to contrast the Irish co-operative movement with continental co-operative movements argue that Irish success fell short of its objectives.[21] In Denmark, where questions of land ownership were resolved before the nineteenth century and which enjoyed high levels of educational literacy the results proved far more successful.

However, the type of state that functioned in Ireland presented more obstacles to the Irish co-operator. Remedial legislation to solve the intractable land question and expand educational provision occurred in the period, but in many ways, what one can see in the IAOS's efforts to build a more co-operative economy is also far-reaching experiment in building up the capabilities of the state. The time taken to offer farmers agricultural instruction by the IAOS's team of organisers anticipated work later conducted by the first Department of Agriculture; another agency founded by Horace Plunkett. The Congested Districts Board also performed some of these functions along Ireland's western seaboard, but the co-operative movement can claim responsibility for an immense amount of theoretical and practical experimentation that occurred in the Irish economy from the late nineteenth century onwards.[22]

Chapters 2 and 3 examines how the co-operative movement set out to develop the Irish economy and population stood out against the backdrop of political ferment in the years before independence. Before the First World War, the much-debated Irish Question turned on whether legislation for an autonomous Irish parliament might be enacted and what powers such a body might wield. Horace Plunkett approached Ireland's problems from a different starting position. He, and other like-minded individuals sympathetic to his arguments, re-framed the Irish Question as social and economic in nature with the improvement of rural living conditions as the central concern.[23] In the late nineteenth century, the phenomenon of widespread emigration alongside the present spectre of famine led Plunkett to conclude that rural Ireland stood on the precipice of a demographic catastrophe. The Great Famine of the mid-nineteenth century was a recent cata-strophic event and the threat of a repeat food shortage remained a threat. The process of national decline also appeared apparent in the habitual process of emigration from rural Ireland. Plunkett argued that emigration indicated a 'low national vitality' with one of the most worrying symptoms shown in 'the physical and moral effects of the drain … on youth, strength, and energy of the com-munity'.[24] Throughout his career, Plunkett argued that only a thorough co-operative reorganisation of the Irish countryside would raise living standards and stem the flow of emigration.

Economic and political cultures are inseparable. A history of co-operation provides detailed insight into the mundane concerns and priorities that mattered to people. Co-operative societies provide an entry point into complex agrarian situations whereby 'many questions of economy, politics, society, and culture were debated'. Co-operatives provide an insight into the implications of these debates for rural society at a local level, while demonstrating how they instigated monumental change on a national level.[25] The potential for historians to use the site of co-operatives to illuminate the complexity of rural society in Ireland remains under-utilised. In contrast, historians of British co-operation, which has received much recent attention, have argued that the Manchester-based Co-operative Wholesale Society (CWS) made important interventions in British political culture.[26] Peter Gurney's seminal study argued that British co-operation constituted 'a particular mode of consumption [that] generated fierce and protracted social conflicts'. Co-operation represented an alternative paradigm for consumption to that offered by capitalist entrepreneurs. By generating debate and conflict around the sphere of consumption, the co-operative movement shaped modern British society.[27] Manu Goswami argues how, in colonial India, a discursive construction of national identity articulated the position of a community unevenly incorporated into an imperial economy. Economic ideas that offered a critique of prevailing socio-political conditions allowed anti-colonial activists to become the 'authors of the political economy of nationhood'.[28] Some of the most effective authors of a national political economy in Ireland emerged from the co-operative movement. Irish co-operators differed from their counterparts in Britain in that they were more concerned with a culture of production over consumption. While the CWS served the interests of its members, which were the working-class consumers from industrial cities, the IAOS focused instead on the interests of rural producers.

This book highlights why it is important to understand the role played by co-operatives in shaping Irish political culture. The Irish co-operative movement occupied an ambiguous, yet formative, governmental position that changed radically across the period covered. The IAOS diffused an ideology of co-operation that emerged interstitially, and which was 'elaborated along networks distinct from but nevertheless dependent upon the official circuits of power'.[29] This study redresses this gap in the historiography of the Irish state, arguing that Irish co-operators co-ordinated a serious developmental effort during the early twentieth century despite existing outside these official circuits of power. For example, the movement's relationship with the Department of Agriculture oscillated between acting as a vital instrument for rural development to an unwanted and alternative source of expertise. The complex and incongruous relationship between the voluntary co-operative movement and the state became a site of political conflict, which left an indelible mark upon Irish institutions. Despite a turbulent relationship with government institutions, the movement remained a legitimate source of authority for farmers as IAOS organisers incorporated new techniques and farming methods into their industry. By following the thread of co-operative modernisation, it is argued that the movement contributed to an Irish form of rule.

The importance of the co-operative movement, then, resided in its ability to conjure up a practical sense of what constituted the nation, while simultaneously organising the resources and ideas that helped assemble the state in Ireland. The co-operator's desire to re-make the countryside produced a reservoir of detailed economic information produced by a sprawling network of local institutions across the country and which informed subsequent legislation. The start of the First World War placed these efforts in jeopardy and in Ireland, the violent aftermath of that conflict led into a violent campaign for independence and eventual civil war. Chapters 4 and 5 examine the ways in which the movement's officials navigated these years of violence and kept the movement afloat. The establishment of an independent Irish Free State in 1922 represented a political compromise that proved unsatisfactory for many nationalists and led to civil war during 1922–23. Nevertheless, by the 1920s, a partitioned, agricultural nation-state is precisely what emerged and having gained prominence during a period of cultural renaissance, co-operative ideas found a receptive audience among the generation of nationalists that took power after independence. The final chapter argues that co-operative societies provided an important source of continuity across rural Ireland. The changing *dramatis personae* of Irish political administrations mattered less than the organisation of local resources to people who utilised co-operative societies on a frequent basis. As a result, co-operative organisation provided one means of ensuring that the Irish Free State experienced a degree of political and economic stability in the aftermath of revolution.

An overarching argument contained in this book is that the co-operative movement authored a specific type of 'imagined community' and ushered it into practical existence across the Irish countryside through its network of societies. By the 1930s, analyses of Irish independence emphasised agriculture's importance to Irish national identity. Leo Kohn, a constitutional expert on Ireland, portrayed agriculture as 'the principal industry of the country, and it has behind it a tradition of administration which is at once more comprehensive *and more Irish* than that of any other government service' (emphasis added).[30] The organisation of Irish producers along co-operative lines granted them a platform to influence the development of an emergent nation-state. Co-operative organisation played a fundamental role in shaping Ireland's political culture. The Irish reconfigured co-operation to favour the interests of rural producers and in the process differenti-ated their version from a British conception of co-operative organisation. The IAOS's reorganisation of rural society helped link Irish political culture to the interests of producers. Moreover, as a result of this practical experimentation, the ideas associated with the co-operative economy promoted by the IAOS, were taken up by separatist nationalists and found eventual legislative expression in the Irish Free State's Agricultural Commission after independence.

Although tempting to write a history that solely concentrates on the attractive and curious personalities of those who led the co-operative movement, close examination is given to the work of the IAOS's team of organisers, employees and local figures who coalesced around the site of the co-operative. Taken together these co-operative experts played a vitally important role in engineering the form taken by the Irish state in the countryside as co-operative creameries, credit societies and other businesses resulted in a new institutional landscape. Although I examine co-operative development in different parts of the country, in later chapters I have focused in particular on the movement's experiences in County Kerry. Located in the south-west of Ireland, Kerry represented an ideal target for IAOS organisers being within the dairying heartlands that made up a region that produced key Irish exports. Many of the changes that affected rural areas in the period covered, such as land ownership reform, emigration and political violence occurred in County Kerry.[31] Many of the challenges that faced new co-operative societies played out in Kerry, as did many of the innovations derived from creamery production of butter and distribution. A local analysis highlights the varied forms of resistance to co-operative expansion, which acted as a major frustration to the IAOS's attempts to organise the county's farmers. This resistance ranged from butter traders who viewed the introduction of co-operative creameries as a threat to their living, private creamery owners, and competition from the CWS who targeted the same market as the IAOS. The ways in which IAOS organisers overcame these forces to create a nationwide network of dairying and agricultural societies determined the structure of Ireland's rural economy and helped define the political climate of the early twentieth century.

The IAOS promoted a vision of an idealised community based upon reciprocity and mutual concern. The concentration upon social and economic aspects of rural life did not isolate co-operators from the contemporary debate about Ireland's political future. Rather, such a position formed an important counterpoint. The book's periodisation reflects a decision to take analysis of the co-operative movement from its emergence during the cultural revival in the 1890s through to the end of the first years of independence. This emphasises the importance of co-operation to rural people's everyday lives throughout a period that encompassed the rise of cultural nationalism, world war and revolution. Competing ideologies of nationalism and unionism did not monopolise contemporary debate. The book shows how the sustained advocacy of co-operation by the IAOS through its efforts to reorganise rural society mattered a great deal as it moulded historical understandings of Irish nationhood and identity, which still resonates today.

Notes

1 Irish Agricultural Organisation Society, *Report of the Irish Agricultural Organisation Society for the period from 1st July 1914 to the 31st March 1915* (Dublin: Sackville Press, 1916), 24. [Hereafter, all reports are referred to as IAOS, *Annual Report, 19XX*].

2 For example see UN Secretary-General's Report, *Co-operatives in Social Development*, A/70/161 (2015), http://undocs.org/A/70/161 [accessed 10 October 2017].

3 Richard Sennett, *Together: The Rituals, Pleasures and Politics of Co-operation* (London: Allen Lane, 2012).

4 Trevor West, *Horace Plunkett, Co-operation and Politics* (Gerrard's Cross, Bucks.: Colin Smythe, 1986), 3.

5 IAOS, *Annual Report, 1921*, 7.

6 Kevin H. O'Rourke, 'Culture, Conflict and Cooperation: Irish Dairying Before the Great War', *Economic Journal*, 117 (2007), 1357–1379.

7 Philip Bull, *Land, Politics and Nationalism: A Study of the Irish Land Question* (Dublin: Gill and Macmillan, 1996); James S Donnelly, Jr, *The Land and the People of Nineteenth-Century Cork* (London: Routledge & Kegan Paul, 1975).

8 Anthony Webster, 'Co-operatives and the State in Burma/Myanmar, 1900–2012: A Case-Study of Failed Top-Down Co-operative Development Models?' in Rajeswary Ampalavanar Brown and Justin Pierce (eds), *Charities in the Non-Western World: The Development and Regulation of Indigenous and Islamic Charities* (New York: Routledge, 2013), 65–87.

9 Robert Kane, *The Industrial Resources of Ireland* (Dublin: Hodges and Smith, 1845), 423.

10 R.F. Foster, *Modern Ireland, 1600–1972* (London: Penguin, 1989), 569.

11 Joseph Lee, *The Modernisation of Irish Society, 1848–1918*, 3rd edn (Dublin: Gill & Macmillan, 2008); J.J. Lee, *Ireland, 1912–1985: Politics and Society* (Cambridge: Cambridge University Press, 1989).

12 Oliver MacDonagh, *States of Mind: Two Centuries of Anglo-Irish Conflict, 1780–1980* (London: Pimlico, 1992), 50–51. Also Conrad M. Arensberg, *The Irish Countryman*, 2nd edn (Garden City, N.Y.: The Natural History Press, 1968); Conrad Arensberg and Solon T. Kimball, *Family and Community in Ireland*, 2nd edn (Gloucester, Mass.: Peter Smith, 1961).

13 Patricia Clavin, *Securing the World's Economy: The Reinvention of the League of Nations, 1920–1946* (Oxford: Oxford University Press, 2013).

14 UN Secretary-General, *Co-operatives in Social Development*.

15 Akhil Gupta, *Postcolonial Developments: Agriculture in the Making of Modern India* (London: Duke University Press, 1998), 38.

16 Rita Rhodes, *Empire and Co-operation: How the British Empire used Co-operatives in its Development Strategies, 1900–1970* (Edinburgh: John Donald, 2012).

17 Amartya Sen, *Development as Freedom* (Oxford: Oxford University Press, 1999).

18 Tom Garvin, *News from a New Republic: Ireland in the 1950s* (Dublin: Gill & Macmillan, 2011), 13.

19 Bryan Fanning, *Irish Adventures in Nation-Building* (Manchester: Manchester University Press, 2016), 1–16.

20 Seán Ó Riain, 'The Flexible Developmental State: Globalisation, Information Technology and the "Celtic Tiger"', *Politics and Society*, 28.2 (2000), 157–193; Emma Heffernan, John McHale and Niamh Moore-Cherry (eds), *Debating Austerity in Ireland: Crisis, Experience and Recovery* (Dublin: Royal Irish Academy, 2017).
21 Timothy W. Guinnane, 'A Failed Institutional Transplant: Raiffeisen's Credit Cooperatives in Ireland, 1894–1914', *Explorations in Economic History*, 31 (1994), 38–61; Carla King, 'The Early Development of Agricultural Cooperation: Some French and Irish Comparisons', *Proceedings of the Royal Irish Academy*, 96C.3 (1996), 67–86; O'Rourke, 'Culture, Conflict and Co-operation'.
22 Ciara Breathnach, *The Congested Districts Board of Ireland, 1891–1923: Poverty and Development in the West of Ireland* (Dublin: Four Courts Press, 2005).
23 Patrick Mary Doyle, 'Reframing the "Irish Question": the Role of the Co-operative Movement in the Formation of Irish Nationalism, 1900–1922', *Irish Studies Review*, 22.3 (2014), 267–284.
24 Horace Plunkett, *Ireland in the New Century: with an Epilogue in Answer to Some Critics* (London: John Murray, 1905), 33.
25 Yannis Kotsonis, *Making Peasants Backward: Agricultural Cooperatives and the Agrarian Question in Russia, 1861–1914* (Houndmills: Macmillan Press Ltd, 1999), 4–8.
26 John F. Wilson, Anthony Webster and Rachael Vorberg-Rugh, *Building Co-operation: A Business History of the Co-operative Group, 1863–2013* (Oxford: Oxford University Press, 2013).
27 Peter Gurney, *Co-operative Culture and the Politics of Consumption in England, 1870–1930* (Manchester: Manchester University Press, 1996), 22. Other works highlighting how co-operatives organised political culture in the twentieth century include Lawrence Black and Nicole Robertson (eds), *Consumerism and the Co-operative Movement in Modern British History: Taking Stock* (Manchester: Manchester University Press, 2009); Mary Hilson, Pirjo Markkola and Ann-Catrin Ostman (eds), *Co-operatives and the Social Question: The Co-operative Movement in Northern and Eastern Europe (1880–1950)* (Cardiff: Welsh Academic Press, 2012); Nicole Robertson, *The Co-operative Movement and Communities in Britain, 1914–1960: Minding their Own Business* (Farnham: Ashgate, 2010); Anthony Webster, Alyson Brown, David Stewart, John K. Walton and Linda Shaw (eds), *The Hidden Alternative: Co-operative Values, Past, Present and Future* (Manchester: Manchester University Press, 2011).
28 Manu Goswami, *Producing India: From Colonial Economy to National Space* (Chicago: University of Chicago Press, 2004), 279.
29 William H. Sewell Jr, *Logics of History: Social Theory and Social Transformation* (Chicago: The University of Chicago Press, 2005), 119. For an analysis of interstitial ideologies as sources of social power see Michael Mann, *The Sources of Social Power, Volume I: A History of Power from the Beginning to A.D. 1760* (Cambridge: Cambridge University Press, 1986), 15–19.
30 Leo Kohn, *The Constitution of the Irish Free State* (London: George Allen & Unwin, 1932), 312.
31 Donnacha Seán Lucey, *Land, Popular Politics and Agrarian Violence in Ireland: The Case of County Kerry, 1872–1886* (Dublin: University College Dublin Press, 2011).

1

The origins of co-operation in Ireland

The establishment of the Irish Agricultural Organisation Society (IAOS) in Dublin in April 1894 marked a milestone in the emergence of the modern Irish nation-state. The new society offered leadership to the co-operative societies formed over the previous five years that aimed to improve the state of Irish agriculture. Presided over by Horace Plunkett, the Anglo-Irish agricultural reformer and Unionist MP for South Dublin, the IAOS aimed to inject a new spirit of vitality and innovation across rural Ireland. Plunkett outlined a hopeful vision for the IAOS that saw people of all political and religious stripes united behind a project to promote 'the welfare of the agricultural classes'. Plunkett's appeal for cross-societal support to spread the principle of co-operation stood out in a context of fractious debates about what direction Ireland's political future should take. As someone who studied the condition of Irish agriculture, Plunkett concluded that farmers worked within an exploitative system. Farmers bought too dear and sold too cheap; transport costs remained too high; inadequate credit provision existed; and an under-utilisation of resources saw farmers fall short of their potential. The Irish situation stood in sharp contrast to other countries where farming communities overcame some of these challenges. However, he continued, 'wherever such progress has been made, the means by which the improvement has been effected has been the same, namely, *organisation*'.[1]

If, as James Scott has argued, the condition of modernity is the organisation of knowledge and resources to overcome economic and social problems, such as the production of food, then the IAOS can claim to have left a long-lasting legacy in modern Ireland. Modernising projects, so frequently associated with processes of urbanisation, can equally apply to developmental strategies in the rural sphere and agriculture.[2] The originality of the IAOS's intervention resided in its efforts to organise the constituents of rural society around a network of co-operative creameries, credit societies and agricultural societies. The principle of co-operation underpinned and unified the new rural movement. Yet despite the emphasis on cross-communal support and encouragement of active participation among its supporters, perhaps because of it, it provoked huge controversy upon its introduction to rural Ireland.

The aim of this chapter is to establish how the concept of co-operation applied to Ireland at the end of the nineteenth century. Before examining the extent to which farmers embraced co-operative ideas, and the challenges placed in the way of this radical new form of economic organisation, it is necessary to outline the social, economic and political conditions under which co-operative activists promoted their ideas among Irish farmers. Ireland experienced tumultuous political and social change in the second half of nineteenth century because of devastating famine. The co-operative movement's introduction at the end of the nineteenth century represented a rigorous attempt to deal with the worst effects of rural instability. But the introduction of co-operative ideas also pointed to the significance of the transnational intellectual currents that shaped the state of modern Ireland.

As well as outlining general conditions in Ireland, it is important to understand how Plunkett and others arrived at the conclusion that co-operative principles would best serve Irish economic interests. Accordingly, the second object of this chapter is to locate Irish co-operation within this wider milieu. Enthusiasts for the co-operative idea studied the example of co-operative experts at work in countries such as Britain, Germany and Denmark. The existence of a large multinational, consumer-oriented co-operative organisation in Britain proved to be influential in deciding the form which mainstream co-operation in Ireland took. The final section of the chapter examines how the early efforts of IAOS organisers challenged a British model of co-operation. The tension generated between the Irish and British movements is analysed and shown to define the Irish co-operative project by the early twentieth century. The challenge presented by a consumer-oriented movement forced the IAOS to emphasise its own producer credentials. This conflict helped define Irish economic identity as one that revolved around agricultural producers. This battle to promote one conception of co-operation over another helped set the terms of Irish economic development for decades.

Rural Ireland in the late nineteenth century

Horace Plunkett presented a pessimistic portrait of the countryside in his book *Ireland in the New Century*. He viewed the source of social and political grievance within the country primarily as economic in nature. High levels of emigration offered a chief symptom of both a 'low national vitality' and what he termed the 'problem of rural life'. To reverse this process he argued that to 'keep the people at home we have got to construct a national life with ... a secure basis of physical comfort and decency. This life must have a character, a dignity, an outlook of its own.'[3] Plunkett played many roles throughout his life – agricultural reformer, parliamentarian and philanthropist – but each venture upon which he embarked attempted to answer the question about how one might construct a new type of national life. It was in his role as founder and leader of Ireland's co-operative movement that he achieved his greatest degree of success in resolving this issue.

Plunkett's promotion of the co-operative principle offered a response to what he understood as a deep crisis of Irish agriculture, one that only accelerated throughout the nineteenth century. Competition from large-scale farming outfits in America and more organised competitors on the continent stressed the need for reform. Co-operative societies acted as agents of 'social and economic progress' by creating bonds of mutuality and cohesion between farmers and prepared them for the great struggle of international competition.[4] The movement's efforts to revitalise rural life happened at the end of a century in which a devastating famine fundamentally restructured social, economic and demographic conditions.[5] The Great Famine of 1845–51 resulted in the death of an estimated 1.1 million people and the emigration of some 2.1 million in the decade after 1845.[6] Three important features of rural life crystallised in the aftermath. First, high levels of emigration out of Ireland, particularly from rural regions, became a normalised feature of everyday life. As Enda Delaney highlighted, almost as many people born in Ireland lived outside the country as in it by the end of the nineteenth century.[7] The impact of this movement of people profoundly shaped Irish society in many ways. Emigration provided a recurring source of anxiety throughout the nineteenth and twentieth centuries and posed a series of social, economic and moral questions for Ireland's political and spiritual leaders.[8]

The longer-term economic trajectory saw increased pressures placed on Ireland's farmers, typified by an agricultural depression in the early 1880s. The value of agricultural output in 1886 stood at 64 per cent of its 1876 value and, meanwhile, international competition only increased.[9] The timing of this depression compounded another problem for Irish farmers engaged in dairy production. For much of the nineteenth century, Ireland enjoyed a position as one of the pre-eminent suppliers of butter to Britain. Butter production took place within the home, by women who worked the product by hand.[10] This butter would be sold to merchants who supplied one of the markets in Ireland, or sent on to Britain where it formed an important source of nutrition for the industrial workforce. The invention of the creamery separator in the late 1870s revolutionised the butter industry. Before this invention, producers placed milk in containers and waited for the cream required for the manufacturing process to separate gradually. The mechanical creamery separator accelerated the separation process and extracted a higher proportion of cream from the milk.

The swift diffusion of the new separation technology in Denmark gave dairy farmers in that country a distinct competitive advantage over their Irish counterparts.[11] Throughout the 1880s Irish butter producers lost their pre-eminent position in the British marketplace to their better-organised Danish rivals. The widespread establishment of co-operatively organised creameries placed ownership over the separator in the hands of many Danish farmers.[12] Reform-minded individuals such as Plunkett noted that the diffusion of new technology and the manufacture of an improved product occurred through co-operative endeavour.

A third feature saw the persistence of rural unrest that revolved around the vexed question of land ownership and what constituted a fair rent for farmers. A series of legislative land reforms from 1870 onwards sought to achieve the gradual transfer of land ownership from the landlords to tenant farmers. A series of poor harvests throughout the 1870s saw an increase in rural unrest and violence. The establishment of the Land League by Michael Davitt in 1879 and the election of Charles Stewart Parnell, leader of the Irish Parliamentary Party (IPP), as President of the League saw a political campaign for land reform aligned to a social movement that promoted agitation. The Land League's demands the 'Three Fs' – fair rent, fixity of tenure and fair sale – shaped the terms of Gladstone's 1881 Land Act. The 1881 Land Act formed the Liberal Government's response to the rural discontent that was the Land War. The Act established a Land Court empowered to control rents, with the result that over the next two decades almost two-thirds of land occupiers experienced an average rent reduction of 22 per cent.[13] Despite legislative changes to land ownership and tenant rights imposed by Gladstone's Government, a sense of unfinished business around the issue remained in place. This incomplete settlement of the land question at the end of the nineteenth century ushered in a temporary cessation of rural violence that allowed the co-operative movement to flourish. However, practices of land redistribution continued long into the twentieth century and remained an emotive political issue beyond independence.[14]

Plunkett believed that 'the spread of agricultural co-operation through voluntary associations' was required to overcome practical problems that affected Irish farming's international reputation and also offered a way to more effectively exploit national resources. He argued that co-operative societies represented an 'agency of social and economic progress' without which:

> [s]mall landholders will be but a body of isolated units, having all the drawbacks of individualism and none of its virtues, unorganised and singularly ill-equipped for that great international struggle of our time, which we know as agricultural competition.[15]

The concern for the 'men of small means' remained a feature of co-operative rhetoric throughout the early twentieth century. In a letter addressed to Fr Tom Finlay, the IAOS's vice-president, Plunkett argued that the early experience of the co-operative movement 'united men of the utmost diversity of position, circumstance, interest and opinion'.[16] Ireland's ongoing transition from 'landlordism to a peasant proprietary' deprived them of a semblance of social cohesion.[17] Co-operative organisations offered a means to create social cohesion and provided a platform for small farmers to contribute more effectively to national development.

The emergence and growth of the co-operative movement within the Irish context occurred as an attempt to both stem the flow of outward rural migration and to marshal an efficient use of agricultural resources. A new caste of co-operative expert appeared in the countryside devoted to revolving issues around the production and distribution of agricultural goods, and in the process to establish a new form of political economy in Ireland. The cataclysmic shock of the Great Famine placed new pressures on Irish society that fundamentally shaped the emergent modern nation-state. Joseph Lee has argued that Irish modernisation, understood as a movement away from a peasant-based society resulted from slow improvements to farming, combined with concurrent processes of depopulation and infrastructural reform throughout the second half of the nineteenth century.[18] The decades after the famine saw a growth in agricultural productivity caused by the decrease in the number of agricultural holdings smaller than one acre from 570,338 in 1851 to 485,455 in 1911. This reduction in farmers cleared the land of smaller occupiers as reflected in the fact that the percentage of holdings under 15 acres dropped from 49 to 40 per cent in the same period.[19] In the midst of the changes to land holding sizes and incremental increases in agricultural output, the interventions of organisers sent by the IAOS to visit farmers engaged in new co-operative businesses helped to develop new forms of agricultural knowledge from the 1890s onwards.

An Irish economic revival

The introduction of co-operative farming methods instigated by Plunkett in the 1890s happened as part of a wider process of cultural reconfiguration within Ireland. The Irish Revival of the late nineteenth century established a 'new "self-help" consensus' and provided space for new cultural projects to emerge. As Senia Paseta argues, the cultural revival's 'amorphousness' allowed it to be 'a rallying point for various political and social causes, and facilitated the fraternisation of individuals as diverse as Douglas Hyde, Eoin MacNeill, Horace Plunkett and George Russell'.[20] At the same time, the Irish Revival benefited from the perceived irrelevance of constitutional politics. Irish nationalism lost momentum after the death of Charles Stewart Parnell and the consequent split in the IPP in the 1890s.[21] The second Home Rule Bill's failure in 1893 side-lined the debate over Ireland's constitutional status.[22] As a result, the cultural sphere provided the most dynamic arena in which to articulate Irish values and demonstrate the vitality of national life.

Rural co-operation provided the economic corollary to the new Irish dramatic, linguistic and sporting movements that emerged in the period. A plethora of cultural organisations sprang up that included W.B. Yeats's National Literary Society in 1892 and the Gaelic League by Douglas Hyde in 1893, which indicated support for Irish forms of cultural expression in the arts and language.[23]

These cultural initiatives coincided with the emergence of the new form of rural economics pioneered by Plunkett. Plunkett founded the IAOS in 1894 as a co-ordinating body to direct a fast-growing economic movement. The work of P.J. Mathews has made apparent the importance of mutual support that individuals from one revival movement offered to others. These revivalists shared an enthusiasm for a self-help ethos and a belief in the necessity for Irish modes of cultural, social and economic expression – as indicated by Plunkett's endorsement of the Gaelic League.[24] In turn, support from literary quarters aided the initial growth of new co-operative societies as demonstrated by Lady Gregory's involvement in the successful effort to establish a co-operative society in her village.[25]

Under Plunkett's stewardship, the co-operative movement galvanised enough support to drive the expansion of this project until it wove various social, economic and political threads together to create a distinct Irish culture. Stephen Gwynn later reflected upon the centrality of the economic aspect to the Revival, which proved decisive in the creation of Ireland's 'strong culture'. A former Nationalist MP, Gwynn identified many contributors to this cultural milieu which included the Gaelic League, the literary movement and Sinn Féin 'in its earlier more purely intellectual phase'. However, the most important social force that contributed to a modern Irish culture proved to be the co-operative movement:

> All these separate activities were in touch with one another … but Sir Horace Plunkett perhaps more than anyone else helped to create out of these a central culture. His wide sympathies drew about him a group of young men and women concerned generally for the welfare of Ireland… As a result, Irish thought began to be taken seriously wherever there was interest in ideas, and gained dignity in the process.[26]

Gwynn saw the co-operative movement as one significant network around which cultural and social expressions of Irishness cohered in the early twentieth century.

Plunkett's effort to popularise co-operative solutions to rural problems fixated on the larger question of national character. The problems that afflicted Ireland also possessed a moral quality according to his analysis. The 'national habit of living in the past' only served to provide 'a present without achievement, a future without hope'. If the plays of literary revivalists were intended to stage new forms of Irishness for audiences to consume, then Plunkett hoped that the co-operative society might serve as a stage on which a new rural subjectivity could be performed. Writing fifteen years after the establishment of the first co-operative creamery, Plunkett admitted that:

> The conclusion was long ago forced upon me that whatever may have been true of the past, the chief responsibility for the remoulding of our national life rests now with ourselves, and in the last analysis the problem of Irish ineffectiveness at home is in the main a problem of character – and of Irish character.[27]

The co-operative movement aimed at more than economic modernisation – it aimed to inculcate a new Irish subject characterised by a more co-operative outlook on social and political matters.

Intellectual origins and early developments

The agricultural co-operative movement that emerged in Ireland had complex and varied origins. Plunkett is recognised as the major conduit through which modern co-operative ideas as applied to agriculture came to Ireland. Plunkett proved to be a curious, outward-looking individual who saw the potential offered by the successful application of co-operative principles employed in other countries. Possessing the conviction of the convert, he yearned to replicate some of these effects in Ireland and his enthusiasm proved infectious as he recruited sympathetic support from a range of talented individuals. The dissemination and application of co-operation relied upon a network of supporters that increased and tied themselves to Plunkett's co-operative project. Without the assistance of Robert Anderson, the land agent from Cork, Fr T.A. Finlay the Jesuit economist, and George Russell (better known by his pen name Æ), along with the professional co-operative organisers who travelled the country, the spread of co-operation would have remained a sporadic isolated affair rather than the expansive network it grew into.

The history of co-operation in Ireland has a longer genealogy that predates the emergence of the agricultural co-operative movement in the 1880s. The continuation of some elements of a traditional farming system continued to exist well into the twentieth century. Folklorists and anthropologists identified a co-operative model of farming whereby the rural population shared in the performance of work across ties of family and kinship, although this communal form of labour, known as the *meitheal*, had been in decline since the Great Famine.[28] More formalised co-operative experiments inspired by the ideas of Robert Owen also occurred in the early nineteenth century. During the 1830s, co-operative retail societies appeared across Ulster; also in Ralahine, County Clare, a co-operative commune appeared on the Vandeleur estate. Individuals who supported Robert Owen's economic ideas founded these societies, but they failed to convert such enthusiasm into long-term success and within a few years, these experimental societies disappeared.[29] Although their existence offered only minor inspiration for Plunkett and his group gathered around the IAOS, the Ralahine experiment provided inspiration for Irish socialists. James Connolly believed that the Ralahine experiment represented 'an Irish point of interrogation erected amidst the wilderness of capitalist thought and feudal practice'. In Connolly's 'rejuvenated Ireland of the future' Ralahine's peasants 'will be dwelt upon with admiration as a great and important landmark in the march of the human race towards its complete social emancipation'.[30] Connolly's use of the Ralahine co-operative commune showed how co-operative ideas proved adaptable and ready to be championed by a diverse range of political and economic thinkers. This intellectual versatility proved to be one of factors behind the longevity of the co-operative ideal.

The modern Irish co-operative movement that grew out of the febrile cultural and intellectual atmosphere of the late nineteenth century drew upon co-operative precedents expressed elsewhere. This outside influence was crucial. The Danish uptake of creamery technology proved to be a formative example for Irish co-operators. Denmark's creamery sector grew rapidly in the 1880s and this successful uptake was ascribed to the co-operative business model that aided this diffusion. Throughout the late nineteenth and early twentieth centuries, attempts to implant Danish innovations into the Irish context ensued as Irish agronomists, representatives from the co-operative movement and some politicians visited the dairying Valhalla.[31] The Irish movement also looked to implant some of the continental advances in the field of co-operative finance to a cash-poor rural economy. The Raiffeisen co-operative rural banks established across Germany aimed to prevent small farmers prone to usurious practices from falling into a debt trap. Henry Wolff, the English expert on agricultural credit and a student of the Raiffeisen movement, proved to be a key expert in this field. Wolff's work popularised co-operative financial institutions across the English-speaking world. Plunkett read Wolff's *People's Banks*, and led the author to recount how 'having, as [Plunkett] put it – been "converted" by what I had written, in 1894 … [he] invited me over to Dublin to "convert" his colleagues as well'.[32]

However, the presence of the Manchester-originated Co-operative Wholesale Society (CWS) in Ireland proved to be the most direct influence over Irish co-operative development. Close proximity and shared language enhanced the transfer of ideas in the short term. The CWS, established in 1863, formed a leading component of the British co-operative retail movement. The society acted as the primary wholesale agent for the movement and sold commodities to individual co-operative retail societies, which in turn sold on to their members primarily located in the urban centres throughout England. The purchase of foodstuffs formed the largest part of their business and the importance of items such as butter, eggs and other agricultural foodstuffs saw the CWS expand their presence across Ireland. The CWS opened large depots in Limerick, Armagh, Waterford, Tralee and Cork between 1868 and 1877.[33] Furthermore, they employed their own agents in these towns in order to monitor and ensure the supply of foodstuffs.

The British co-operative movement's primary aim was to supply its industrial working-class membership base with high-quality, unadulterated foodstuffs at a cheap price. Securing a dependable supply of butter proved critical as it formed a staple part of the British diet. Irish dairy produce represented a propitious and important resource. In the mid-nineteenth century, unorganised dairy farmers supplied the CWS, which acquired Irish butter for its members living in industrial towns and cities. The CWS acquired a prominent position in the Irish dairy industry as it employed experienced buyers who attended the country's major butter markets and operated 'under the immediate and direct control of the Society – not merely being employed as agents or buyers on commission'. Their buyers took up residence close to the great butter markets in Ireland located primarily in the region of fertile dairy plains of south-west Ireland – Cork, Limerick and Tralee.[34] As the CWS extended its presence in Ireland a British newspaper, the *Co-operative News*, summarised its spread as an attempt

> to bring the producer and the consumer together, to so organise labour as to produce for known wants, and to serve the consumer as nearly as possible at cost price on condition that he finds the necessary capital in the first instead of the last instance ... It is really a *find*, and not an effort to him.[35]

Percy Redfern commented that the CWS 'grew fat on butter... [and] Ireland was the source of the supply'. The stated aim of the CWS, to harmonise the respective interests of consumer and producer, justified their initial extension into Ireland during the 1870s.[36] The introduction of the creamery separator and competition from farmers in Denmark incentivised the CWS's greater involvement in the production process in order to benefit their membership base. Thus, the first co-operative creamery was organised on behalf of the CWS in Drumcollogher, County Limerick, in 1889. The principal figures behind its establishment were W.L. Stokes, who worked as the CWS's Limerick agent, and butter merchant, Robert Gibson.[37] The CWS focused on securing the highest quality butter at the best possible price for the consumer. Although not its aim, the CWS played a crucial and controversial part in delineating a new variant of co-operative organisation that eventually took root in Ireland. When Plunkett and his followers began to organise their creameries during the 1890s, their focus on securing the highest price for the producer placed the two co-operative movements at philosophical odds.

When Horace Plunkett initiated his campaign to build a movement of rural co-operatives, it occurred within a broader international uptake of the co-operative model. In many ways, the adoption of co-operative organisation as a way to meet Irish farmers' social and economic challenges reflected the cosmopolitanism of the movement's founder. The modern co-operative principles that became rooted in the Irish movement had complex, international origins. Plunkett spent his young adult life conducting experiments in agricultural methods on the plains of Wyoming.[38] Although initially living there for health reasons related to lung problems he spent time farming and conducting his own agronomical experiments. Plunkett returned to Ireland after his father's death in 1889 and quickly threw his energy behind the creation of a rural co-operative movement. Although not involved in the establishment of Ireland's first co-operative creamery, his interest in economic co-operation emerged at the same time. A diary entry dated 24

January 1889 recorded a discussion on 'my co-operative hobby', but there is little evidence before this to suggest how he became attracted to the study of mutual economics.[39]

The successful example of co-operative stores in England piqued Plunkett's initial interest in co-operative economics. The formation of the Rochdale Equitable Pioneers Society in the north-west of England in 1844 represented a response to an economic depression. The Rochdale society served the working classes in an industrial cotton town that experienced a long-term downturn in living standards. This retail society marked a breakthrough in the modern co-operative movement. Other retail societies modelled on Rochdale were founded over the following years. The 'Rochdale Principles' also served as a template for other co-operatives that emerged around the globe in subsequent decades. At the heart of the modern co-operative model sat the democratic principle that entitled one member to one vote, irrespective of wealth, status or size of investment in the business. Open membership combined with political and religious tolerance formed another important feature of the model.[40]

The history of the co-operative movement in England raised the possibility that an opportunity existed to transplant the experiment in Ireland and animated Plunkett's first public intervention on the subject. In an article published in *Nineteenth Century* in 1888, he outlined the impoverished state of rural life and argued that the country's population 'are not able to obtain a fair exchange in commodities for what money they expend'. A solution that provided people access to reasonably priced goods required a form of social organisation such as 'the "Co-operative Store Society", an institution hitherto almost exclusively English'.[41] Fr Thomas Finlay SJ emphasised the importance of Plunkett's attendance at the 1889 Co-operative Congress in England, which allowed him to make 'a new and deeper study of the principles of co-operation, and [he] came back resolved to apply them on a large scale at home'.[42] Plunkett attended the Congress at Ipswich where he 'met the leading men of the co-operative movement & at once plunged into co-operative thought'.[43] After the first day of the conference, he recorded in his diary 'I was greatly impressed with the tone of the arguments used by the representatives of the working men ... I never before realised how much the working man is doing for himself compared with what is being done for him.'[44]

The Ipswich Congress left an immediate impression with the young Irish reformer. Plunkett met and discussed co-operative principles with intellectual luminaries such as Alfred Marshall and Beatrice Potter. Enthused by the conversations that took place, Plunkett returned to Ireland with a plan. He travelled to Doneraile in County Cork that July, where he discussed with local dignitaries the new ideas he picked up and 'the feasibility of starting a cooperative movement in this district'.[45] He returned in November along with J.C. Gray, who worked for the Co-operative Union, an organisation designed to promote co-operatives in all sectors of the economy. Plunkett's first foray in economic co-operation saw him attempt to transplant the consumer model adopted by the British co-operative movement. The proposed co-operative society was to be established along the lines of the English retail societies. He held two meetings at Doneraile courthouse on 21 November attended by a few local Protestants and some labourers, but without the support of local Catholic farmers and business, who Plunkett referred to as the 'R.C. squireens', which hinted at the future resistance efforts to establish co-operative societies would face.[46] Doneraile Co-operative Society was established and affiliated to the Co-operative Union. Although an initial success, the society ceased trading as a co-operative after changes in management. Nevertheless, other local traders responded to the business through improved services and the experiment helped create a climate that led to the creation of the Doneraile Co-operative Credit Society in 1894.[47]

Two important incidents occurred in Doneraile that influenced the development of the co-operative movement. First, Plunkett met a young land agent named Robert Anderson. Their mutual friend Alexis Roche introduced Anderson to Plunkett. In his memoir, Anderson recalled being 'abysmally ignorant of what a co-operative store was like or how it might succeed', but based on the meeting he offered to assist Plunkett in his new work.[48] Anderson went on to forge a close working relationship with Plunkett throughout his life and served as the IAOS's first Secretary. Second, Plunkett's visit to the south-west of Ireland exposed him to the condition of the country's dairying heartlands. Anderson described this as the moment when Plunkett realised the problems that faced Irish dairying. Although then 'uninformed of the great revolution which had begun in Scandinavia, he divined the cause of the Irish dairying *débacle* and had designed a remedy for it'. The proximity of the CWS creamery in Drumcollogher awakened Plunkett's interest in the potential that co-operative creameries possessed for the improvement of rural Ireland and provided Plunkett with the raw material that became his 'more ambitious programme'.[49] From this point onward, the creamery society became the primary vehicle for the expansion of Irish co-operation. As Plunkett's enthusiasm for the spread of creameries grew the example of Denmark moved evermore to the fore. In an address to the dairy farmers of Ireland, he cited Denmark as the important influence: 'To the organisation of Co-operative Creameries [in Ireland] is largely due the success of the Danish butter, the most formidable rival of our own product in the English markets.'[50]

During 1890, Plunkett travelled throughout Ireland to encourage farmers to take on the responsibility of organising and administering their own creamery. On 28 April 1890, he drove with Anderson to Buttevant, County Cork, to convince the committee of a joint stock creamery, then in construction, to convert the business into a co-operative affair: 'Hard work. But the seed was sown, as the missionaries say.'[51] In these early years of organisation, the workload of promotion fell upon the shoulders of Plunkett and Anderson, as the pair visited districts

across the country to address meetings of local farmers about the benefits attached
to establishing their own creamery. Despite his 'halting delivery' the substance
of his speeches remained 'admirable, clear, and logical' as he expanded upon
co-operative principles and how they would be applied. Anderson in turn offered
advice on how to arrange finance, milk payments and duties for the committee.[52]
Despite the limited resources at their disposal, the employment of a few organisers
trained to conduct visits and expound on the virtue of co-operation did draw
results. After five years, thirty-three co-operative dairy societies existed – all
located in the dairying heartland of the south-west.[53]

The Irish Agricultural Organisation Society

The year 1894 remains a landmark year in the emergence of the modern Irish
nation-state. The foundation of the IAOS saw an immediate professionalisation
of efforts to reorganise rural society and spread the co-operative principle. The
IAOS provided a locus of leadership for a growing movement of agricultural
societies and proposed a direction for future growth informed by the study of
co-operation in other countries. At the well-attended inaugural meeting held on
the 18 April 1894 at the Antient Concert Rooms in Dublin, Plunkett addressed
an audience drawn from a cross-section of influential Irish society: the Lord
Mayor of Dublin; members of the Anglo-Irish gentry; leading industrialists and
business people; and representatives from other state and voluntary organisations.
Letters of support from the likes of the Catholic Archbishop of Dublin and
Nationalist MPs signalled initial widespread support for the venture. Plunkett's
speech that day offered a manifesto for rural renewal. He set out that the IAOS
represented a 'new departure in the development of our national resources' – one
which dealt directly 'only with the rural population of Ireland. I proceed upon
the assumption that the chief wealth of Ireland thus limited is, and must ever
be, almost agricultural.' Plunkett argued that agriculture could only achieve the
necessary transformation if farmers acted in combination with one another. The
influence of Scandinavia, Germany and Russia was highlighted as Plunkett
emphasised that the IAOS looked to 'bring to the help of those whose life is
passed in the quiet of the field the experience which belongs to wider opportunities
of observation and a large acquaintance with commercial and industrial affairs'.[54]
The IAOS's role would be to act as an important conduit for new ideas and
agricultural innovations between farmers and the outside world.

The IAOS played a crucial role in shaping the form of co-operation that spread
across Ireland in the following years. The foothold made into the creamery
industry in the first few years provided Plunkett and his supporters with strong
evidence against the idea 'that farmers were incontrovertible atoms'. Instead,
farmers were capable of communitarian organisation. The IAOS would facilitate
this further act of combination through the employment of paid organisers whose

job would be to visit co-operative societies 'and generally to instruct the farming community upon what can be done by co-operation'.[55] Plunkett presided over the IAOS and Robert Anderson provided able administrative assistance as the Secretary. The Jesuit economist, Fr Thomas Finlay, joined the executive as Vice-President and offered the movement a public association with a leading intellectual voice from the Catholic Church. George William Russell, better known as Æ, joined the IAOS, first as an organiser, and worked as editor of the movement's weekly newspaper the *Irish Homestead*. The newspaper played an important role in the propagandist aspect of the IAOS and provided a forum for Æ – a polymath poet, theosophist and co-operative economist from Lurgan, County Armagh – to develop his own theories and practices of co-operative action for Ireland. The *Homestead* frequently published literary pieces that placed it firmly within the wider firmament of cultural revivalism. Most importantly, the newspaper circulated ideas about how to create a more co-operative economy, and debates of a social and political nature played out in its pages.

Organisation became the watchword of the co-operative movement and the IAOS acted as an important harbinger of Irish modernity as it strove to reorganise the countryside. The IAOS embarked upon the creation of a detailed study of the countryside as it strove to know as much about the rural population and its socio-economic conditions as possible. The IAOS's annual reports contained a reservoir of information related to each co-operative society. The publication of individual society accounts created a transparent audit of agricultural activity on a national level. These reports also included minutes of Annual General Meetings, membership figures for each society, and a statistical breakdown for co-operation in each county.[56] The IAOS tracked social and economic trends affecting the produce that its members dealt in, which allowed organisers to provide precise instructions and market intelligence to help co-operative farmers prosper. In addition, the IAOS mapped and detailed an extraordinary amount of detail about economic activity across the countryside (see figure 1.1). Sat at the apex of a network of co-operative societies, the IAOS generated an insight into the condition of life, work and productivity, which could be used to direct targeted interventions towards individual societies when required. This information could also be utilised by government departments, which is what eventually occurred.

The co-operative movement asserted itself as a force for progress. The movement's leaders saw the IAOS as a means to 'fulfil their role as cultural and intellectual leaders'. One outcome of contemporary land reforms was that various social and cultural actors from Anglo-Irish backgrounds asserted their relevance as moral leaders in lieu of the connection between landlord and tenant that had prevailed in the nineteenth century. The IAOS represented one way in which a farmer might be morally reconstituted as a 'noble peasant of the cultural revival'.[57] Plunkett's social status led to accusations that he served as a representative of the

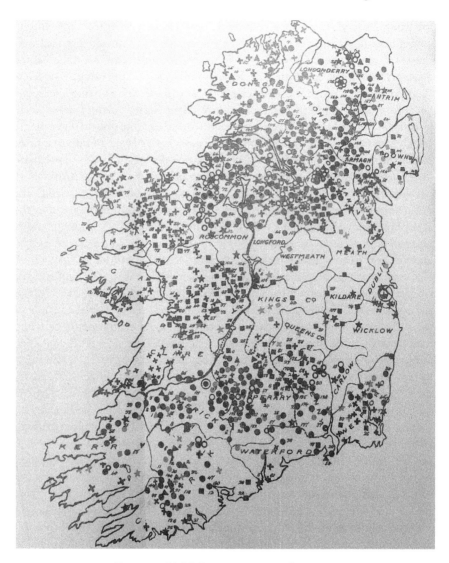

Figure 1.1 IAOS Co-operative network in 1902
Dairy and agricultural societies ●
Auxiliaries ○
Agricultural societies ■
Co-operative banks ✚
Poultry societies ▲
Miscellaneous ★
Federations ◉
Societies registered prior to 31 December 1902 are printed in black.
Societies formed during 1903 are printed in grey.

landlords in their attempt to assert moral leadership over farmers. Having Fr Thomas Finlay on side helped to counter criticisms from some nationalists that the IAOS represented a front for continuing traditional Anglo-Irish influence. Furthermore, members of the Catholic clergy helped to establish the co-operative movement at a local level. Parish priests and curates played an important brokerage role when they worked to create local support for a proposed creamery or credit society. In effect, the IAOS formed a site for a new co-operative élite to discuss the implications of its movement's project.

Keen observers of rural developments outside Ireland watched the unfolding agrarian experiment taking place with great interest. The IAOS represented one of the most prominent agrarian development organisations on the international stage at the start of the twentieth century – a point emphasised further by its almost unique stature within the Anglophone world. The attention and treatment given to questions of rural economy and agricultural modernisation meant that the Irish movement played a key role in influencing the establishment of similarly focused movements elsewhere. On the IAOS's twentieth anniversary, Horace Plunkett referred to the organisation as the 'parent' of similar bodies that had been founded in England and Scotland, as well as in the United States and Finland.[58] Finnish farmers proved to be among the first of the new farmers' movements to take their lead from the Irish. The Pellervo Society, founded in 1899, drew heavily upon the precedent set by the IAOS, which its founding president, Hannes Gebhard, admitted to adopting as his model:

> Co-operation in Ireland is of special interest for us, not only because the political position of that country and the poverty of its rural population resemble Finnish conditions, but principally for the reason that the origin and management of the co-operative movement there resemble more closely than those of any other country the origin and development of our own co-operation.[59]

The following year English agriculturalists established the Agricultural Organisation Society 'on the model of the Irish Agricultural Organisation Society',[60] and a Scottish Agricultural Organisation Society followed in 1905.[61]

The IAOS's organisational efforts quickly bore fruit as a sophisticated network of co-operative societies was established by the start of the twentieth century. The IAOS employed a small team of organisers who proved crucial to this process. These organisers' duties shifted from initial work mustering support for a potential society through to guiding the movement's wider development through policing societies. They regularly visited societies, assessed their output, and observed their adherence to IAOS rules. Organisers offered the following services: the provision of architectural and engineering advice; the provision of financial and account-keeping expertise; identifying potential customers; and encouraged the diffusion of new technologies such as farm and dairy machinery. Organisers also attended

local society Annual General Meetings and reported to Dublin on the spirit of
co-operation throughout the districts. The establishment of a co-operative society
encouraged dairy farmers to shed antiquated methods of production, and organisers
reinforced ideal behaviours in order to nurture a co-operative population. When
the IAOS expressed disquiet at the practice of creameries renewing informal
loans to members, it fell to the organiser to discourage this behaviour. In 1907,
for example, the IAOS emphasised that:

> Every effort is being made by our Organisers to discourage this practice ... The
> uses and abuses of credit are being brought home to borrowers both at meetings
> of Societies, and through the Organisers' visits of inspection.[62]

The co-operative society had an innovative effect upon a local community, which
was at once technological and democratic. Robert Anderson highlighted how a
member's attendance at a society meeting made the movement's transformation
instantly apparent. These meetings occurred against the backdrop of modern
buildings that housed the new 'steam-driven separators, butter-workers, and
churns, and all sorts of scientific appliances unavailable to the isolated farmer'.
These rural enterprises were administered by a democratically elected committee, upon which 'the best business-men in the community' sat, whether
'landlord or tenant, Protestant or Roman Catholic, Unionist or Nationalist'.[63]
Often the presence of leading figures on these committees reflected an individual's status within a locality. However, the communal enterprise helped to
introduce technological improvements to many localities through the collective
purchase of machinery. Via the democratic process and governance structures
in place, members theoretically could hold to account those who made business
decisions.

Communication between the IAOS in Dublin and co-operative societies
throughout Ireland formed a central feature of the strategy to nurture a modern
countryside. The role of the IAOS organiser proved vital to the growth of the
movement. The IAOS Secretary, Robert Anderson, recounted that his experience
as an organiser consisted of long, strenuous days in order 'to bring unbeliev-
ing and tight-fisted farmers into the co-operative fold'.[64] Organisers needed
to convince an array of opponents that included shopkeepers, butter traders,
private creamery owners and local politicians who viewed these new businesses
as threats to their own interests.[65] As a result, the organiser became the target of
local opposition to the introduction of co-operative societies and meetings often
descended into boisterous events. At one meeting in County Clare, Anderson
recalled how he fled the village because of threats by local opponents to 'cut
the "livers"' out of him.[66] As examined in later chapters various impediments
stood between the IAOS's blueprint of a fully co-operative agricultural landscape
and the reality of implementation. However, in the immediate aftermath of the
IAOS's foundation the most potent threat to the continued existence of the Irish

movement emanated from another source of co-operative organisational expertise –
the CWS.

The Irish Agricultural Organisation Society and the Co-operative Wholesale Society

The establishment of the IAOS in 1894 represented a seismic shift in the relationship between Irish and British co-operators. Its emergence challenged CWS
interests in Ireland and offered an alternative paradigm for co-operative development. The CWS attempted to organise Irish farmers as suppliers to their co-
operative depots and creameries with the objective of placing the interest of
consumers above producers. Plunkett's effort to establish creameries at the end
of the nineteenth century prioritised the interests and maximised the profits for
the farmer. Plunkett described the IAOS's focus upon the producer as one of
'the newer tendencies in full work in this outpost of the co-operative world'.[67]
It certainly represented one of the most prominent international producer co-
operative movements in the early twentieth century. The IAOS capitalised upon
the opportunity presented by the invention of creamery separators and sought
to re-make the character of Irish farmers by providing access and ownership over
this new technology. The CWS had acquiesced in its role as a butter buyer for
most of the late nineteenth century. However, the modernisation of dairying
combined with the IAOS's emergence as a new force in Irish dairying saw the
CWS assume an enthusiasm for the creamery project and the potential for profit
in butter manufacturing.

A vigorous debate about the future of co-operation in Ireland erupted within
a year of the IAOS's establishment. As the IAOS and CWS began to organise
creameries that placed different emphases on the interests of the farmers a flurry
of correspondence on the issue about how best to organise a co-operative infrastructure over Irish butter production appeared in the pages of the *Co-operative
News*. Henry Youngs, a correspondent from Norwich Co-operative Society in
England, argued that 'it was the *duty* of the Wholesale Board … to carry on the
great work which it has in part proved itself so well able to do, not only in the
collection and distributing of goods … but in the production of same wherever
possible when it is the advantage of its members' (emphasis added). He argued
specifically in relation to the production of butter 'that if this policy is continued,
not only in England but in Ireland we shall all as co-operators be benefitted'. A
letter by Plunkett appeared alongside Youngs in which he offered an alternative
view. Plunkett argued that the 'whole trouble between [the IAOS] and the
Wholesale has … arisen from the fact that co-operators do not understand
farming, and the farming classes do not understand co-operation'. He highlighted
the CWS's failure to organise any farming societies of their own in England as
evidence of this fact. Plunkett believed the IAOS 'can solve this part of the

co-operative problem'. However, he also warned that a rupture between the Irish and British movements appeared unavoidable

> and if the spirit you arouse against us makes it better for us to sever our connection for a while with those who cannot trust us to look after the interests of co-operation in Ireland, I am confident that a few years will find English and Irish co-operators again joining hands across the Channel.[68]

As the IAOS and CWS championed their respective ideas for co-operative dairying, the strained relationship possessed important implications for the continued evolution of co-operation in Ireland that reflected an underlying tension between different co-operative organisations at the international level. In the late nineteenth century co-operative movements emerged across the globe to mediate economic effects upon consumers and producers. In 1895, the International Co-operative Alliance (ICA) was founded to co-ordinate the growth of these national movements. However, from the outset it was clear to onlookers that the CWS drove the direction of travel within this body.[69] The French economist, Charles Gide, noted that agricultural and credit co-operatives, 'frightened by the imperialist ambitions of the consumers' societies, are gradually leaving the [International Co-operative] Alliance'.[70] The IAOS chose to remain outside the ICA. Indeed, the Irish were not alone in this, as producer movements elsewhere failed to integrate into the international organisation. Owing to the ICA's focus on consumers' interests, Irish co-operators concluded that the pursuit of the farmers' interests required the movement to maintain a national focus. The proximity of the CWS more directly affected the IAOS's development as an attendant rivalry, hinted at on the level of international co-operative relations, played out vociferously in the south-west of Ireland.

In the earliest days of creamery organisation, the Irish organisers and the CWS seemingly worked in harmony as they looked to provide farmers with access to creamery separators and an improved product. Now, Irish co-operators retreated from a formal cross-movement alliance with British co-operators and focused more specifically on their movement within a national context. The difference over whether to prioritise the interests of the farmer or the consumer created a philosophical impasse that grew into an irresolvable economic conflict. Robert Anderson later described the resultant economic divergence that occurred in south-western Ireland as 'Civil War'.[71] To dairy farmers, the CWS operated Irish creameries along similar lines to other privately operated creameries – that of an individual supplier to a business with little or no say over how the business was run. Critics held that the CWS encouraged a culture of dependency among Irish dairy farmers who relied upon milk payments from a CWS creamery committee, which they could not hold to account. This stood in stark contrast to farmers who supplied IAOS creameries. These farmers owned the creamery and shared in any profits.[72] The IAOS aimed to safeguard its position as the most important instrument of co-operation in Ireland by exuding a popular appeal capable of countering the huge resources at the disposal of the CWS. The IAOS utilised one of its most potent tools – rhetoric. The agricultural co-operative movement claimed to work for the national interest and the fact the CWS originated from Manchester made it vulnerable to attack in a period of increased nationalistic sentiment. Described by one contemporary as 'avowedly non-political', the IAOS nevertheless employed the discursive tools of Irish nationalism to oust its competition.[73]

Five of the CWS's six pre-1874 trade depots were located in the south-western province of Munster, which is where the economic conflict between the two co-operative bodies played out most viciously. The CWS expanded its size rapidly. In 1897, the CWS employed 91 employees throughout Ireland, of which 38 worked in the creameries.[74] By 1900, 384 CWS employees worked in Ireland and its creameries accounted for 305 of this number.[75] The CWS annual report for that year described the situation with satisfaction:

> The Wholesale has now 35 creameries working, with 28 auxiliaries, chiefly in the south-western counties, and has been very successful in the attempt at butter-making. No expense was spared that the creameries might compete successfully with the well-equipped Danish creameries.[76]

The same report made no mention of the presence of IAOS creameries, which provided a closer competitor than the Danish creameries. By 1900 the number of IAOS creameries competing with the CWS stood at 153, with a further 38 auxiliary societies that captured milk supply from more remote farmers and which they then transported to a central society.[77]

By 1900, the CWS and IAOS were locked into an aggressive competition to organise the dairy industry. The Co-operative Congress, the conference held for all co-operative movements on the British Isles, endorsed the CWS's decision to establish its own creameries in Ireland. In response, the IAOS withdrew their representatives from the Co-operative Union – a body founded to co-ordinate the promotion of all co-operative societies. In August 1901, Plunkett used his address as that year's President of the National Co-operative Festival to justify this decision and their subsequent struggle to control the Irish creamery industry. In front of delegates gathered from across the United Kingdom, Plunkett argued that the British version of creamery organisation offered little in the way of the co-operative spirit when applied to Ireland. Co-operative principles needed to be judged by 'the effect which they produce upon the character of the individual and the extent to which they elevate the social and improve the material well-being of the community'. On this criterion, the CWS failed to apply co-operation in business with Irish farmers. The creameries operated by the CWS saw 'farmers supply their milk as they do to any other capitalist who gives them their price, but in which they have no share in either management or profit, in which they take no pride, in which they learn no lesson'. The Co-operative Congress's decision to endorse the extension of the CWS in the creamery industry forced the Irish movement into a position of 'co-operative Home Rule'.[78] The speech accused the CWS of failing to act in a co-operative fashion and publicly signalled the deterioration in relations between the Irish and British movements. The *Co-operative News* ran reports of Plunkett's speech 'on the trend of co-operation' as a 'criticism of the English Wholesale Society'.[79] When he reflected on the speech, Plunkett admitted that 'I "went for" the Wholesale Society and it appears that they so absolutely dominate the movement that I may have done so unwisely – perhaps I am in for a libel action'.[80]

The enmity provoked by the economic conflict between the two movements manifested at a local level. County Kerry represented a target area for co-operative extension as it possessed a 90 per cent rural population and formed an integral part of the dairying heartlands.[81] In north Kerry, competition over the milk supply proved fierce, as the struggle to organise the region's dairying sector grew especially aggressive due to extra competition from a robust private creamery sector. However, the IAOS viewed the CWS creameries as the immediate threat due to their description as co-operative enterprises. Charles Riddall, the chief IAOS organiser for the south-west, found the majority of his workload for the 1900s consisted of nullifying the threat posed by the CWS as each movement tried to squeeze the other organisation out of business. The CWS's venture into creamery ownership reached a peak in 1906 when relations between the two movements became critical. At this point, the CWS possessed 38 central creameries and 47 auxiliaries across Ireland, but mainly located in the province of Munster. Nine of these central creameries operated in County Kerry.[82] The number of IAOS creameries continued to rise in the first decade of the twentieth century as it attempted to squeeze out the CWS. In 1900, only five creameries aligned to the Irish movement operated in County Kerry. By 1912, this number stood at 14 (see table 1.1). This seemed small when compared to the number of co-operative creameries in other counties. However, Kerry possessed a higher number of member-owners per society than any other co-operative creamery in Munster. In Kerry, the average number of members per society stood at 125, while the provincial average was 71.

How the co-operative principle ought to be applied to agriculture posed a specific iteration of the Irish Question – whether the principal subject to be considered in economic development plans should be the producer or the consumer. In August 1907 the Vice-President of the CWS, Thomas Tweddell, made his views on the matter clear in a paper entitled 'Co-operation of Consumers' delivered to a meeting of the British Association. Tweddell argued that the organisation of consumers represented the most beneficial form of co-operative organisation. Despite initially stating that time prevented him from concentrating upon co-operative production, Tweddell broke away from his putative subject to comment

Table 1.1 Provincial statistics for IAOS creameries

Province and county	No. of IAOS creameries	No. of shareholders on 31 December 1912	Lbs. of butter made
Clare	1	99	74,306
Cork	21	876	1,589,479
Kerry	*14*	*1,749*	*2,363,799*
Limerick	55	3,258	9,591,092
Tipperary	51	4,150	6,719,417
Waterford	2	128	151,576
MUNSTER	**144**	**10,260**	**20,489,669**

Source: IAOS, *Annual Report, 1913.*

upon the Irish situation. The work of the CWS in pursuit of the consumers' interest placed the organisation firmly in a respected historical co-operative tradition as it represented 'Robert Owen's ideal, viz., the abolition of profit in all the wide ramifications of trade'. Tweddell considered it a misfortune, therefore, that instead of concentrating upon this work, their movement, 'should have spent so much of its time and energy in contending and disputing over it instead, but so it has been; this subject has been the Irish question of the Co-operative movement – insoluble, interminable'.[83]

The 'interminable' aspect of this conflict emanated from the IAOS's implicit rejection of consumer-focused economics. The question of where the profits from the butter industry ended up remained a point of contention. One journalist for the *Southern Star* reported on the visit of a CWS deputation from Bristol to examine the butter industry of Ireland and its potential profitability. However, while the deputation enjoyed the profits, the journalist acerbically remarked that 'profits are always made out of somebody'. That 'somebody' included the farmers of counties Limerick, Cork and Kerry who supplied CWS creameries. The author resented the fact that that the CWS described itself as a 'co-operative' business in Ireland and stripped the farmer of profits he might otherwise hold if 'he worked the creamery as a real co-operative concern':

> The fountain which gives forth bitter water as well as sweet is a less misleading institution than the 'co-operative' society which co-operates in Bristol to exploit in Kerry. The only claim the Wholesale has to be co-operative in Ireland is that it co-operates the potential profits of the farmer's industry away from him.[84]

By 1907, any possibility of *détente* between the Irish and British movements grew evermore distant. Knocknagoshel, a village just outside Tralee and close to the CWS depot, provided a practical example of the toxicity that characterised the relationship between the two organisations. That year, the IAOS applied pressure upon the CWS to relinquish control of its creamery in Knocknagoshel to local farmers. This accorded with previous claims by the CWS to relinquish ownership if local farmers demonstrated an appetite to operate their own business.[85] Writing in the *Irish Homestead*, Æ argued that the farmers of Knocknagoshel enjoyed enough cross-community support to establish their own producer-oriented co-operative society, and lobbied the CWS to sell them the local creamery premises. However, the CWS demonstrated no desire to relinquish control. Æ criticised the refusal to sell and branded the CWS as an organisation that, 'only took up the creamery business in Ireland because of the backward state of civilisation'. Æ understood the CWS's modernisation programme as one defined in opposition to the rural project undertaken by the IAOS. He acidly argued that conditions in Kerry showed that 'civilisation is not in such a backward state … and that the creamery might safely be sold to the local farmers without their lapsing back into barbarism'. Furthermore, the dispute at Knocknagoshel allowed Æ to define the CWS as a usurious presence in Ireland: 'Their game – let us put it plainly – has been in Ireland the game played by any gombeen trader, who lets his customers have credit so that they may remain on his books'.[86]

By likening the CWS to traditional enemies of farmers – private interests, publicans and gombeen men – and combining this with their status as an exploiter of Irish producers, Æ and the IAOS crafted a powerful discourse that tapped into popular sentiment that undermined the popular appeal of the CWS. Furthermore, Æ located his attack within a language of nationalism, accusing the CWS of pursuing the 'bondage' of Irish farmers so that 'the English working man may get cheaper butter at our expense'.[87] This binary of producer and consumer helped co-operators define their early twentieth-century Irish subject as something antithetical from the (English) consumer.

IAOS organisers utilised similar arguments to extend their movement's appeal at a local level. In 1907, local farmers had lobbied the Rural District Council to promote a co-operative bacon-curing plant in the north Kerry market town of Listowel in order 'to divert some of the big profits of the Bacon trade here from three or four large firms, into the hands of the producers – the farmers and labourers – and to give employment'.[88] In the end, the plant never materialised due to opposition and in spite of support given by Horace Plunkett.[89] In December 1908, Charles Riddall arrived in Listowel to persuade locals of the benefits of organising their own creamery along IAOS-oriented lines. The local newspaper recorded Riddall's speech to the farmers around Listowel, which made a scathing attack upon the CWS:

> This English Co-operative Society was … thoroughly co-operative in England, but in Ireland it stood on the very same level as a proprietary creamery. In Knocknagoshel, one of the principal points to be got over in regard to the people's connection with the English concern was the fact that the farmers … were tied hand and foot in the English institution, and it then became the task of farmers in that locality to

liberate themselves from the hands of those English persons who came over to Ireland some twenty years ago posing … in many cases as philanthropists, but who had proved to be in many cases the exact opposite.[90]

This verbal assault sounded the decline of the CWS's efforts to organise Irish dairying.

In January 1909, the CWS ceded the co-operative territory around creameries to the IAOS, having shared 'the common experience of those Englishmen who seek to pave the bogs of Ireland with good intentions'.[91] By the end of that decade, the CWS ceased establishing creameries and sold off most of its concerns to local farmers or creamery proprietors retaining only three creameries and six auxiliaries.[92] In Knocknagoshel, farmers assumed control of the local creamery premises. Riddall argued that the prosperity of Irish farmers relied upon their 'liberation' from an English institution, thereby linking the IAOS and co-operative farmers in Kerry to larger processes of social change and intensified nationalism that underpinned this period. The outcome of this conflict held important consequences for the continued development of co-operative organisation in Ireland. The IAOS became bound up within economic debates about what direction to take national development. The idealisation of the Irish producer as opposed to the British consumer affected not only the development of the Irish co-operative movement, but also the entire socio-economic development of Ireland.

Throughout the 1890s, the CWS established creameries in Ireland that privileged the interests of consumer-members over those of farmer-producers. Percy Redfern, the CWS's official historian, wrote in 1913 in summation of this situation that 'the CWS sought to provide the English co-operative consumer with a British-made alternative equal in quality to Danish butter'. By establishing creameries in Ireland, the CWS hoped to become less reliant on purchasing highly priced butter from Denmark through the organisation and control of the means of production in Ireland. Such a policy, the IAOS maintained, did not serve the interests of their members. In a sign that the competition between the CWS and the IAOS still rankled, Redfern characterised the IAOS position as one in which:

> The [CWS] was charged with desiring to make of the Irish 'a stick to beat the Danes.' Irishmen have not the character of being averse to sticks and beatings, but in this case they wanted for themselves as producers the full rewards of victory.[93]

Throughout the early twentieth century, the co-operative movement played a prominent role in the conception and definition of the Irish nation – in particular the economics of the Irish nation. The crucial outcome in the economic war between the CWS and the IAOS resided in the fact that in championing its own model of economic co-operation, the IAOS made the Irish farmer-producer the central economic unit of its plans for co-operative development. Moreover, the economic arguments made by IAOS employees fed into a wider nationalist critique that existed outside the traditional forums of parliamentary debates around Home Rule and political autonomy. As shown in their speeches, Irish co-operative organisers frequently deployed a nationalist-infused rhetoric when they appealed to farmers to establish a co-operative society along the IAOS principle rather than the CWS. As the two co-operative organisations strove for dominance of the creamery sector, the IAOS's support for rural producers led to a differentiation in Irish and English identities primarily articulated in the sphere of economics. The efforts to establish itself as the pre-eminent co-operative movement among the Irish farmers proved to be a time-consuming and costly challenge for the IAOS in its formative years. However, it faced many other challenges to promote its co-operative movement across rural Ireland – but despite this the IAOS also managed to build an institutional legacy that helped to establish a long-term developmental plan for a new and modern Ireland.

Notes

1 Horace Plunkett, 'The Irish Agricultural Organisation Society, Limited – What it is and What it Does', in Irish Agricultural Organisation Society, *Annual Report, 1895* (Dublin: Sealy, Bryers and Walker, 1895), 17–18 (p. 17).

2 James C. Scott, *Seeing Like a State: How Certain Schemes to Improve the Human Condition Have Failed* (London: Yale University Press, 1998).

3 Horace Plunkett, *Ireland in the New Century: with an Epilogue in Answer to Some Critics* (London: John Murray, 1905), 40–41.

4 Plunkett, *Ireland in the New Century*, 44–45.

5 Mary E. Daly, *The Famine in Ireland* (Dundalk: Dundalgen Press, 1986); James S. Donnelly, Jr, *The Great Irish Potato Famine* (Stroud: Sutton, 2001). Cormac Ó Gráda, *Black '47 and Beyond: The Great Irish Famine in History, Economy, and Memory* (Princeton: Princeton University Press, 1999).

6 K. Theodore Hoppen, *Governing Hibernia: British Politicians and Ireland 1800–1921* (Oxford: Oxford University Press, 2016), 128.

7 Enda Delaney, 'Our Island Story? Towards a Transnational History of Late Modern Ireland', *Irish Historical Studies*, 37 (2011), 599–621 (pp. 601–602).

8 Sarah Roddy, *Population, Providence and Empire: The Churches and Emigration from Nineteenth-Century Ireland* (Manchester: Manchester University Press, 2014).

9 Barbara Lewis Solow, *The Land Question and the Irish Economy* (Cambridge, Mass.: Harvard University Press, 1971), 171–173.

10 Joanna Bourke, *Husbandry to Housewifery: Women, Economic Change and Housework in Ireland, 1890–1914* (Oxford: Clarendon Press, 1993), 85.

11 Kevin O'Rourke, 'Property Rights, Politics and Innovation: Creamery Diffusion in pre-1914 Ireland', *European Review of Economic History*, 11 (2007), 395–417.

12 Ingrid Henriksen, 'Avoiding Lock-In: Co-operative Creameries in Denmark, 1882–1903', *European Review of Economic History*, 3.1 (1999), 57–78; Ingrid Henriksen and Kevin H. O'Rourke, 'Incentives, Technology and the Shift to Year-Round Dairying in Late Nineteenth Century Denmark', *Economic History Review*, 58.3 (2005), 520–554.

Cormac Ó Gráda, *Ireland: A New Economic History, 1780*–1939 (Oxford: Clarendon Press, 1994), 259–262.

13 Hoppen, *Governing Hibernia*, 219–222; Virginia Crossman, *Politics, Pauperism and Power in Late Nineteenth-Century Ireland* (Manchester: Manchester University Press, 2006); Ó Gráda, *Black '47 and Beyond*, 104–114.

14 Terence Dooley, 'Land and Politics in Independent Ireland, 1923–1948: The Case for Reappraisal', *Irish Historical Studies*, 34.134 (2004), 175–197; Dooley, *'The Land for the People': The Land Question in Independent Ireland* (Dublin: University College Dublin Press, 2004).

15 Plunkett, *Ireland in the New Century*, 44.

16 NLI, Ms 49,803/44/2, Horace Plunkett to Fr Finlay, December 1909,

17 Plunkett, *Ireland in the New Century*, 44.

18 Joseph Lee, *The Modernisation of Irish Society, 1848–1918*, 3rd edn (Dublin: Gill & Macmillan, 2008).

19 Ó Gráda, *Ireland: A New Economic History*, 259.

20 Senia Paseta, *Before the Revolution: Nationalism, Social Change and Ireland's Catholic Élite, 1879–1922* (Cork: Cork University Press, 1999), 153.

21 Paul Bew, *Enigma: A New Life of Charles Stewart Parnell* (Dublin: Gill & Macmillan, 2012), chapters 6 and 7.

22 Alvin Jackson, *Home Rule: An Irish History, 1800–2000* (Oxford: Oxford University Press, 2003), 80–85.

23 P.J. Mathews, *Revival: the Abbey Theatre, Sinn Féin, the Gaelic League and the Co-operative Movement* (Cork: Cork University Press, 2003).

24 Mathews, *Revival*, p. 30.

25 Augusta Gregory, 'Ireland, Real and Ideal', *Nineteenth Century*, 44.261 (1898), 769–782 (pp. 771–773); Mathews, *Revival*, p. 5; John Hutchinson, *The Dynamics of Cultural Nationalism: The Gaelic Revival and the Creation of the Irish Nation State* (London: Allen & Unwin, 1987).

26 Stephen Gwynn, *Ireland* (London: Ernest Benn, 1924), 118–119.

27 Plunkett, *Ireland in the New Century*, p. 32.

28 Conrad M. Arensberg, *The Irish Countryman*, 2nd edn (Garden City, New York: Natural History Press, 1968); Conrad Arensberg and Solon T. Kimball, *Family and Community in Ireland*, 2nd edn (Gloucester, Massachusetts: Peter Smith, 1961); Anne O'Dowd, *Meitheal: A Study of Co-operative Rural Labour* (Dublin: Comhairle Bhéaloideas Éireann, 1981); Breandán Mac Suibhne, *The End of Outrage: Post-Famine Adjustment in Rural Ireland* (Oxford: Oxford University Press, 2017), 97–98.

29 Vincent Geoghegan, 'Robert Owen, Co-operation and Ulster in the 1830s', in *Politics and the Irish Working Class, 1830–1945* (Houndmills, Basingstoke: Palgrave Macmillan, 2005), 6–26; E.T. Craig, *An Irish Commune: The History of Ralahine* (Dublin: M. Lester, 1920).

30 James Connolly, *Labour in Ireland: Labour in Irish History; The Re-conquest of Ireland* (Dublin: Maunsel & Roberts Ltd, 1922), 143.

31 Henriksen, 'Avoiding Lock-In'; Thomas O'Donnell, *A Trip to Denmark* (Dublin: Gill & Macmillan, 1908); Ó Gráda, *Ireland*, 259–262.

32 Henry W. Wolff, *People's Banks: A Record of Social and Economic Success*, 3rd edn (London: P.S. King and Son, 1910 [1893]), 558.

33 Anthony Webster, 'Building the Wholesale: The Development of the English CWS and British Co-operative Business 1863–90', *Business History*, 54.6 (2012), 883–904.

34 CWS, *Annual 1897* (Manchester: CWS, 1897), 16.

35 *Co-operative News*, 23 May 1874, cited in Percy Redfern, *The Story of the CWS: The Jubilee History of the Co-operative Wholesale Society Limited. 1863–1913* (Manchester: CWS, 1913), 95.

36 Redfern, *Story of the CWS*, 95–96.

37 Carla King, 'The Early Development of Agricultural Co-operation: Some French and Irish Comparisons', in *Proceedings of the Royal Irish Academy: Archaeology, Culture, History, Literature*, 96C. 3 (1996), 67–86 (p. 70).

38 Lawrence M. Woods, *Horace Plunkett in America: An Irish Aristocrat on the Wyoming Range* (Norman, Oklahoma: Arthur H. Clarke Co., 2010).

39 NLI, Horace Plunkett Diary, 24 January 1889.

40 John F. Wilson, Anthony Webster and Rachel Vorberg-Rugh, *Building Co-operation: A Business History of the Co-operative Group, 1863–2013* (Oxford: Oxford University Press, 2013), 34–42.

41 Horace Curzon Plunkett, 'Co-operative Stores for Ireland', *Nineteenth Century*, 24.139 (1888), 410–418 (p. 411).

42 T.A. Finlay, 'Agricultural Co-operation in Ireland', *Economic Journal*, 6.22 (1896), 204–211 (p. 205).

43 Horace Plunkett Diary, 9 June 1889.

44 Horace Plunkett Diary, 10 June 1889.

45 Horace Plunkett Diary, 18 July 1889.

46 Horace Plunkett Diary, 21 November 1889.

47 Patrick Bolger, *The Irish Co-operative Movement: Its History and Development* (Dublin: Institute of Public Administration, 1977), 59.

48 R.A. Anderson, *With Horace Plunkett in Ireland: The Co-op Organisers' Story* (London: Macmillan and Co., 1935), 1–2.

49 Anderson, *With Horace Plunkett*, 6–7.

50 Horace Curzon Plunkett, *Co-operative Dairying: an Address to the Farmers of the Dairy Districts of Ireland* (Manchester: Co-operative Union Limited, 1890), 6–7.

51 Horace Plunkett Diary, 28 April 1890.

52 Anderson, *With Horace Plunkett*, 12.

53 IAOS, *Annual Report, 1895* (Dublin: Sealy, Bryers and Walker), 11.

54 'Irish Agricultural Organisation Society', *Irish Times*, 19 April 1894, 5.

55 Horace Plunkett, 'The Aims of the Co-operative Movement (1894)', in Declan Kiberd and P.J. Mathews (eds), *Handbook of the Irish Revival: An Anthology of Irish Cultural and Political Writings 1891–1922* (Dublin: Abbey Theatre Press, 2015), 90.

56 For example see, IAOS, *Annual Report, 1914*, appendices.

57 Leeann Lane, '"It is in the Cottages and Farmers' Houses that the Nation is Born": Æ's "Irish Homestead" and the Cultural Revival', *Irish University Review*, 33.1 (2003), 165–181 (p. 167).

58 Irish Agricultural Organisation Society, *Report of the Irish Agricultural Organisation Society for the period from 1st July 1914 to the 31st March 1915* (Dublin: The Sackville Press, 1916), 40.

59 Hannes Gebhard, *Co-operation in Finland* (London: Williams and Norgate, 1916), 35.
60 'Agricultural Reform', *Co-operative News*, 19 May 1900, 507.
61 John Morley, *British Agricultural Co-operatives* (London: Hutchinson Bentham, 1975), 20–22; Malcolm Sargent, *Agricultural Co-operation* (Aldershot, Hampshire: Gower, 1982), 18–19.
62 IAOS, *Annual Report, 1907*, 8–9.
63 R.A. Anderson, 'Agricultural Co-operation in Ireland', in *Ireland: Industrial and Agricultural*, ed. by Department of Agriculture and Technical Instruction (Dublin: Brown and Nolan, Limited, 1902), 218–234 (p. 232).
64 Anderson, *With Horace Plunkett*, 30.
65 Líam Kennedy, 'Farmers, Traders and Agricultural Politics in Pre-Independence Ireland', in *Irish Peasants: Violence and Political Unrest, 1780–1914*, ed. by James S. Donnelly Jr and Samuel Clark (Manchester: Manchester University Press, 1983), 339–373.
66 Anderson, *With Horace Plunkett*, 20.
67 Anderson, 'Agricultural Co-operation', 232.
68 Henry Youngs and Horace Plunkett, 'The Wholesale and Irish Agricultural Organisation Society', *Co-operative News*, 29 June 1895, 695–697.
69 Johnston Birchall, *The International Co-operative Movement* (Manchester: Manchester University Press, 1997).
70 Charles Gide, *Consumers' Co-operative Societies* (Manchester: Co-operative Union Limited, 1921), 140.
71 Anderson, *With Horace Plunkett*, 76–85.
72 Louis P.F. Smith, *The Evolution of Agricultural Co-operation* (Oxford: Blackwell, 1961), 195.
73 Stephen Gwynn, *The History of Ireland* (New York: The Macmillan Company, 1923), 492.
74 CWS, *Annual Report, 1899* (Manchester: CWS, 1897), 7.
75 CWS, *Annual Report, 1900* (Manchester: CWS, 1900), 7.
76 CWS, *Annual Report, 1900*, 16.
77 IAOS, *Annual Report, 1899* (Dublin: Sealy, Bryers and Walker, 1899), 9.
78 Horace Plunkett, *The Trend of Co-operation in Great Britain and Ireland* (Dublin; n.p., 1902), 3, 13.
79 'National Co-operative Festival', *Co-operative News*, 24 August 1901, 1023–1024.
80 Horace Plunkett Diary, 16 August 1901.
81 Desmond A. Gillmor, 'Agriculture', *Irish Resources and Land Use*, ed. by D.A. Gillmor (Dublin: Institute of Public Administration, 1979), 109–137 (pp. 119–122); Desmond Gillmor, 'Land and People, *c.*1926', in *A New History of Ireland, Volume VII: Ireland, 1921–84*, ed. by J.R. Hill (Oxford: Oxford University Press, 2003), 62–85 (p. 84).
82 CWS, *Annual 1906* (Manchester: CWS, 1906), 3.
83 CWS, *Annual 1908* (Manchester: CWS, 1908), 140.
84 'Practical Farming: The Profits of Butter-making', *Southern Star*, 4 August 1906, 3.
85 CWS, *Report and Balance Sheet for Half Year Ending June 1903* (Manchester: Co-operative Union, 1903).

86 'Gombeen' is a pejorative term that referred to an individual who made money at other people's expense and misfortune. The term possessed usurious overtones and co-operators applied the term to economic rivals. Peter Gibbon and M.D. Higgins, 'Patronage, Tradition and Modernisation: The Case of the Irish "Gombeenman"', *Economic and Social Review*, 6.1 (1974), 27–44.

87 'Why the Traders Leave the CWS Alone', *Irish Homestead*, 19 January 1907.

88 Kerry Local History Archive (KLHA), Minute Book of Listowel District, Rural District Council, 'Proposed Co-operative Bacon Curing Plant', 31 October 1907.

89 'The Co-operative Movement in North Kerry: The Proposed Bacon Factory', *Kerry Sentinel*, 22 February 1908.

90 'Proposed Co-operative Creamery for Listowel', *Kerry Sentinel*, 2 December 1908.

91 Redfern, *Story of the CWS*, 303.

92 Bolger, *The Irish Co-operative Movement*, 198.

93 Redfern, *Story of the CWS*, 296.

2

A civilisation among the fields

'Co-operation is gradually altering the character of Irish rural life,' Æ opined in a 1905 *Irish Homestead* editorial, 'but we are only at the beginning'. Rural Irish communities possessed the potential to bring about a new type of economy whereby 'everybody and every industry connected with agriculture' formed the foundations of a 'co-operative state'. A far from impartial observer on this matter, Æ envisaged that a co-operative commonwealth might be brought about through the expansion of co-operative societies so they might eventually produce and distribute all goods for market. Æ's work for the IAOS, first as an organiser of credit societies and subsequently *Homestead* editor, trained him to leaven his idealism with pragmatism when it came to the hard work required to win farmers over to the co-operative model. As he wrote: 'we don't believe the last day will come, or any new Jerusalem appear in the heavens until men have made the most there is to be made out of this old world'. The establishment of a co-operative society represented an occasion pregnant with possibility, as it formed a nucleus from which a reinvigorated local community might flourish. At the centre of each village would be 'the co-operative creamery, with the manager's house beside it ... There will be a village hall where committee meetings will be held, lectures delivered, dramatic performances, concerts, and dances.'[1] The dissemination of the co-operative principle among the farmers of Ireland amounted to a concerted attempt to nurture and build a new type of state in Ireland – one incubated within the rural community.

Co-operative activists viewed their task as the creation of a modern, dynamic 'civilisation among the fields', as they looked to conduct social change.[2] This chapter recovers the lost ideological thread of Irish co-operation and argues that the IAOS's influence over the countryside generated new forms of agricultural knowledge and expertise that went on to shape the nature of the Irish state. Under the IAOS's direction, the numbers of co-operative societies increased over the next twenty years – a mixture of co-operative creameries, agricultural stores, credit societies and poultry societies. The resultant portrait of the co-operative movement is one of a voluntary, nominally non-state organisation that exerted considerable influence over the economy and character of an emergent nation-state.

I start with an examination of the IAOS leadership and the focus then moves between the national and local layers of the co-operative movement from the 1890s onwards. In this latter regard, understanding the role of the co-operative organiser is crucial. The IAOS's Executive Committee consisted of landlords, Catholic clergy, industrialists, Unionists and Nationalists. However, the prominence of landlords left the executive vulnerable to criticism in its earliest years, which in turn limited the effectiveness of the organiser in the field. In order for a new society to be established and succeed, it was crucial that support came from across the local community. While the establishment of new societies relied upon the support granted by traditional authority figures such as the priest and landlord, the co-operative society also contributed to the creation of a new social caste of managers and administrators.[3] The work of professional co-operative organisers proved to be of particular importance as these, more than any other individual, shaped the growth of the movement. Organisers constantly moved between the national and local levels of the co-operative organisation and therefore played a critical role in connecting the leadership to the members. They policed individual societies through visits and inspections, communicated new ideas associated with agriculture, and produced reports on individual societies for the Dublin head-quarters. Although few in number organisers acted as the crucial figures that moved between and linked together the network of societies.

The idea that the co-operative principle's introduction offered both an opportunity and means to achieve a positive transformation in the Irish countryside appeared obvious to visitors who wished to understand the peculiar social and political conditions of the country. In autumn 1897, the American Progressive and muckraking journalist, Henry Demarest Lloyd, toured Ireland and Britain to witness the work conducted 'in the field of production by co-operative societies'. Lloyd's fierce reputation as an investigative journalist stemmed from his publication of articles that warned against the dangers of unrestrained corporate power and monopolistic capitalism in the 1880s and 1890s. When Lloyd arrived, he expected scenes that fitted Ireland's reputation as 'the most distressing country in Europe ... with its sad faces by the roadside'. Instead, he encountered a country undergoing profound social change. The economic leadership shown by Plunkett and the IAOS left Lloyd impressed. He credited the improvements he witnessed to 'the light of co-operation ... one now finds Ireland – the land of famines and evictions ... further advanced in the organization of agricultural co-operation than England'.[4] Similarly, Louis Paul-Dubois's 1908 travelogue cited the co-operative movement as a major source for potential national regeneration. The French sociologist viewed the movement as a key agent of education for Irish farmers and emphasised the co-operative movement's role in striving for social improvement. He believed it exerted a positive moral effect upon the population, inculcating values such as discipline, and the powerful notion of 'self-help by mutual help'.[5] This curious social phenomenon of rural co-operation noticed by international visitors such as Paul-Dubois and Lloyd reflected the conscious effort to reorganise Irish society completely, starting with the peasant and moving up through all levels of Irish social and political life.

As Leeann Lane has argued, the IAOS represented one way in which farmers might be morally reconstituted as a 'noble peasant of the cultural revival'.[6] Success in this mission required co-operators to fashion a coalition of interests that carried influence and authority with the rural population. Plunkett summarised this objective with an aphorism later adopted by rural reformers elsewhere: 'better farming, better business, better living'. By this, he meant that 'agriculture must be regarded as an industry, as a business, and as a life'. The most important of these maxims for the co-operative activist was the third. The improvement of agriculture through enhanced farming and business methods mattered as a 'means to better living'. Co-operative activists envisaged an ideal rural community where 'every member ... can be satisfied that remaining on the land does not imply being in the backwater of modern progress'.[7] In the end, supporters believed the IAOS network contained the potential to revitalise rural communities and help prepare a new form of economic organisation to animate the Irish nation.

The national organisation

The IAOS's establishment led to the formation of a new coalition that played a prominent role in the direction of Irish social politics at the end of the nineteenth and early twentieth centuries. Plunkett wanted the IAOS to be a home for those who wanted to harmonise Irish society's diverse interest groups into a practical reality; a place where landlord and farmer, Nationalist and Unionist, rural and urban inhabitants worked towards a common goal of a more co-operative economy. Economic co-operation then, was more than just a business model. It offered a means through which social and political harmonisation might occur. The coalition that grew out of the labours to build a more co-operative country remained in constant flux, owing to the many controversies that affected the co-operative movement. At a local level, the societies under the IAOS umbrella consisted mainly of farmers, but also included landlords, clergy and new authority figures such as creamery managers and itinerant co-operative organisers who linked the co-operative network together.

Horace Plunkett remained intimately associated throughout his life with the organisation he started. He served as the first president of the IAOS from 1894 until his death in 1932, outside of a seven-year period when he served as Vice-President of the Department of Agriculture and Technical Instruction (DATI). Ever the patrician, Plunkett remained an unapologetic defender of the role played by members of the landlord class in the regeneration of Irish soil and society. His faith in the innate moral and intellectual superiority of his class made Plunkett a somewhat problematic leader for a movement committed to the pursuit of non-political interventions. The composition of the IAOS Executive was certainly an obvious target for criticism, although the story proved more complex at a local level. Plunkett's public statements on how landlords needed to retain a leadership role made this case easier. An outcome of land reforms enacted over previous decades saw the connection between tenant farmers and landlords weakened. Plunkett argued that 'the abolition of landlordism, so far from destroying the usefulness of the Irish gentry, really gives them their first opportunity, within the memory of living men, to fulfil the true functions of the aristocracy'. The gentry might no longer claim mastery of the land, but by virtue of their education and wealth they possessed special advantages they should use to promote socially harmonised rural communities in pursuit of common goals.[8]

The repeated assertion of such *noblesse oblige* made it easy for critics of co-operation to attack the IAOS as a site of elitist politicking as Plunkett provided enemies with an easily caricatured stereotype of Irish landlords who looked to assert their superiority over farmers. Certainly, landlords dominated the IAOS leadership. Other members of the landlord class succeeded as IAOS president when Plunkett stepped down to serve as Vice-President of the DATI in 1900 – first Lord Monteagle and then Colonel Nugent Everard – until Plunkett returned to the position once again in 1907.

Despite the prominence given to landlords, the foundation of the IAOS did mark an attempt to fashion a new type of social partnership that ignored traditional lines of sectarian and political identities. Fr Thomas Finlay served as the Vice-President and actively promoted co-operative projects across Ireland. As a recognis-able public intellectual, Finlay lent a cerebral credibility to the movement as he frequently engaged in debates with critics of the co-operative system, offered evidence to parliamentary inquiries on issues such as the provision of rural credit, engaged in labour politics and worked as Professor of Economics at University College Dublin. He also contributed to the vibrant journal culture of that period via a number of publications, as well as conceiving of the *Irish Homestead*. As someone well connected to members of the clergy throughout Ireland and with a reputation as a vocal nationalist Finlay helped to counter criticisms that the IAOS promoted the continuation of traditional Anglo-Irish influence.[9] The make-up of the rest of the IAOS Committee reflected the effort to include a range of political and social opinions as Plunkett aimed to ensure nationalists occupied a place on the Executive. Alongside landlords such as Lord Monteagle and Walter MacMorrough Kavanagh were grandees drawn from the Irish Par-liamentary Party tradition such as Thomas Sexton and Arthur Moore and also included, albeit briefly, the prominent MP and later Nationalist Party leader, John Redmond.[10] However, Redmond resigned his position on the committee after a year when his brother, Willie, replaced him.

Catholicism and co-operation

Plunkett immediately looked to attract the support of the Catholic hierarchy as a crucial step to win over the large numbers of Catholic farmers. An endorsement from the bishops might counter criticisms that the IAOS represented a landlord's league. Plunkett recognised the temporal power of the Catholic clergy during the time he worked for the Congested Districts Board (CDB) and the early years promoting co-operation for farmers.[11] On the eve of the IAOS launch Plunkett aimed to secure the support of Archbishop William Walsh of Dublin for the venture. The timing was propitious. The IAOS's establishment occurred three years after the appearance of Pope Leo XIII's Papal Encyclical, *Rerum Novarum*. Pope Leo pleaded for greater Catholic engagement with social and economic issues. The inequalities created by capitalism and the threat posed by socialism threatened to tear apart modern society and an application of Catholic social teachings was required to mediate between these two forces. In an argument that appealed to the sensibilities of co-operators, *Rerum Novarum* outlined a moral vision in which all classes 'should dwell in harmony and agreement, so as to maintain the balance of the body politic'.[12] This statement accorded with the principle of mutual economic interest across rural classes promoted by the IAOS. In April 1894, Plunkett thanked Walsh for his 'kind support of my new project' and pointed to the IAOS's compatibility with Catholic social teaching when he stated, 'I am sure that the principles we have laid down will harmonise with your Lordship's views upon economic and industrial questions in Ireland.'[13] The support granted to the work of co-operative organisation by prominent religious figures such as Walsh proved to be a useful tool for organisers to combat attacks. For example, in a dispute with a trader opposed to the extension of co-operative dairying in Tralee, Robert Anderson pointed to the fact Archbishop Walsh supported the extension of co-operation when he offered the farmers of Inch, County Wexford, a £100 interest-free loan towards the establishment of a co-operative creamery.[14]

The courting of sympathetic bishops remained part of Plunkett's long-term strategy. In a letter to the Catholic Bishop of Elphin, John Clancy, Plunkett argued that 'the moral and social justification of the co-operative creamery is that its successful working calls for the exercise by the participants in the undertaking of certain qualities which we all wish to promote in Ireland'.[15] In making this point, Plunkett attempted to stress the interest that all parties, both secular and religious, shared in the spread of co-operative businesses. What Plunkett viewed as the development of rural character might also be interpreted as the moral improvement of the bishop's Catholic subjects.

Attitudes towards co-operation among the hierarchy and the clergy proved uneven and remained ambiguous or even hostile. At a meeting of the bishops on 30 April 1895 the question over what extent 'priests should take an active part in the formation of Co-operative Creameries' was discussed. The bishops reached no definitive conclusion except for a deferred decision to prepare a memorandum of guidance at some stage in the future.[16] As an indication of interest in the new movement, Bishop Patrick O'Donnell of Raphoe sat on the early IAOS Executive Committee. O'Donnell had ascended to the bishopric aged 32 and worked previously with Plunkett on the executive of the CDB, where they both shared an interest in ways to regenerate the economy to counteract poverty and emigration. Another important ally in the church was Bishop O'Dwyer of Limerick – a diocese where co-operative creameries managed to spread with great success.[17] At a national level, the support of the clergy for the IAOS helped to broaden the appeal of economic co-operation. Yet tensions between the IAOS and the Church always threatened to surface. Although an architect of the fragile coalition between the Church and co-operative movement, Plunkett also proved himself a liability in upsetting this finely balanced alliance.

Ireland in the new century

Plunkett provided the IAOS's animating spirit but also acted as a weathervane for political controversy. He worked hard to bring along as many shades of political and social opinion behind the banner of the IAOS, but equally showed a tendency to squander this hard-earned goodwill. In 1904, he completed his major literary work, *Ireland in the New Century*. The book's publication became a source of substantial controversy that placed Plunkett and his movement within a maelstrom of highly publicised invective. In this work, one can find a distillation of Plunkett's idiosyncratic social, economic and political views. He offered readers a literary exposition of many of the familiar themes with which he was associated in public, such as emigration, rural decline and the need for a radical approach to agricultural modernisation. No one who followed Plunkett's past statements would have been shocked by his outline of the Irish Question as a social and economic matter rather than a political one. However, one chapter in the book criticised the malign economic effects of the Catholic Church in Ireland. Plunkett argued that a primary motivation for his belief in co-operative organisation resided in its capacity to affect improvement in the character of those whom it incorporated. He contrasted this with a prevalent Irish Catholic culture that prevented progress and denied prosperity. In particular, he criticised the 'excessive and extravagant church-building ... at the expense of poor communities'.[18] Friends recommended Plunkett not to publish this section of the book. Tenacious and convinced of his argument's correctness, Plunkett published the book with the chapter intact. When it appeared, it 'aroused a fierce and sometimes ill-informed controversy'.[19]

The controversy damaged many of the relationships, which Plunkett spent a great deal of time and energy to put in place. Any goodwill that existed between

Plunkett and the IPP's leadership evaporated immediately. John Redmond, who worked fruitfully alongside Plunkett on the Recess Committee of 1896, launched a stinging attack upon the author in March 1904 while on a fundraising tour of the United States. Redmond claimed that Plunkett's plans for an industrial revival in Ireland amounted to 'quackery' and the book represented 'nothing more or less than an insidious effort to undermine the Home Rule movement'.[20] The fallout with the Nationalist leader proved so toxic that Redmond wrote to the IAOS Secretary to 'remove his name from the list of past and present members of the Society … and to assure him that no other use has been made of his name since his resignation'.[21] Thus ended any hope of a rapprochement between the IAOS and the leaders of nationalist sentiment represented by the IPP.

Relations between Plunkett and sympathetic allies in the Church did survive in certain instances. For example, Bishop O'Dwyer's interest in questions about educational provision in Ireland brought him into regular correspondence with Plunkett. However, *Ireland in the New Century* placed a strain on this relationship. Plunkett defended his book to the Bishop of Limerick on the grounds that his 'attitude towards Catholicism has been profoundly misunderstood' and 'any careful reader of my book will see that, in view of the low economic state of our country and its high spiritual aspirations, my desire is to get the Catholic Church recognised as a powerful auxiliary to economic progress'.[22] Perhaps sincere in this view the fact remained that Plunkett's unrestrained criticism of the Church's influence over economic matters belied his undiplomatic side and tendency to provoke hostility. When they met in person, Plunkett found that the book 'made [O'Dwyer] very sore. But he remains generously friendly'.[23] Plunkett also received private expressions of support from Dr Sheehan, the Bishop of Waterford, but 'nothing which could be taken as expressing approval of my views which he admits in private'.[24]

Despite occasions of support, the critical tone of *Ireland in the New Century* primarily unleashed controversy. Fr Barry, parish priest for Oldcastle, County Meath, attacked the book as 'rather the drivel of a charlatan than a university-trained thinker' in the nationalist newspaper, *Freeman's Journal*. He called Plunkett's work 'mean and insidious' and set a template for further attacks from Catholic hierarchy and clergy.[25] Barry's broadside precipitated Cardinal Logue's Pastoral in which the leader of the Irish Catholic Church condemned the book 'though he admits he has not read it'.[26] Several months later, the rector of the Irish College in Rome, Monsignor Michael O'Riordan, responded to the controversial chapter of the book with the epic *Catholicity and Progress in Ireland*, which prolonged the controversy further. The controversy weakened Plunkett's authority at the DATI and provided further ammunition for those critics strongly opposed to the extension of the IAOS and the co-operative movement. Even Bishop O'Donnell, once a prominent champion of the IAOS, grew estranged from the movement as his relationship with Plunkett broke down.[27] As Robert Anderson pithily recalled three decades after its publication, 'it cannot be said that the book made the task for us organisers any easier'.[28]

The Irish Homestead

The IAOS established *The Irish Homestead* to propagandise the objectives and ideas of the co-operative movement. This proved to be a vital medium in countering the effects of bad publicity that co-operation and its advocates attracted. The first issue launched on the 9 March 1895 under Fr Tom Finlay's editorship. Already an experienced editor of journals such as the *Lyceum* and the *New Ireland Review*, he established the *Homestead* with finance obtained by Plunkett. Finlay edited the newspaper for its first two years with the aim to document 'the progress of agricultural co-operation' and provide readers with the unfolding 'chapters of the economic history of Ireland'.[29] The *Homestead* offered readers a lively commentary on a wide range of social and political topics that ranged from instructive pieces on the importance of winter dairying to editorials on the Russian Revolution. The paper maintained an eclectic focus that encompassed national and international news, instruction on innovative farming methods, information about agricultural markets and news about individual societies, as well as literary pages that placed the journal within the contemporary cultural revival. *The Irish Homestead* was a weekly publication to which all societies were encouraged to subscribe as it provided news stories on agricultural innovations in other countries and thereby formed a vital link to a global co-operative forum. In its first years the IAOS subsidised the *Homestead*, but by 1904 the newspaper paid its own way and – besides subscribers from its own societies – attracted an overseas readership in countries such as France, Germany, Finland, Canada, New Zealand and the United States.[30]

The growth of the movement during the 1890s led to conflict with economic opponents who published their attacks in the press. Fr Finlay understood the importance of a newspaper to promote the movement's progress and offer a public rebuke to such attacks in media. For example, a report on 'Horace Plunkett's Disorganization Society' in the *Skibbereen Eagle* described the movement as a 'scheme for the introduction of continental socialism'. The author advised farmers not to support the IAOS, which amounted to 'a mockery, a delusion, a snare' whose 'plain object' was 'to abolish shopkeepers, pig-buyers, cattle-dealers and the like'.[31] The first editorial explained that the decision to publish a new journal stemmed from the fact that 'there is hardly any interest worth representing before the public which has not its organ in the Press ... A movement which is not supported by its own newspaper is in danger of being thought insignificant. If it cannot publish its message through the medium of its own press, it is in danger of not being listened to at all.'[32] The establishment of a co-operative society undoubtedly affected the interests of these listed professions as they were intended to act as a point for farmers to purchase farming necessities at wholesale prices and a means through which to sell their produce to customers at value closer to retail price. As outlined in the first issue of the *Homestead*:

> No new movement of importance can make way without provoking hostility. It must necessarily affect the privileges of existing interests, and must expect to be denounced accordingly ... We take it as a sign of its progress that [the co-operative movement] is vehemently condemned by certain critics who have no share in its benefits. And we are prepared to gauge its progress by the violence of its opponents.[33]

Several editors worked on the paper in the decade before Plunkett appointed Æ to carry out the duty in August 1905. Æ brought to the task an intellectual curiosity and poetic sensibility that made him an ideal candidate for the propagandist role. As recollected by George Moore in his irreverent memoir *Hail and Farewell*, Plunkett came to understand that 'a poet was necessary. ... If they could get a poet with some knowledge of detail (Plunkett reserved the right to dream to himself), the country might be awakened to the advantages of co-operation.' W.B. Yeats introduced Plunkett to the 'poet-accountant' who then offered Æ a job as an organiser of credit societies. Æ accepted, along with the present of a bicycle.[34] Æ's grounding in the IAOS's practical work, in which he travelled across Ireland on his bicycle, made him intimately familiar with the conditions of rural Ireland, which intensified his belief in the necessity for a co-operative reorganisation of the economy. However, Æ's most important work for the IAOS occurred during his time at the helm of the *Irish Homestead*, which continued until the journal's incorporation within the *Irish Statesman* in 1922. His organisational experience grounded the theorising and arguments about Irish social affairs, economics and politics with which he filled the *Homestead's* pages. Under Æ's editorship, the *Irish Homestead* became a key part of the IAOS's strategy to promote its message among current and potential supporters. As Nicholas Allen observed, while Plunkett conceived of the *Homestead* as a platform to further the ideals of co-operation 'Russell's genius was to make this task intrinsic to a commentary on Irish life'.[35]

Co-operation and the changing role of women

The *Homestead* proved a highly provocative paper under Æ's editorship. One area in which he used the *Homestead* to spark a public debate was on the role of women in efforts to reorganise the countryside. The spread of the co-operative movement played a significant role in redrawing the working lives of rural women. In its earlier years the IAOS concentrated upon the spread of its societies, particularly creameries, and found little space to discuss and debate the transformations the co-operative system exerted upon the role of female labour. Throughout the nineteenth century, butter production was primarily a female-dominated industry. Production occurred in the home where it was either consumed or sold on to butter merchants. The introduction of creameries in the late nineteenth century immediately lowered female employment, with the co-operative system heavily implicated in the shift of butter making from a domestic industry into the new modern separating factory at the heart of a parish. Women remained largely absent within the labour structure of the creamery, rarely held a position on the committees, and were in a tiny minority of named shareholders. In effect, the introduction of the creamery very quickly converted the practice of butter making into a masculine occupation.[36]

In 1908, a damning indictment of the IAOS's failure to address the issue of female rural employment came from a former supporter of the movement. Fr Terence Connolly of Manorhamilton provided evidence to a royal inquiry in which he apologised for his role in starting co-operative creameries, on account of the fact he and others who supported the creamery failed to provide an alternative source of employment: 'where a girl was deprived of the industry of churning … the idea was that she … would be turned over at once to a cottage industry like lacemaking or sprigging or something of that kind. I think the issue has not been sufficiently followed up.'[37]

The poultry industry represented another source of traditional female employment affected by the efforts to reorganise the countryside's economy. Poultry work was often a secondary occupation for the farm wife but it provided an important income stream. Joanna Bourke has highlighted an increase in poultry rearing between 1901 and 1911 by almost 20 per cent.[38] However, these efforts to reorganise the poultry aspect of Irish agriculture often occurred without reference or regard to the interests of women. Women interpreted the IAOS's promotion of poultry co-operative societies as a means to convert egg production into another sphere of masculine influence. As Robert Anderson admitted in a speech delivered at the DATI's Poultry Conference in 1911, the IAOS:

> was stupid enough to ignore the women and to attempt to secure an egg supply to a society composed of 'mere men.' In its early days (and we are still, alas! In those early days) every form of co-operative organisation came in for trade opposition. The Poultry-keepers' Societies were no exception to the rule. The womenkind resented the invasion of their domain by the men, and their passive resistance provided the egg dealers with the best possible weapon wherewith to attack this particular form of 'Plunkettism.'[39]

Some co-operative societies offered limited employment roles as dairymaids, as shown in the photograph of the staff at Achonry Co-operative Society (figure 2.1). However, competition for positions proved fierce and a potential employee needed to demonstrate excellent credentials in order to avail of these opportunities. Sometimes those who applied for these positions did so out of frustration borne of a lack of work opportunities elsewhere. However, these positions remained scarce and could not meet the demand that existed among young women to move into employment. Debra Lyons of Dromahair, County Leitrim, had waited

Figure 2.1 Employees outside Achonry Co-operative Creamery, ca. 1909

four years for an appointment as a female warder in the Irish prisons service but, owing to high demand in that sector, desired to retrain in dairying at Glasnevin. As she lacked the experience and money to enter the Glasnevin training institute she wrote to Josslyn Gore-Booth with his 'great interest in creameries' for help to obtain a position as an assistant dairymaid so that she might gain experience and income to support her application for the next intake. She explained that her father had died and she had no brother, and only she and two sisters lived on the farm. Enclosed testimonials from the local parish priest, rector, magistrate and Justice of the Peace acknowledged Lyons's 'steady, prudent, and industrious' character, but also suggested that the pursuit of such positions remained highly competitive and open only to those who could demonstrate a certain level of social respectability.[40]

Despite the inroads made by the creamery system, its concentration in the major dairying regions of Counties Limerick, Tipperary, Kilkenny, Sligo, Cavan, Monaghan, Cork, Leitrim, Kerry and Waterford meant that areas remained where the practice of home dairying continued into the twentieth century. The persistence of this older method of production provided scope for a leading female role in shaping the terms of modern butter production outside of the creamery system. During the 1900s, the DATI (see chapter 3) employed dairy instructors to travel to areas where hand dairying still proliferated. An instructor demonstrated modern methods in butter preparation to her audience, but as well as this, she performed an important role in the dissemination of public health information. The spread of tuberculosis remained a constant source of anxiety across Ireland throughout the early twentieth century and public health experts viewed the dairy industry as one culprit in the spread of that disease. Ellie Doyle was one such instructor who lectured dairymaids on how to manufacture and improve the quality of butter produced in the home so that they might compete with foreign butter producers. Doyle also provided instructive examples about how easily diseases like tuberculosis tainted milk and became 'very rapidly disseminated by the agency of impure milk; and how in each and every act performed by the dairymaid, the most scrupulous attention to cleanliness should be rigidly observed'.[41]

The role of women within the co-operative movement moved to centre stage following the publication of Æ's article 'Migration of Irishwomen from the Farm'. In that piece Æ asked his readers to consider the reasons why Irish women emigrate from the countryside and controversially observed that 'while man's voice is uplifted loudly announcing his grievances, woman's voice is silent … In Ireland women have hardly ever appeared on the political platform or added their diagnosis of what is wrong with us to the Irish man's loudly expressed tribulations.'[42] The article prompted a vocal response from female readers who castigated Æ for speaking 'blather' with the added rejoinder 'cheap talk is what you are best at these times'.[43] In April 1910 one correspondent, Ellice Pilkington, responded to Æ's provocation with a hope 'that you won't close your columns to "fair, fierce women," while you keep them open to – fierce men, who try to annihilate you. A great step is gained already as you are prepared to grant us "equality"'.[44]

Later that year, Pilkington availed herself of an opportunity to address that year's IAOS conference on the women's question in the rural economy. The organisation, United Irishwomen (UI) was founded in the aftermath to direct the support women could offer to the extension of the co-operative movement. The first meeting of the new body took place in Bree, County Wexford on 30 September and Anita Lett was elected the first president.[45] The UI aimed to work to prevent the continuation of female emigration out of Ireland. In a statement of the UI's working objectives, Pilkington argued along lines expressed by Plunkett in the past that the rural population 'must remain on the land, happily occupied, well employed, socially and intellectually developed. Here is permanent work for women to do.'[46] Pilkington viewed the UI as an auxiliary organisation to the IAOS and did not perceive of the role of the female in society in any revolutionary sense. Instead, she argued that among the UI 'none of us aspired to reform society or preach any gospel but that of domestic economy, good comradeship, and truth'.[47]

The UI did perform important organisational work neglected by the IAOS. Miss Reynolds transferred from the IAOS to become the chief organiser on the UI staff. In this role, she worked to promote a more efficient distribution of milk to districts where 'it is impossible to procure even the most meagre supply for the children and babies, who are fed instead on black tea and bread'. In 1912, Reynolds established a UI branch in Fenit, County Kerry, which established a regular supply of milk for customers guaranteed by a local farmer. The average weekly amount delivered in November of that year was 112 gallons. She also established milk depots in Carlow and Omagh the same year. These depots immediately increased the circulation of milk in these undersupplied areas. In Omagh, the UI report noted that 'women from the country have walked 2 to 3 miles to buy the milk'.[48] In taking up the work of milk supply, instructing members in matters of domestic economy and organising social events, the UI provided another agency in the reorganisation of rural life.

The effect of the co-operative movement upon the culture of female work proved double-edged. On the one hand, the movement contributed to an ongoing process of reducing opportunities for female employment, particularly in dairying. Furthermore, the failure to address the question of female work at the level of the IAOS represented an institutional limitation that reflected the male composition of the movement's leadership. However, this resentment led to a serious if belated engagement with the question of the gendered structure of labour in the rural economy and led to women taking up the blunt and somewhat patronising challenge posed by Æ in the *Homestead*. Despite this genesis, the opportunity to put forward the voice of women within a wider discussion of co-operation was seized by individuals such as Ellice Pilkington. Rural emigration remained a perennial problem, and the UI did little to change a popular perception that women should occupy a supporting role within the farm economy. Yet the foundation of the UI in 1910, although somewhat conservative in its views, represented an important landmark in a gendered approach to resolving socio-economic questions. The organisation's existence, alongside the instructive work of female instructors, showed how women did influence the timbre of farm work, and provided an important platform for women to engage in debates about the condition of rural life.

The IAOS and the generation of knowledge

By the end of the nineteenth century, the co-operative movement established itself as the pre-eminent agent for agricultural modernisation. Despite instances of public outcry levelled at the IAOS on a national level, the movement remained a highly effective agent in promoting its agenda of rural reform. The IAOS's efforts to organise the people and resources of rural Ireland pointed to what Michel Foucault referred to as *raison d'état*. By this he meant 'a practice, or rather the rationalization of a practice, which places itself between a state presented as given and a state presented as having to be constructed and built'.[49] To build an economy in which all future production and distribution would take place through co-operative businesses required the creation of new institutions supplemented with the propagation of new types of knowledge. From its inception the IAOS endeavoured to know as much about the countryside as possible. The IAOS obsessively measured and mapped the increase of co-operative activity in the reports that it published each year. Each report contained a detailed analytical breakdown for individual societies including where they were located, the size of membership, paid-up share capital, available loan capital and turnover. With the information generated, resources and support could be directed throughout the social network to rectify problems and shortcomings with a sophisticated degree of precision. Under Robert Anderson's guidance, a team of organisers, auditors, accountants, engineers and lecturers assisted the staff of the individual societies to ensure their business was administered effectively. As the movement expanded, the more detailed its portrait of rural life became and the more the responsibilities that rested with the IAOS staff grew. The organisers' reports provided the Dublin headquarters with detailed information about the condition of societies throughout Ireland. This allowed the IAOS to map a network of co-operative societies with a statistical breakdown of activity that made these transparent units eligible for purposes of statecraft. The annual reports of co-operative economic activity provided useful progress updates for those interested in the measurement and co-ordination of agricultural activity.

After the establishment of the DATI in 1899, the co-operative movement served as an important ally to state-led efforts aimed at the reform of the rural economy. The IAOS employed agricultural lecturers as part of its team of experts who imparted information about new agricultural techniques to members. Frequent inspections of creameries by organisers provided the IAOS headquarters in Dublin with a detailed snapshot of the condition of co-operative agriculture in practice. Within a few years, the IAOS proclaimed the 'progressive character' of their dairying societies that became centres of a scientific and rational approach to agricultural production: 'lectures given to Dairy Societies are crowded, the ordinary general meetings are well attended, experimental work is carefully watched, and its teaching intelligently applied'.[50] The close relationship between the DATI and IAOS embodied by Horace Plunkett's leadership caused problems for the co-operative movement as it came under attack from traders, private creamery proprietors and Nationalist politicians who accused Plunkett of an abuse of power.[51] Nevertheless, in the first six years of the DATI's existence, the IAOS's prominence in agricultural politics grew to such a level that it appeared inseparable from the Department.

Co-operative efforts in agrarian education produced important results over time and helped to foster a particular type of expertise focused around the site of the local co-operative creamery or agricultural society. Before the DATI started work the IAOS delivered a great deal of the technical instruction in agricultural matters, with instructors sent out to provide lessons on butter making, egg production, poultry rearing and other matters. This educational function of co-operation predated the DATI's work and the state department for agriculture represented an extension of the type of scientific progress pioneered by the IAOS – albeit an extension backed by public funds. This technical instruction continued after the DATI's establishment and the IAOS continued to disseminate information through the publication of leaflets. During 1903–04, the IAOS published eleven different leaflets, addressing a number of topics relevant to farmers' business. The subjects included information to encourage the building up of co-operative trade federations, cleanliness in the dairy, instructions on taking minutes and account keeping, and advice for the management committees. The instructive literature also contributed to the growing literature in the Irish language. That same year an Irish essay competition took place, in which participants wrote on the subject of co-operation, with the winning entry translated into English for the benefit of non-Irish speaking members.[52] The educational impulse attached to the extension of co-operative farming allowed for the dissemination of farming methods to be trialled in a way that complemented later state expansion in the same field.

If the IAOS can be described as exhibiting a *raison d'état* then the chief figure in the performance of this was the organiser. The IAOS organiser proved vital to the growth of the movement. The demands placed upon the IAOS's limited financial resources meant that the body found itself 'compelled to refuse applications for organisers in many instances'. Nevertheless, from the outset organisers proved crucial to the achievement of the movement's sense of mission. When funds improved, the IAOS aimed to increase numbers of organisers 'to give the young Societies all the help needed during the first year or two, and to superintend the organisation of new societies'.[53] In its first twelve months, the IAOS's organisers addressed 315 meetings, out of which thirty-four societies were established.[54] Plunkett addressed the fifth annual conference of the IAOS, satisfied with the figure of 40,000 farmers who 'accepted the self-help doctrine we have preached'.[55]

The work to establish a new co-operative society started with an organiser's visit to address a local meeting of farmers and argue for the benefits of co-operation in business. This work required patience, tenacity and a thick skin as organisers faced a spectrum of interests opposed to the establishment of co-operative creameries or credit societies. These opponents included shopkeepers, butter merchants, private creamery owners and local politicians who viewed these new businesses as threats to their livelihoods.[56] The co-operative organiser aimed to reorganise the countryside by encouraging farmers to act in concert to protect one another from the threat of these so-called 'gombeen-men'. The organiser's identification of the presence of an exploitative class in the Irish countryside mirrored a trope repeatedly found in the writings of Irish cultural revivalists. John Millington Synge unflatteringly characterised this class of individual in a letter to his friend Stephen MacKenna:

> There are sides of all that western life the groggy-patriot-publican-general shop-man who is married to the priest's half sister and is second cousin once-removed of the dispensary doctor, that are horrible and awful. This is the type that is running the present United Irish League anti-grazier campaign while they're swindling the people themselves in a dozen ways and then buying out their holdings and packing off whole families to America.[57]

As the public face of the IAOS, the organiser met with this local opposition. A local meeting organised for the purpose of a new society could expose and trigger a raft of local social conflicts. At Tralee in February 1895, Robert Anderson's efforts to exhort local farmers to establish a co-operative creamery met with stubborn resistance from one trader. Anderson delivered his pitch that the IAOS empowered farmers to engage in modern agricultural methods 'with the very smallest of expenditure and the maximum of profit'. The IAOS placed no money into the society but promised 'to supply all information to farmers starting the co-operative system'. After the meeting, a trader named Moynihan criticised Anderson in the press for misleading farmers. Moynihan argued vehemently against the co-operative creamery system as he claimed it produced an inferior product compared to 'well-made hand butter' and stated that a market 'glutted with creameries' will lead to the product 'sold at the price of grease'. The protest claimed that new creamery technology reduced the need for labour and thereby co-operation achieved the opposite intention its supporters claimed as it increased emigration and destroyed existent native industry. Moynihan argued that traders who 'supplied and backed up farmers in their times of adversity' received no recompense from the co-operative; and he asked 'how many men, how many trades, how many industries will be pauperised, and crippled out of existence?' Anderson tackled all of Moynihan's points in a reply published in the *Kerry Sentinel* and labelled Moynihan as someone who ostensibly wrote 'in the interest of the farming community' but more accurately appeared as 'a special pleader for the middleman'.[58] Despite Anderson's efforts, Moynihan held back the co-operative movement in the market town – although societies were established in surrounding townlands in later years. Such frustrations occurred frequently for the IAOS organiser.

If a society was established then organisers regularly visited their assigned districts to inspect the performance of the co-operative businesses there. Whenever a society experienced any problems through a lack of knowledge, or a dispute arose between members, or if advice was required to pioneer a new branch of business the IAOS sent an organiser to facilitate. Therefore, it was essential that each organiser possessed an intimate understanding of the specific social and economic circumstances in each district to perform this role effectively:

> It will be his business to have all kinds of local information at his fingers' ends – to know where the priest is friendly and where he is not, where the schoolmaster is competent, and where the gombeen-man is threatening. He must also know the weak points of the societies, and so be able to locate trouble without waste of time.[59]

Communication between the IAOS in Dublin and co-operative societies throughout Ireland formed an integral feature of efforts to nurture a new civilisation.

The establishment of a creamery in this period did not mean that the form it took needed to be co-operative. As Cormac Ó Gráda and William Jenkins have pointed out, privately operated creameries proved to be the most numerous at the outset of the transformation of Irish dairying and maintained a source of fierce competition with the IAOS right through to the 1920s.[60] Large dairying companies such as the Condensed Milk Company of Ireland had a sizeable market share of the dairying industry, particularly in Munster.[61] The antagonism that existed between representatives of the IAOS and the private creameries spurred on the competition over the milk suppliers of the Irish dairying heartlands.

The charismatic organiser

Co-operative organisers drove economic development in Ireland by the creation of local networks of support. Geniality and personality proved major assets. The success or failure of an organiser's efforts partly reflected their ability to draw together figures of local influence and encourage new members to join a fledgling society. In some areas landlords still led the way. One notable landlord was Josslyn Gore-Booth of Lissadell, County Sligo. He came to Plunkett's attention in 1895 as a volunteer IAOS organiser for the Sligo area.[62] Gore-Booth represented the type of progressive landlord that appealed to Plunkett's sensibilities – one who demonstrated concern and empathy for the welfare of his tenants. As one local newspaper reported, Gore-Booth led in the establishment of Drumcliffe Co-operative Society and 'ever since its inception worked incessantly for its success. Everything that a man could do has been done by this gentleman to improve the condition of the Drumcliffe people.'[63] As President of Drumcliffe Co-operative Society Gore-Booth championed the IAOS in the north-western region and was involved in the establishment of several other societies that included the Sligo District Co-operative Society, the Ballintrillick Co-operative Stores and the Irish Beekeepers' Association. He developed a close working relationship with other influencers, which included members of the clergy, and grew into a recognised source of intelligence on the development of the regional co-operative movement.

In the north-west of Ireland, competition between the IAOS and the private creameries created plenty of work for the co-operative organiser in the area, Henry Shaw. Counties Sligo, Roscommon and Leitrim had emerged as a bat-tleground between the IAOS and the creamery firm, Lonsdale and Company, at the end of the nineteenth century. Shaw cultivated important relations with landlords and members of the Catholic clergy and hierarchy in order to promote the co-operative cause. During the summer of 1900, Lonsdale threatened to undermine co-operative creameries already established. Shaw used his contacts with creamery managers and employees in the region to keep abreast of Lonsdale's efforts to extend their businesses. These efforts included a plan to erect an auxiliary creamery near Achonry Co-operative Dairy Society.[64] In a series of letters to Gore-Booth, Shaw explained his plan to disrupt Lonsdale's expansion. Shaw identified that a key broker in Lonsdale's plans was the local parish priest, Fr Scully, who had shown Lonsdale's agent, Mr Drake, around the region and introduced him to the local farmers. Shaw planned to reverse Scully's influence though his own connection to the Bishop of Achonry 'who is likely to hear something of this as he is very friendly to the movement and myself'.[65] Shaw later attended a meeting at Carrowmore School for the Achonry Coop Society 'to assist them keeping out Lonsdale who had got tenants consent for site (a man named McCann) to erect Auxiliary in the locality'. Shaw informed Gore-Booth that 'as the contemplated site is on Major O'Hara's property I shall have little difficulty in stopping that, and as Lord Harlich and yourself are the other Landlords I think we shall manage to keep them out'.[66] Lonsdale and Company continued to pose a threat to the IAOS in the area, but Achonry Co-operative Society strengthened their position against the company through the establishment of their own Auxiliary in the townland of Ballyara later that year.

The personality of the organiser proved to be an important, if immeasurable, aspect to their duties. In an ebullient passage George Moore described Æ's time in the field as someone who

> rode through Ireland, preaching the doctrine of co-operation and dairy-farming from village to village winning friends to the movement with the personal magnetism which he exercises wherever he goes. As soon as he arrived in a village everybody's heart became a little warmer, a little friendlier; the sensation of isolation and loneliness, which all human beings feel, thawed a little; everybody must have felt happier the night that that kindly man mounted a platform, threw back his long hair, and began to talk to them, giving them shrewd advice and making them feel that he loved them and that they were not unworthy of his love.

To establish a society the organiser relied on his or her ability to foster effective and productive working relationships with individuals who possessed a high degree of social capital in a village. Again, Moore recalled that Æ frequently lodged in the house of the priest when he made trips to address meetings, and his effect was such that

> the lonely village priest, who does not meet a friend with whom he can exchange an idea once every three months, would spend a memorable evening with Æ. ... In the morning the old bicycle would be brought out, and away Æ would go, and the priest, I am sure, looked after him, sorry that he was going.[67]

Although Moore's recollections exhibit some affected exaggeration, members of the clergy proved to be important allies to the organiser. Fr Jeremiah O'Donovan explained how his own introduction to the co-operative movement, which 'he regarded as the most important work being carried on at present in Ireland', occurred when he learned about their work from the organiser P.J. Hannon.[68] Parish priests and curates played an important brokerage role between the IAOS and the farmers. For example, the parish priest, Canon Ryan, chaired an IAOS meeting in the town of Emly, County Tipperary. The meeting 'resulted in those present signing applications for over £500 in shares in a co-operative society, to take over the disused creamery'.[69] At the first meeting of Kilflynn Co-operative Society, the local curate Fr Crimmins was elected the society's chair and promised to make a success of the new society. He commended the shareholders for 'appointing such, good sensible men' and promised the members 'there would be no friction, and that the creamery would be a great success, and would be seen very soon in the improved condition of the people (hear, hear)'.[70]

The involvement of priests in running local societies proved a common feature of co-operative activity. For example, Ballaghderreen Co-operative Society maintained a priest in the positions of both president and vice-president in its formative years. Such tenures provided priests with one way to exert influence over local economic decisions, such as which individuals received positions of paid employment at the society. This authority might also be brought to bear on members' behaviour to increase economic efficiency at the creamery. At a meeting held to set the prices paid to farmers for the milk supplied, Fr Durkin, the vice-president, used his position to ensure the passage of a resolution that punished farmers who supplied low quality milk, potentially due to dilution. The motion threatened suppliers whose milk contained less than 3 per cent fat 'that if their standard does not improve the payment for their milk will be greatly reduced and won't be paid for at the rate of 3d. per Gal. any more'.[71]

A priest's leadership might provide the necessary encouragement that led people to support a co-operative business, but equally priests followed the advice of parishioners towards this direction. Fr James Neary, the parish priest for Frenchpark, responded to a letter from Josslyn Gore-Booth that inquired about the potential for a new creamery in that parish. The proliferation of co-operative creameries and auxiliaries acted as a buttress to contain the expansion of privately owned creameries such as Lonsdale's. Fr Neary possessed no expertise on the matter of economic co-operation before Gore-Booth's contact with him. Neary grew 'anxious to interview some intelligent persons in this Parish & the surrounding Parishes'. When he discovered that all his sources of intelligence supported the co-operative system of dairying, he decided to help establish a new auxiliary society in his parish to supply Farrymount Co-operative Creamery three miles away. As Neary concluded in his letter to Gore-Booth, 'I certainly do not approve of the proprietary system – I am sure also that the people themselves will see that the Co-operative Creameries will be more profitable to them.'[72] The priest, then, could emerge as the most useful convert.

Co-operative society as a site of local power

Organisers frequently negotiated complex social relations to establish a new society. This required a strenuous and often protracted effort on their part as they aided new societies through the initial steps of incorporation and helped explain the rules. The time taken between establishment and a new society beginning its work could stretch to several months. During this transitional period the organiser remained alert and ready to deal with any emergencies that arose (such as mistakes due to lack of business experience among members) and to help defeat any challenges or attacks that might be aimed at the society in the meantime.[73]

Organisers also provided an impetus of leadership at the outset. For instance, at the first meeting of Ballaghderreen Co-operative Society Henry Shaw 'was received with prolonged cheering' when invited by the chairman, Fr O'Connor, to address the shareholders. Shaw outlined the importance of following IAOS procedures, but also offered advice on the character of the men the shareholders needed to elect to the committee, which showed the importance of the organiser in helping to establish the trajectory of these businesses:

> he first reffered [sic] to the financial state of the society which was second to none on Ireland for the very short period working he then reffered [sic] to the election of committees and pointed out that 12 members i.e. – 8 for Ballaghderreen + 4 for Monasteraiden would be sufficient to manage the business of their society + he urged on the shareholders to elect only men of solvency + business tact men that could be relied on and if in cases of emergency secure overdrafts for their society from their Banker.

Shaw's speech provided the perfect introduction for Fr O'Connor, who proceeded to read out a list of men he recommended for the role of committee members. After they were read out a proposal was passed that allowed the names put forth to be accepted at once without going to a formal election.[74]

Co-operative society meetings acquired a notorious reputation. A satirical song entitled 'Tales from A Kerry Creamery' by 'Shemus' revolved around an imagined meeting and captured the colour of one of these events. The song focused upon the details of a meeting, told from a harassed secretary's point of view. Although published as a humorous appraisal of a co-operative meeting, the song suggests that while resentment of the way business was organised existed among certain farmers, sometimes violently expressed, very little happened to reform how societies operated. From the outset, the song's narrator establishes a picture of local disquiet:

Twas the day uv the Gineral Meetin', an' a stormy meeting too,

For we hadn't a pinny profit, an' the shareholders all looked blue;

From answerin' curus queschuns me brain was addled quite –

Sure 'twas only the mercy o' heaven we hadn't a fakshun fight.

Local grievances are aired, accusations are made about the competency of the creamery's staff, and the dairymaid 'got a "rubbin' up" that she'll sartinly raymimber' – a casual indicator of the misogynist attitudes female employees might face at their place of work. However, the song concludes that the members accepted conditions as they existed before the meeting took place. Despite the fear that events might take a nasty turn, the final verse confirms the survival of the society and a return to business as usual: 'the ould Committee's ray-elected, an' the sthaff wor "let off wid a caution"'.[75] Society meetings offered members a local forum whereby dissatisfactions and jealousies were given a public hearing, but where ultimately order would be imposed by the methods prescribed by the society's conventions.

Co-operative societies came to represent sites of local power. Inclusion on the local committee proved an important indicator of an individual's importance within the community. However, committee members became visible targets for local resentment and meetings acquired a reputation as raucous affairs where local grievances were aired. For example, at Ballinclemessig Co-operative Society, one member physically assaulted the chairman. However, the society's solicitor advised the chairman from pursuing a legal action 'even though it would certainly aggravate the offence when the person assaulted was at the time chairman of a lawfully constituted meeting'.[76] From the start of the movement's existence, local co-operative meetings assumed notoriety as lively social occasions and offered an opportunity for communal catharsis.

The co-operative society as civilizing influence

While organisers acted as intermediaries between individual societies and the IAOS, on a local level co-operative societies acted as intermediaries between local farmers and the marketplace. As the local creamery became a common sight across dairying regions, *The Irish Homestead* noted that 'a new rural personality has come into existence. The creamery manager will more and more become an influence in the country.' Managers constituted new rural authority figures on a par with 'the clergyman, the doctor and the schoolmaster'. Their role at the interface between members and the society's committee proved vital. Managers negotiated the short-term interests of the farmer by paying an acceptable 'fair' price for milk supplied, while ensuring the long-term sustainability of the society. The success of co-operation in Ireland relied upon local managers acquitting their duties in accordance with co-operative principles, as

> [h]is employment is of a nature which tends to develop and widen out character. He is brought into contact with hundreds of farmers; and he alone perhaps in the community, through the fact of his being in direct contact with the greatest market in the world, and because he acts on behalf of the greatest industry in Ireland, is enabled to some extent to gauge the probable economic effect of certain political changes.[77]

The creamery manager occupied a unique position in Irish society. As the business's main official the manager acted as the connecting point between a district's butter producers and the marketplace beyond the village. Therefore, the success or failure of a co-operative creamery consisted in the ability to manage the expectations of members and fasten their support to the society, and to ensure that they met the demands of customers. While in early days prominent members of creameries, both co-operative and private, looked 'to get their own immediate friends and relations appointed to the principle positions, such as managers and dairymaids, whether properly qualified or not', this practice soon declined. It quickly became apparent that such appointments sowed discontent among suppliers and created an impression that nepotism and patronage operated at the creamery in a way that benefited some farmers over others. As William Stokes of the CWS noted at the end of the nineteenth century, it almost universally transpired that all appointments were made on merit 'and an unwritten but firmly established rule exists that those selected must have no connection with the locality or with any of the suppliers from the district'.[78]

Ultimately, the co-operative society was a mechanism designed to instigate a revolution of Irish character. In *The National Being*, Æ emphasised the importance of the co-operative society's educational effects upon farmers. He conceived the character of Patrick Moloney in a polemical work that championed the co-operative model as the ideal arrangement for Irish society. Patrick Moloney represented a typical farmer who relied on the co-operative movement in order to shed the traditional superstitions that prevented his transformation into a co-operative subject. An important characteristic of co-operative organisation resided in the educational effect visited upon Patrick through constant interaction with the manager. Æ imagined that such contact encouraged Patrick to become

> a member of a committee getting hints of a strange doctrine called science from his creamery manager. He hears about bacteria, and these dark invisibles replace, as the cause of bad butter-making, the wicked fairies of his childhood.[79]

Working through the co-operative society exposed farmers to arguments and ideas in favour of public health awareness, quality control and efficiency at the expense of the mythic aspects of a popular folk culture that other literary revivalists celebrated.[80] Co-operative managers enlightened farmers about their old, traditional ideas and replaced them with new scientific norms that improved Patrick Moloney's industry.

One important aspect of scientific management resided in proficient numeracy and bookkeeping. The publication of accounts formed a legal requirement stipulated by the Industrial and Provident Societies Act and the task of maintaining a society's accounts fell to the manager. Candidates for managerial posts needed to demonstrate not only their ability to stay abreast of the latest advances in dairying techniques, bacteriology and engineering, but also demonstrate their competence in general business methods.[81] In the early years of the movement's existence, a dearth of numerical and administrative expertise by management affected the performance of the movement. For example in 1905, John O'Connell, a Tralee-based solicitor, returned the business accounts sent for his inspection by the manager of Lixnaw Co-operative Society. O'Connell politely noted that a 'little confusion has arisen in this case owing to the form of the accounts furnished by you which of course no doubt are understood by you but not by everyone'. Helpfully, he wrote the figures in pencil, as he believed they should be presented.[82]

The quality and regularity of statistical returns from individual co-operative societies influenced how the IAOS conducted its work and prioritised its objectives each year. This accumulation of detailed information allowed the co-operative movement's leaders to read the movement and respond to shortcomings across the movement in a more directed and efficient manner. The statistical returns and balance sheets submitted by co-operative societies allowed the IAOS to judge the level of progress made by the movement based on annual year-on-year comparisons. Ten years into the IAOS's existence, the Executive Committee complained of 'the failure of a large number of societies to furnish statistical returns or balance sheet'.[83] For example, fourteen of the thirty-seven registered co-operative creameries in County Limerick returned no statistical data for the year 1903.[84] A decade later, however, the financial practices of societies improved due to regular interventions into society business by IAOS-appointed accountants. From 1907 onwards, the chief accountant, Andrew Swain, trained the other organisers in accountancy so that they could oversee the bookkeeping methods employed by individual societies.[85] While still imperfect, the quality of the accounts submitted at the end of the financial year witnessed a marked improvement, especially in the case of creameries, 'in which the transactions are most numerous and complex and where a very complete and elaborate system of account keeping now prevails'.[86]

However, the IAOS complained that a dearth of good management material in Ireland was due to defects in the educational system. As late as 1922, the IAOS asserted that co-operative societies outnumbered good managerial candidates, 'and pending the cultivation of such a new "race" of managers as is being cultivated in the creameries, a tremendous responsibility is thrown on the IAOS and its staff and on the committees of the societies'.[87] In consequence, the experience of co-operative societies varied from district to district, owing to management decisions taken in regard to determining the quality of milk that farmers brought to the creamery and the prices paid for supplies. Other factors such as the presence of rival creameries affected how individual societies functioned, but a manager's ability to unify the membership behind a single purpose played an important role in the success of a co-operative enterprise.

By the first decade of the twentieth century the local co-operative society became an important site whereby new forms of social life were generated alongside experiments that promoted leisure time as a common good in a locality. To help along the 'brightening of rural life' Plunkett offered £50 prizes in 1901 and 1902 to the co-operative society that worked hardest to 'make their parish a pleasant place to live in, and one which no Irishman would like to emigrate from'. Dromahair Co-operative Society in County Leitrim secured the prize through its efforts to use educational means to raise 'their members to a higher social plane'. The efforts employed by this society over a six-month period saw lectures delivered on subjects such as poultry, horticulture, veterinary science, domestic economy and bee keeping. Attendees to these talks were treated to entertainments such as lantern presentations. A domestic training school for girls opened in the village of Creevelea with an average attendance of 44 girls; and a carpentry class for boys garnered an average attendance of 20. A series of entertainments that included a music festival, a concert and a cinematography exhibition took place and a farmers' circulating library was established. A series of other initiatives also launched in the locality, such as temperance drives, distribution of free flowers and shrubs, and 'a crusade against badly-kept homesteads'.

The IAOS played no direct role in the organisation of these social activities, which they viewed as evidence of 'one of the very best outcomes of the co-operative movement. We would not have achieved any real success if we had only united people for business purposes and they remained solitary and unsocial at heart.'[88] By the end of 1901, about thirty societies formed their own local lending libraries funded by grants offered by the DATI.[89]

Plunkett reflected on the IAOS's first decade in existence as evidence of the movement's success in this direction:

> Those who have known Ireland for the last dozen years cannot have failed to notice the advent of a wholly new spirit, clearly based upon constructive thought, and expressing itself in a wide range of fresh practical activities.

These activities included the co-operative organisation of agriculture and rural credit, efforts to revive and initiate industries, and the creation of the DATI. Taken together, these changes encouraged, 'all that was healthy in the voluntary effort of the people to build up the economic side of their life'.[90] Activity of this type that emerged out of the local co-operative society helped to create a version of an enlivened rural Ireland observed by the likes of Henry Demarest Lloyd and L. Paul-Dubois.

The co-operative society and dissent

Besides nurturing the practical side of co-operation, organisers faced situations whereby they needed to ensure that societies remained solvent in the face of challenges and internal problems. One such figure on the front line of co-operative organisation throughout the early twentieth century was Charles Riddall who worked as the organiser for the south-west of Ireland.[91] Riddall's reports and communiqués formed the basis of the reservoir of detail about the state of agriculture available to the movement's executive in Dublin. Riddall devoted an extraordinary amount of energy to securing the permanence of co-operative organisation in that region and acted as the IAOS's chief negotiator for the takeover of creameries offloaded by the CWS in 1909.[92] Riddall was able to befriend local individuals who could provide the information required to help local societies out of problems. He also demonstrated an earthy use of language in his efforts to commit support for co-operative societies. At Listowel, he addressed a meeting of co-operative supporters and stated that opposition to their proposed creamery came from persons 'tied to the proprietary concerns'. He characterised these people 'as worms rather than men ... [and] hoped, however, that they would soon be in a position to emancipate such unfortunate individuals from their serfdom and slavery'.[93] As the IAOS fell back upon its own resources, the ability of organisers such as Riddall to negotiate compromises and find solutions to a range of problems that affected individual societies proved to be essential for the continuation of agricultural co-operatives during these years.

The prominence and notoriety achieved by co-operative societies meant they could become the recipients of violent attention as tensions bubbled under the surface of the Irish countryside and echoed the agrarian violence of the nineteenth century.[94] One such society that experienced a rather volatile time during the first decade in operation was Ballinclemessig Co-operative Society in County Kerry. Founded in 1902, it started life amid acrimony. The first meeting held on 8 April 1902 immediately split the society on the issue of where the creamery should be located. Ballinclemessig won the support of a slight majority of members over the neighbouring village of Causeway. P.J. Hannon, the organiser present on that occasion, 'announced that any person who wished to withdraw could do so within 6 days' on account of the decision. The presence of a new co-operative could add prestige to the locality where it resided, particularly since a creamery housed modern technology and marked out its locality as a place of relative importance. Accordingly, the decision to locate this creamery in the townland of Ballinclemessig drew resentment from the Causeway inhabitants. The contentious decision led to the exodus of some initial members, including the provisional chairman, Fr McCarthy, and undoubtedly the decision bred resentment towards the new co-operative in its early years.[95] The controversial introduction of the creamery to Ballinclemessig sowed the seeds of outrage against the society several years later. On the evening of 12 December 1908, an arson attack on Ballinclemessig Co-operative Society destroyed the entire premises and a former committee member emerged as the prime suspect for the attack. To compound the problem facing the co-operative farmers in the area, along with the loss of creamery equipment and account books, it emerged the committee had never taken out an insurance policy.

Riddall had fostered a professional relationship with the solicitor John O'Connell in order to keep himself informed of developments that affected the society. O'Connell worked in Tralee and included several of north Kerry's co-operative societies among his clients. He worked with Ballinclemessig Co-operative from its inception and possessed a detailed knowledge with regard to the background, personalities and grievances that characterised the society. O'Connell struggled to make progress with the case due to Ballinclemessig committee's failure to remain in regular communication with him. As a result, he bypassed his clients and contacted their organiser, Riddall, to whom he confided his personal view of the committee members:

> I would request that you should remain in this district working up the case till matter is disposed of. <u>Your assistance would be invaluable.</u> The members of the Committee are very slow. I have heard nothing from them of late. They live a long distance from Tralee + like all men of their class they keep on delaying information … till the last moment. One can hardly blame the poor men as they are mostly old and of very limited ability.[96]

The two men liaised together in order to bring the case to court. O'Connell's decision to approach Riddall shows how the sometimes 'poor men' who administered the society were bypassed in favour of the co-operative expert. O'Connell believed that 'the evidence as to malice is pretty strong'.[97] Charles Riddall went further when he wrote on the subject of Ballinclemessig: 'There is a great dispute between the Ballinclemessig and Causeway people over the purchase of Palmer and Elliott's [a private company] Ballinorig Creamery.'[98] The collapse of the local private creamery run by Palmer and Elliott meant that a new space had opened up in the dairy economy. Since Ballinclemessig's establishment, the co-operative had been involved in a rivalry with the local private concern and Riddall sensed that the collapse of this business related to outrage. Despite strong evidence of a break-in, Ballinclemessig Co-operative Society failed to secure a judgment in its favour and the former committee member was released.

Events like the destruction of a co-operative creamery could produce unexpected effects. At Ballinclemessig, the attack appeared to strengthen co-operative organisation within the community. The local population recognised the importance of the co-operative society to its economic interests and rallied around to ensure its survival. The society provided more than an outlet for milk supplies for local people. A creamery provided local employment and offered a range of services that included the purchase and marketing of local butter and provision of advance payments as a source of credit to farmers in lieu of milk to be received.[99] Furthermore, the arson attack encouraged those people who had previously remained apart from the creamery to join the society. O'Connell noted that 'several persons who had refused to become shareholders before the burning have done so since'.[100] The IAOS used Ballinclemessig in a propaganda exercise to emphasise the vibrancy of the co-operative ethos that existed among farmers in Kerry. The IAOS cited the inhabitants there as people who

> nothing daunted by their misfortunes ... re-erected and re-equipped a most up-to-date creamery in record time ... [T]his example of co-operative determination will be approved throughout the country.[101]

This episode demonstrated how quickly the new co-operative societies could be normalised within a locality such as Ballinclemessig.

Charles Riddall often provided a most valuable service to the IAOS by managing the sometimes contentious and complex local relations that coalesced around the co-operative society. At Newtownsandes Co-operative Society in north Kerry the committee considered the liquidation of the society following a scandal involving the creamery manager, John Houlihan. Before he left the society in January 1916, Houlihan destroyed the account books, which left the society in a precarious financial position. At 'a rather lively meeting' of the membership held to determine the future of the society, two members were ejected by members of the local constabulary who attended to watch over the proceedings. Charles Riddall also attended in an effort to preserve the future of the society. As the society's future hung in the balance Riddall reported to Dublin that members 'recognised however that the Society could not hope to keep its doors open unless the members did something more than give verbal undertaking to support it'. The situation required 'sufficient support in the shape of milk and money should be guaranteed by the members'. At that meeting held on 19 February 1916, forty members present agreed to guarantee an overdraft extension to help the creamery through its immediate financial difficulties as it tried to work out the financial liabilities attached to the business. Furthermore, an advert was placed for a new manager and dairymaid.[102]

At the end of March Riddall returned to the district to ascertain the degree of progress. He discovered that the bank had refused an overdraft due to a lack of clarity on the financial position of Newtownsandes Society. Instead, members came together to agree to sign money bills to support the co-operative and a farmer with a large acreage, who supplied the local private Kerry and Cork

Company's creamery, decided to donate £6 and agree to shift his milk supply to the co-operative. Furthermore, members agreed to forfeit all monies owed to them for December 1915, which amounted to a sum close to £450. Riddall wrote to Robert Anderson to explain that the people realised that the alternative to such measures was liquidation, which meant 'the establishment of another Creamery Proprietor in the district and that Co-operation would become for them a dead letter'. After the financial agreements were put in place the main obstacle to the co-operatives' continuation hinged on the membership's disagreement over the appointment of Thomas de Lacy as the new manager. Riddall refused to endorse de Lacy to the Newtownsandes committee in case he 'might cause dissension and undo all the work of reconstruction that had been so courageously and well done by the people themselves'. However, Riddall believed that de Lacy was the right man and therefore he organised a committee meeting at which he would endorse de Lacy, but before he attended he spoke to the local parish priest and curate. In Fr O'Carroll, the curate, Riddall found 'a sympathetic advisor'. The parish priest, 'an anti-co-operator' prevented Fr O'Carroll from open support for the co-operative society. O'Carroll advised Riddall to speak to other local men who he said would support the de Lacy appointment, and by the time Riddall later attended the committee meeting he found near unanimous support for the new manager.

> Only one member of the Committee opposed this appointment, but after I had given my opinion of Mr de Lacy that member of the Committee proposed his appointment and another member of the Committee whom Father O'Carroll had 'talked round' seconded it and Mr de Lacy was then unanimously offered the position at £120 per annum plus a bonus out of the profits, the amount of which should be left to the discretion of the shareholders. ... The Committee expressed their appreciation of the work we had so far done for them and stated that had it not been for my presence at the meeting of shareholders on 19th February last the Society would certainly have gone into liquidation.[103]

Certainly, in the early decades of the twentieth century the hard, repetitive work of spreading the co-operative gospel led to the creation of resilient socio-economic institutions that characterised a new type of political economy. As new challenges that encompassed war, revolution and bitter communal violence arose over the course of the next decades the commitment of farmers to their societies would be severely tested.

Notes

1 'The Co-operative Village', *Irish Homestead*, 4 November 1905, 801–802.
2 'The Struggle between Country and Town', *Irish Homestead*, 15 August 1908, 645–666.
3 Fergus Campbell, *The Irish Establishment, 1879–1914* (Oxford: Oxford University Press, 2009).

4 Henry Demarest Lloyd, *Labor Copartnership: Notes of a Visit to Co-operative Workshops, Factories and Farms in Great Britain and Ireland, in which Employer, Employé, and Consumer Share in Ownership, Management, and Results* (London: Harper & Brothers Publishers, 1898), 52.

5 L. Paul-Dubois, *Contemporary Ireland* (Dublin: Maunsel & Co., 1908), 451.

6 Leeann Lane, '"It is in the Cottages and Farmers' Houses that the Nation is Born": Æ's "Irish Homestead" and the Cultural Revival', *Irish University Review*, 33.1 (2003), 165–181 (p. 167).

7 Horace Plunkett, 'Rural Regeneration', *North American Review*, 214.791 (1921), 470–476 (p. 474).

8 Horace Plunkett, *Noblesse Oblige: An Irish Rendering* (Dublin: Maunsel & Co., 1908), 26.

9 Thomas J. Morrissey, *Thomas A. Finlay, SJ, 1848–1940: Educationalist, Editor, Social Reformer* (Dublin: Four Courts Press, 2004).

10 IAOS, *Annual Report, 1895*, 3.

11 Líam Kennedy, 'The Early Response of the Irish Catholic Clergy to the Co-operative Movement', *Irish Historical Studies*, 21.81 (1978), 55–74 (p. 60).

12 *Rerum Novarum: Encyclical of Pope Leo XIII on Capital and Labour*, http://w2.vatican.va/content/leo-xiii/en/encyclicals/documents/hf_l-xiii_enc_15051891_rerum-novarum.html. [accessed 14 September 2017].

13 Horace Plunkett, Kildare Street Club to Archbishop Walsh, Dublin, 18 April 1894, Dublin Diocesan Archive (DDA), Walsh Papers, Box 255, 363/3.

14 'Among the Societies', *Irish Homestead*, 9 March 1895, 8.

15 Horace Plunkett, Dublin to Bishop Clancy of Elphin, Sligo, 2 June 1908, NLI, Ms 49,803/31/9.

16 Bishop MacCormack's Notebook, 30 April 1895, Galway Diocesan Archive, Box 22.

17 Kennedy, 'The Early Response', 60.

18 Horace Plunkett, *Ireland in the New Century: with an Epilogue in Answer to Some Critics* (London: John Murray, 1905), 107.

19 R.A. Anderson, *With Horace Plunkett in Ireland: The Co-op Organisers' Story* (London: Macmillan and Co., 1935), 150.

20 Dermot Meleady, *John Redmond: The National Leader* (Dublin: Merrion, 2014), 65.

21 Special Committee Meeting, 25 August 1904, Gore-Booth IAOS Papers, 1904, PRONI, D/4131/M/15.

22 Horace Plunkett, Dublin to Bishop O'Dwyer, Limerick, 8 March 1904, Limerick Diocesan Archive, BI/ET/K.

23 Plunkett Diary, 5 April 1904.

24 Plunkett Diary, 29 March 1904.

25 R. Barry, P.P., 'Sir Horace Plunkett on the Influence of Religion', *Freeman's Journal*, 1 March 1904, 2.

26 Plunkett Diary, 7 March 1904.

27 Plunkett Diaries, 5 April 1910; Kennedy, 'The Early Response', 60.

28 Anderson, *With Horace Plunkett*, 150.

29 Cited in Morrissey, *Thomas A. Finlay*, 95.

30 IAOS, *Annual Report, 1904*, 24–25.
31 'Mr Horace Plunkett's Disorganization Society Limited', *Skibbereen Eagle*, 12 October 1895, 2.
32 'Our Programme', *Irish Homestead*, 9 March 1895, 3–5.
33 'Among the Societies', *Irish Homestead*, 9 March 1895, 6.
34 George Moore, *Hail and Farewell! Ave, Salve, Vale* (Gerrards Cross, Bucks.: Colin Smythe Ltd, 1985 [1911]), 302–303.
35 Nicholas Allen, *George Russell (Æ) and the New Ireland, 1905–30* (Dublin: Four Courts Press, 2003), 27–29.
36 Joanna Bourke, *Husbandry to Housewifery: Women, Economic Change, and Housework in Ireland, 1890–1914* (Oxford: Clarendon Press, 1993), 87–88.
37 Cited in Bourke, *Husbandry to Housewifery*, 102.
38 Bourke, *Husbandry to Housewifery*, 196–197.
39 DATI, *Conference on the Poultry Industry, Dublin, May, 1911: Report of Proceedings* (London: HMSO, 1911), 125.
40 Debra Lyons, Dromahair, to Josslyn Gore-Booth, Lissadell, 24 August 1900, Gore-Booth, Drumcliffe Co-operative Dairy Society and Related Papers, PRONI, D4131/M/11B.
41 'Lecture and Demonstration in Dairying at Kilflynn', *Kerry Sentinel*, 29 June 1904.
42 'Migration of Irish Women from the Farm', *Irish Homestead*, 22 January1910, 61.
43 An Irish Woman of 1910, 'A Castigation', *Irish Homestead*, 5 February 1910, 109–110.
44 Ellice Pilkington, 'The Irish Countrywoman', *Irish Homestead*, 9 April 1910, 294.
45 'United Irishwomen', *Irish Homestead*, 8 October 1910, 844–845.
46 Ellice Pilkington, 'United Irishwomen – Their Work', in Horace Plunkett, Ellice Pilkington and George Russell (eds), *The United Irishwomen: Their Place, Work and Ideals* (Dublin: Maunsel & Co., 1911), 19–35 (p. 20).
47 Ellice Pilkington, 'United Irishwomen – Their Work', 22.
48 The Society of the United Irishwomen, *Annual Report, 1912* (Wexford: The People, 1913), 4.
49 Michel Foucault, *The Birth of Biopolitics: Lectures at the Collège de France, 1978–1979* (Houndmills, Basingstoke: Palgrave Macmillan, 2010), 4.
50 IAOS, *Annual Report, 1901*, 16.
51 Líam Kennedy, 'Farmers, Traders and Agricultural Politics in Pre-Independence Ireland', in *Irish Peasants: Violence and Political Unrest, 1780–1914*, ed. by James S. Donnelly Jr and Samuel Clark (Manchester: Manchester University Press, 1983), 339–373.
52 IAOS, *Annual Report, 1904*, 25.
53 IAOS, *Annual Report, 1895*, 5.
54 Lionel Smith-Gordon and Laurence C. Staples, *Rural Reconstruction in Ireland: A Record of Co-operative Organisation* (London: P.S. King and Son, 1917), 63.
55 IAOS, *Annual Report, 1899*, 7.
56 Kennedy, 'Farmers, Traders and Agricultural Politics'.
57 Ann Saddlemyer (ed.), *The Collected Letters of John Millington Synge: Volume One, 1871–1907* (Oxford: Oxford University Press, 1983), 116.
58 'Among the Societies, Tralee', *Irish Homestead*, 9 March 1895, 6–7. This article republished Moynihan's letters to the *Kerry Sentinel* verbatim.

59 Smith-Gordon and Staples, *Rural Reconstruction*, 67.
60 Cormac Ó Gráda, 'The Beginnings of the Irish Creamery System, 1880–1914', *Economic Review of History*, 30.2 (1977), 284–305; William Jenkins, 'Capitalists and Co-operators: Agricultural Transformation, Contested Space, and Identity Politics in South Tipperary, Ireland, 1890–1914', *Journal of Historical Geography*, 30 (2004), 87–111.
61 Ingrid Henriksen, Eoin McLaughlin and Paul Sharp, 'Contracts and Co-operation: the Relative Failure of the Irish Dairy Industry in the Late Nineteenth Century Reconsidered', *European Review of Economic History*, 19.4 (2015), 412–431.
62 Plunkett Diary, 2 August 1895.
63 *Sligo Independent*, 24 October 1896. Contained in a selection of press extracts kept in Gore-Booth Papers, PRONI, D4131/M/11A.
64 Auxiliaries were smaller societies that sent milk from one area to a larger central creamery.
65 Henry Shaw, Ballymote to Josslyn Gore-Booth, Lisadell, 5 May 1900, PRONI, D4131/M/11B.
66 Henry Shaw, Ballymote to Josslyn Gore-Booth, Lisadell, 11 June 1900, PRONI, D4131/M/11B.
67 Moore, *Hail and Farewell*, 303–304.
68 'Dinner to Mr P.J. Hannon', *Irish Homestead*, 26 August 1905, 647.
69 'From our Organisers' Diaries', *Irish Homestead*, 6 April 1895, 70–71.
70 'Kilflynn Co-operative Dairy Society', *Irish Homestead*, 2 January 1904.
71 Ballaghderreen Co-operative Agricultural and Dairy Society – Minute Book, 7 August 1906, National Archives of Ireland, BR/ROS/12/1.
72 Fr James Neary, Frenchpark to Josslyn Gore-Booth, Lissadell, 24 April 1899, Gore-Booth Papers, PRONI, D4131/M/11B.
73 Smith-Gordon and Staples, *Rural Reconstruction*, 66.
74 First General Meeting of shareholders, Ballaghderreen Courthouse. Ballaghderreen Co-operative Agricultural and Dairy Society – Minute Book, 11 January 1900, National Archives Ireland [NAI] BR/ROS/12/1.
75 Shemus, 'Tales of a Kerry Creamery', in *A Celtic Christmas: The Irish Homestead Christmas Number*, ed. by H.F. Norman (Dublin: Irish Agricultural Organisation Society, 1898), 17–18.
76 John O'Connell, Tralee, to the Michael O'Connor, Secretary, Ballinclemessig Co-operative Dairy Society, 12 October 1910, KLHA, O'Connell Papers.
77 'Creamery Managers', *Irish Homestead*, 9 December 1905, 883.
78 W.L. Stokes, 'Irish Creameries', in CWS, *Annual Report, 1897* (Manchester: CWS, 1897), 419–449 (p. 426).
79 Æ, *The National Being: Some Thoughts on an Irish Polity* (Dublin: Maunsel & Co., 1916), 25.
80 Yeats was criticised for celebrating the peasant belief in fairies. He defended literal belief in such phenomena, citing rationalism as the 'great sin against art'. R.F. Foster, *W.B. Yeats: A Life, I: The Apprentice Mage, 1865–1914* (Oxford: Oxford University Press, 1997), 77.
81 Creamery Managers, Sample Examination Timetable, March 1919, NAI/AGF/92/2/1573.

82 John O'Connell, Tralee, to the Manager of Lixnaw Co-operative Society Dairy Society, 4 February 1905, KLHA, O'Connell Papers.
83 IAOS, *Annual Report, 1904*, 10.
84 IAOS, *Annual Report, 1904*, 76–77.
85 IAOS, *Annual Report, 1907*, 15.
86 IAOS, *Annual Report, 1914*, 6.
87 IAOS, *Annual Report, 1922*, 15.
88 IAOS, *Annual Report, 1901*, 39–41.
89 IAOS, *Annual Report, 1901*, 42
90 Plunkett, *Ireland in the New Century*, viii.
91 IAOS, *Annual Report, 1907*, 15–16.
92 IAOS, *Annual Report, 1909*, 6.
93 *Kerry Sentinel*, 20 January 1909.
94 Margaret O'Callaghan, *British High Politics and a Nationalist Ireland: Criminality, Land and the Law under Forester and Balfour* (Cork: Cork University Press, 1994).
95 Undated note, *c*.1902, detailing observations about first meeting of Ballinclemessig Co-operative Society, KLHA, O'Connell Papers.
96 John O'Connell to C.C. Riddall, 20 January 1909, KLHA, O'Connell Papers.
97 John O'Connell, Tralee to Michael O'Connell, Causeway, 15 February 1909, KLHA, O'Connell Papers.
98 C.C. Riddall to R.S. Tarrant, Dublin, 6 March 1909, NAI 1088/800/2.
99 John O'Connell, Tralee to Michael O'Connor, Rathmorrel, 24 September 1907, KLHA, O'Connell Papers.
100 John O'Connell, Tralee to Registrar of Friendly Societies, Dublin, 6 April 1909, KLHA, O'Connell Papers.
101 IAOS, *Annual Report, 1909*, 9.
102 C.C. Riddall's Report of Visit to Newtownsandes Co-operative Society, 10 March 1916, NAI 1088/751/3.
103 C.C. Riddall's Report of Visit to Newtownsandes Co-operative Society, 28 March 1916, NAI 1088/751/3.

3

Ireland in the new century

At the IAOS's 1909 annual conference, Æ delivered an extraordinary speech in which he accused the movement of lacking 'the vital heat' displayed by nationalist and unionist political organisations at work in Ireland. Fifteen years after the first gathering of delegates Æ used this opportunity to challenge those assembled to consider and question what values initially drew them into the co-operative movement:

> We want to find our ideal – the synthesis of all these co-operative efforts. Butter especially when it is good, is a pleasant thing to think about; but you cannot inspire a national movement by calling out, 'Really choicest butter'. Eggs, when they are fresh are a delightful food; but they will not help much to form national ideals, though they may occasionally help to mar them – at election times. So we are driven from the actual character of our rural industries to consider the men who carry them on. It is in our men and in the object of their great endeavours we must find ideals.[1]

Æ stated the profound dilemma that faced Irish co-operators. As editor of the *Irish Homestead* he possessed a detailed awareness of the impediments and challenges that co-operators encountered at a national and local level. A decade and a half spent promoting the movement and its brand of economic reform saw the enthusiasm for the hard work of social reform replaced by discussions about the quality of produce. That an apparent short supply of idealism existed among members provided a cause for deep concern.

The IAOS's conference occurred on the eve of a general election campaign that revolved around the issue of Home Rule as the question of Ireland's constitutional status within the United Kingdom dominated public debate. Political opinion in Ireland polarised between those who supported nationalist claims for an autonomous Irish parliament in Dublin and unionists who argued for the country's retention within the United Kingdom.[2] Those who attended the nationwide meetings, which discussed Home Rule, managed 'to lose themselves in their varying ideals of Ireland and Empire'.[3] These political debates drowned out arguments about the need to concentrate upon social and economic questions as well as political ones. The production of agricultural food such as butter and eggs remained an immediate aim of co-operative societies, but if co-operators wished to be heard above the political mêlée they needed to stand for more than an improvement in farming methods. If co-operators wanted to retain their relevance they needed to rediscover their sense of missionary purpose or risk marginalisation. Signs of weariness were apparent after a generation of endeavour that saw the co-operative movement grow from a few businesses to a network of societies drawn across rural Ireland. The IAOS's intervention into the rural economy provoked conflict with traders, private dairy businesses and the CWS and this competition cost money. The establishment of the Irish Department for Agriculture and Technical Instruction (DATI) in 1900 provided a welcome source of support in the guise of an annual state subsidy. However, by the time of Æ's speech a breakdown in relations meant that the removal of a state subsidy on which the IAOS had grown reliant threatened to derail the co-operative experiment and undo the previous fifteen years of progress. Shortly before the annual conference, Horace Plunkett wrote to Fr Tom Finlay to emphasise 'the urgent need' that existed 'for a more rapid development of our Movement'.[4]

The conflict between these two leading agencies of rural development, one voluntary and the other governmental, possessed a particular irony as the DATI owed its existence to Plunkett who lobbied and legislated for its establishment in 1900. Plunkett resigned from the IAOS presidency to act as the DATI's first vice-president – the equivalent of departmental head – from 1900 until 1907. As leader of the DATI, Plunkett remained committed to the promotion of co-operation in agriculture and looked to unite the resources of the two institutions to direct agricultural development. As Plunkett's first biographer noted, 'the basic idea underlying the IAOS and the Department had been that they were twin institutions, complementary to one another'.[5]

The co-operative movement emerged as a state-building force in Ireland during the first decade of the twentieth century – one that directly influenced new political institutions. The work to embed a co-operative social blueprint during the 1890s led to the creation of the DATI, which represented the most dynamic institutional development in Ireland before political independence. Moreover, an examination of the relationship between the IAOS and DATI highlights an important way in which co-operators helped to define agricultural policymaking in Ireland. However, this work exposed tensions within the movement about what constituted an acceptable level of collaborative effort with the state – tensions that remained unresolved in this period. The fallout from Plunkett's removal from the DATI proved toxic and sparked a bitter public row between co-operators and departmental officials in the lead-up to the political crisis created by the third Home Rule Bill. The central issue about whether, or not, to support the co-operative movement with public funds became an emotive one around which new political identities coalesced. The hostility shown towards Plunkett and the

IAOS by the IPP helped a new generation of nationalists define their embryonic political project in opposition to the parliamentary tradition. An attitude expressed in support of the co-operative movement could serve as a proxy for whether someone supported an alternative national project to that put forward by the constitutional nationalists; what Roy Foster termed 'new nationalism'.[6]

The efforts of co-operative activists to re-make Irish society have repeatedly been overshadowed within the historiography by a focus upon the 'white heat' caused by dramatic political and military developments. Although these developments were eye-catching, this focus overlooks the way in which radical change had been gestating at the mundane level at which the co-operative movement primarily operated and through which it contributed to a new nationalist political economy. The split between the DATI and IAOS highlighted the intersection of political and economic ideas within Irish nationalism that became more prominent after the 1916 Easter Rising. The nominal wrangle over funding exposed two incompatible governmental visions for rural development at play before the outbreak of the First World War. The social conflict generated by co-operative economics held repercussions beyond the battle to define a template for agricultural progress. Instead, co-operative ideas fed directly into a wider process of nationalist renewal.

The Department of Agriculture and Technical Instruction for Ireland

The relationship between co-operative movements and the state frequently provoked debates about what constituted a proper relationship. Co-operative activists maintain that an ethos of self-help promoted a spirit of economic autonomy among members. However, some co-operators argue that co-ordinated state support can amplify the effectiveness of co-operative activities, while others view the state as a threat to the voluntary nature of co-operation. For Lionel Smith-Gordon, who conducted a review of co-operation across different national contexts for the Irish movement, the success of the Danish co-operative dairying sector provided 'an example of the right way of combining State encouragement with the principle of self-help'. The Danish state exercised 'its authority only to give effect to what is already the policy approved by the organised co-operators. It gives a legal sanction to what the co-operators have already decided.'[7] This belief animated the work of Horace Plunkett in the early twentieth century, but it was a statist enthusiasm not shared by many of his allies.

The politics of co-operation and state assistance acted as a source of long-standing controversy in Ireland during the first decades of the twentieth century. For his part, Plunkett stressed the importance of 'the resources of self-help' in furthering co-operation. However, he tempered this view on account of continued vigorous competition from foreign producers, which meant that the movement needed its 'voluntary efforts supplemented with a reasonable measure of State aid'.[8] More importantly, the co-operative movement generated a momentum that influenced the way in which the state functioned in rural Ireland. As the American economist David McCabe observed, the existence of the IAOS 'led directly to the creation of a Department of Agriculture and Technical Instruction for Ireland by voicing the demand for such a department, and organizing the farmers in a way to enable them to take full advantage of state aid to their industry'.[9]

The type of developmental work undertaken by Irish co-operators at the end of the nineteenth century saw it act as a surrogate for the state. The IAOS carved out a role whereby it augmented the work of existent state bodies to deliver under-resourced services. For example, the IAOS looked to improve the levels of education among the agricultural classes. The IAOS petitioned the government in 1896 to instruct the Commissioners of National Education to appoint a travelling Dairy Expert, but the position remained unfilled.[10] Already IAOS organisers partly provided such a function as they 'found it necessary to undertake a good deal of directly educational work, including a considerable system of Technical Instruction, in order that the Societies … may be properly able to fulfil the industrial purposes for which they have been formed'.[11] From the start the IAOS looked to harmonise its organisational work with the Congested Districts Board (CDB), which was designed to deal with rural poverty and improve social and economic conditions along the western seaboard.[12] Plunkett served as a member of the CDB and facilitated collaboration. In 1895, the CDB subscribed £200 to the IAOS 'for the purpose of organising Agricultural Co-operative Societies in Congested Districts'. CDB inspectors could help with the initial stages of co-operative organisation. One CDB inspector, Major W.P. Gaskell, engaged in co-operative work and although he 'encountered very great difficulties… [he] succeeded in forming two Societies at Bohola and Killasser, both in the Swinford Union'.[13]

A year after the IAOS's foundation Plunkett looked to build upon that achievement by engineering political agreement over the devolution of agricultural policymaking from Westminster to Dublin. The subsequent foundation of the DATI in 1899 represented a landmark in Ireland's political history and evidence of Plunkett's tenacity as he introduced a second major agency of agricultural progress to Ireland. Although described by critics as 'the Institution that teaches hens how to lay eggs', the Department helped to develop the theory and practice of Irish agriculture.[14] Plunkett used his influence as IAOS President and MP to fashion a coalition of political interests that established the DATI. His first step was to establish the Recess Committee of 1896, which he chaired. The Recess Committee sat as an informal, ad hoc cross-party group of parliamentarians who agreed to discuss the possibility of a separate Irish Board for Agriculture. The deliberations brought together nationalists and unionists and committed no party to any particular policy. John Redmond, the leader of the IPP's Parnellite faction, participated on the understanding that its findings might strengthen demands for Home Rule in the long term.[15] The Committee issued a final report which advocated the transfer of political powers over agricultural and educational legislation from Westminster to a department in Dublin. An Act of Parliament passed in 1899 created the DATI for this purpose.[16] Plunkett found himself pushing at an open door in his campaign to devolve the powers of agricultural policymaking. As Theodore Hoppen argued, the incumbent Conservative administration tended to 'prop up Irish policy upon cushions of government cash'.[17] Some observers argued that the decision amounted to Home Rule for Ireland in agricultural policy, while others saw the decision in keeping with a wider policy programme which consisted of 'an integrated doctrine of strong government and social amelioration'.[18]

The DATI opened on 1 April 1900 and assumed responsibility for a number of tasks: the collection of agricultural statistics; the regulation of markets, fairs and fisheries; monitoring animal diseases; and the administration of the National Library, National Museum, National Botanic Gardens, Geological Survey and Metropolitan School of Art. The major advancement concerned new powers to introduce measures to stimulate agriculture, technical instruction and rural industry. A capital sum of £200,000 and an annual endowment of £166,000 gave the new department significant leeway to effect wide-ranging agricultural reforms.[19] Moreover, for the first time Irish politicians possessed real political power to dictate substantive policy in the field of rural development. Plunkett's reward saw him appointed as Vice-President of the DATI (effectively the departmental head as the presidency remained a ceremonial title reserved for Ireland's Chief Secretary). Prior to 1900 Plunkett used his position as Recess Committee Chair to argue that co-operation proved the most effective agent of agricultural improvement, with his movement identified as 'the chief lever of progress'.[20] Horace Plunkett led the DATI between 1900 and 1907, which marked the start of a collaborative relationship between the state and the co-operative movement to reorganise the Irish countryside.

The DATI immediately asserted its position as an autonomous voice for Irish industrial development by taking part in the 1901 International Exhibition in Glasgow. The Department erected an Irish pavilion at the exhibition which displayed 'a representative selection of the characteristic products of Irish Industry'. A handbook that highlighted Irish industrial and natural potential accompanied the exhibition. In his preface to the collection, the head of the DATI's Statistics and Intelligence Branch, William Coyne, singled out 'the splendid work done by some of the great voluntary associations of Ireland in developing the material resources of this country'.[21] The wide-ranging collection of essays included pieces on co-operative dairying and credit.

The DATI and IAOS co-ordinated workloads under Plunkett's influence. For example, the DATI assumed responsibility for the practice of surprise butter competitions which saw inspectors take samples of butter from random creameries to test.[22] Such practices encouraged creamery managers to promote high-quality butter manufacturing and farmers to supply unadulterated milk. The experience of early fruitful collaboration convinced Plunkett of the function of the state as a crucial component of fuller co-operation. In a speech to the National Co-operative Festival held at Crystal Palace, London, in August 1901, Plunkett conceded the need for a strategic relationship between co-operators and the state. The leadership of the Irish co-operative movement realised that 'in addition to organised self-help ... the economic condition of the country required a measure of State aid'. Plunkett viewed this 'not ... as a substitute for, but as a stimulant and supplement to, associated effort. The DATI provided a potent instrument to achieve the dissemination of this idea.' One such economic condition was that of rural emigration, which required serious action. Plunkett contrasted Irish population decline with that of mainland Britain, telling British co-operative delegates that 'our population is melting away as fast as yours is being reinforced'.

However, the problem proved more serious than numerical decline, as Plunkett outlined: 'the drain from Ireland is worse from the standpoint of quality ... The active and the enterprising leave us with an undue proportion of the very old and very young, of the mentally and physically unsound.'[23] This linkage of population decline to the physical and psychological atrophy of the rural population would remain part of the critical discourse about emigration throughout the twentieth century.[24] By strengthening a co-operative economy, Plunkett hoped that enough Irish people would remain to work in a more industrious countryside.

The DATI's second Annual General Report officially recognised 'the great importance, for the development of agriculture and industries and the improvement of social life in Ireland, of Co-operative Societies of farmers and other producers'.[25] The arrangement between state and co-operative sector provided the IAOS with opportunities to supplement the organisation's income. In 1902, P.J. Hannon and Æ earned 'a considerable sum over and above their salaries' for the IAOS by taking part in the DATI's Pioneer Lecture Scheme.[26] The presence of co-operative societies provided a platform through which information about legislation and agronomical science could be disseminated to large numbers of farmers. Lectures by agricultural experts were organised with the assistance of local societies. For example, in 1904 the IAOS distributed a series of circulars to its societies that informed members about a range of official matters. These included: changes to regulations relevant to co-operative credit societies and the payment of stamp duty; recommendations about obtaining fire insurance for co-operative buildings; directions to IAOS creamery managers to ensure they met a certain level of qualifications and book-keeping standards; and intelligence reports on butter prices and markets.[27]

Some viewed the IAOS and DATI as inseparable. In July 1902, Lismore Rural District Council in County Waterford passed a resolution whereby it endorsed the work of the IAOS and recommended farmers in the district to start their own co-operative creameries and corn stores. The Council passed a resolution that requested both the 'Irish Agricultural Organisation Society and the Department of Agriculture be requested to send down lecturers to point out to the farmers of the district the advantages of co-operation when they are properly organised'. The IAOS agreed to offer its assistance to the farmers of Lismore after the Council's invitation. The request for such assistance opened up new possibilities for co-operative development as Robert Anderson used this opportunity to write to all Rural District Councils 'to take up similar work elsewhere'.[28] The IAOS's association with the DATI provided the movement with a new official prominence.

The collaboration between voluntary and state agencies bore some extraordinary results. In 1905, the establishment of a Home Industries Co-operative Society and Gaelic League branch in the village of Dromore, County Tyrone, provided evidence of the efficacy that co-operation between different organisations provided in the efforts to revitalise communities. Praising Plunkett, *The Irish Homestead* reported that:

> we doubt whether even he saw so deeply into Irish necessities as when, in conjunction with [local priest] Father Maguire, he undertook to make one parish in Ireland a model parish, and let loose three great agencies, the IAOS, the Gaelic League, and the Department upon the work.

Diffusion of the co-operative model required concerted action between not only national agents such as the IAOS and Gaelic League, but also local influential brokers such as the clergy. On occasion this social co-operation produced cordial relations that transcended traditional sectarian divisions. To highlight this effect, the *Homestead*'s report on Dromore concluded with an incident that demonstrated mutual respect between local nationalists and unionists: 'We are credibly informed that at the last twelfth of July celebrations the Orangemen of Dromore asked for the loan of some Nationalist drums and their use was cheerfully allowed for the occasion.'[29]

However, if the principle of co-operation enabled warm relations across some local communities, these effects did not extend across the political sphere. As joint action bore some results the IAOS published a leaflet titled 'Home Rule in the Dairy'.[30] The appropriation of nationalist rhetoric provided constitutional nationalists with an uncomfortable reminder that Plunkett, a one-time Unionist MP, achieved a significant degree of political devolution for Ireland which they had yet to do. Plunkett was a figure of contempt for many nationalists. John Dillon, a leading Nationalist MP, pursued a campaign against the co-operative movement, and Plunkett in particular, in Parliament. Dillon believed the movement's attempts to attain social and economic improvements eroded 'the very substance of the nationalist movement'. It did this by concentrating upon improving material conditions for rural people and weakening demand for an Irish Parliament.

Any attempts to further the co-operative movement's influence – which, Dillon argued, the DATI achieved – should be resisted.[31]

In 1906, the IAOS came under severe scrutiny at an agricultural inquiry organised by the government in response to pressure from Nationalist MPs. The report sought to resolve the anomaly of the Vice-President of the DATI sitting in office without a parliamentary seat. The final report concluded that 'while it is necessary that the Department should be represented in Parliament it is neither necessary nor desirable that it should be represented by the Vice-President'.[32] However, the inquiry revealed the vulnerability of Plunkett's position. Opponents to co-operation used the occasion to criticise how the relationship between the DATI and IAOS unfairly placed public funds at the disposal of the co-operative movement. At the session held in Limerick on 3 July 1906, a sequence of witnesses drawn from local government and business lined up to highlight the damaging effect levelled at private agricultural businesses by the IAOS. William McDonnell JP, Alexander Shaw JP and Thomas Cleeve from Limerick's Chamber of Commerce, Patrick Vaughan JP and Chairman of Limerick County Council, and J. McInerney from the Board of Guardians all attacked the IAOS and criticised the DATI's provision of a state grant to the co-operative movement. Thomas Cleeve, a Canadian businessman who owned the Condensed Milk Company based in Limerick and with over fifty branches throughout the south-west of the country, argued that 'it is regarded as unfortunate to traders and proprietors that Sir Horace Plunkett was appointed Vice-President' of the DATI. The fact he 'was so strong on co-operation' meant that he placed 'in at least second place the industries long in existence before his advent as the chief of the Irish Agricultural Organisation Society'. Plunkett used this position to promote a 'programme of co-operation before all others. It is truly a lamentable state of things that in the 20th century Great Britain would lend herself indirectly to the long-continued failing she had of destroying our established industries'.[33]

In response, the Inquiry provoked a strong reaction from many co-operative societies who publicly moved to defend their umbrella organisation. One such resolution, published by the committee of Abbeydorney Co-operative Society in north Kerry, summarised the positive effects co-operative organisation brought to the farmers of the district:

1   It has raised the value of our produce fully 25 per cent, as compared with Cork market prices, which we had to depend on formerly.
2   That the co-operative creameries have both improved the quality and increased the quantity of our butter.
3   That by co-operation we have been brought into touch with the best markets for our produce, and have thus secured a very good, if not the top, price.
4   That if by any misfortune, while the movement is still young, it should be deprived of the benefits of co-operative organisation and left to the tender mercies of the merchants as formerly, we believe prices would fall heavily, and our industry be ruined in a short time.[34]

The spread of co-operative principles brought technological improvements and expert guidance in a way many farmers recognised. One troubling implication of the breakdown in the IAOS and DATI's relationship was that co-operators would be forced to rely more upon their own resources.

From the outset, Plunkett demonstrated an awareness of the shaky foundation of his position at the helm of the DATI. Plunkett's leadership relied upon the Westminster government's discretion as he lost his parliamentary seat at the 1900 general election. He explained this loss on 'the fact that co-operative education has so demoralised my politics that I am a political outcast'.[35] Plunkett's time as Departmental head saw him attract severe criticism. As discussed earlier, the publication of *Ireland in the New Century* generated a public backlash against Plunkett that further weakened his position at the DATI.[36] His lack of a parliamentary seat left him vulnerable to attack from rivals. Dillon criticised the link between the IAOS and DATI, and questioned the Attorney-General over 'what steps he proposes to take to prevent the continuance of this illegal action'.[37] The Attorney-General confirmed the legality of the relationship, but politically, Plunkett's position proved untenable. The collaboration between the IAOS and the DATI ended in 1907, when Plunkett's political opponents forced him from office.[38]

The Department of Agriculture and Technical Instruction after Plunkett

Any attempt to create a rural hegemonic project around the twin pillars of the IAOS and DATI stalled in 1907 with the replacement of Plunkett by Thomas Wallace Russell as Vice-President of the DATI. Russell was a Liberal Unionist MP from Tyrone who supported tenant farmers' rights. With the passage of Wyndham's Land Act in 1903 and John Redmond's pro-imperialist leadership of the IPP, Russell's opposition to Home Rule softened. He represented a palatable candidate for the departmental leader and received the support of the IPP in this role.[39] Russell directed the DATI for the next eleven years until his retirement after the First World War and implemented policies that improved Irish fisheries, conducted forestry research and experimentation and counteracted a widespread outbreak of foot-and-mouth disease in 1912.[40]

Plunkett's removal from the DATI provoked consternation among local co-operative societies and committees across the country published resolutions that highlighted widespread dismay at the severed connection between the IAOS and DATI. One co-operative society encapsulated a mood that the rupture ended a period of vital state support for the movement:

> That in a country so educationally backward as Ireland, the spontaneous growth of self-help cannot be expected as yet; we therefore consider that it is the duty of the Department of Agriculture to provide the means for extending the co-operative principle among farmers, it having proved to be the most effective form of practical education.[41]

While the end to the IAOS and DATI's partnership demoralised Plunkett, others welcomed the separation. At the 1907 Annual General Meeting Fr Finlay declared that the movement now went forward 'imbued with the proper spirit – the spirit of co-operation applied on the scale on which federations were built up'. Finlay argued that organisers needed to restrict their focus to societies already in existence to guarantee co-operation carried on in the 'proper spirit'.[42] In response, the IAOS directed its resources towards the consolidation of current position, which bred a more conservative movement unwilling to risk expansion.

The separation also encouraged members to express their enthusiasm for new-found economic autonomy in highly nationalistic terms. Mr Scully, a delegate from Clonlisk, County Offaly, viewed the separation of the IAOS and DATI as an opportunity to demonstrate the movement's strength:

> They were too long begging and craving from the Government, and that was what left Irishmen as they are. (Laughter) It was time the co-operators of Ireland began to do their own business. Let them prove to the department and to their enemies that they were able to do it (hear, hear), and when their enemies saw that they were able to do for themselves those enemies would become their friends.[43]

Scully exemplified a view among co-operators that the IAOS's relationship with the state eroded the self-reliance principle and viewed the DATI's interference as inimical to the long-term realisation of the movement's goals. A suspicion of the British state in Ireland began to creep into the attitudes of Irish co-operators over the next decade.

T.W. Russell's appointment created immediate friction between the IAOS and DATI. With Russell at the helm of agricultural development, critics of the co-operative movements such as IPP representatives and traders looked to force a retreat of the co-operative sector's role in agricultural production and distribution. Robert Anderson described Russell as an individual who 'hated the IAOS because his trader and political allies feared it'.[44] *The Times* described Russell, while in office, as someone who 'fought the [Irish Agricultural Organisation] Society with extraordinary bitterness and has shown much perverted ingenuity in opposing its claims and crippling its work'.[45] Russell made his antipathy towards the co-operative movement clear from the start and stressed that, under his leadership, 'there would be no partnership between the IAOS and the Department' and he instituted a policy of 'non-controversial co-operation'.[46] The 'non-controversial' part of this policy referred to the official objective that co-operative societies should continue to trade only if they refrained from harming the interests of local independent and private operators.[47]

On 19 November 1907, Russell delivered his first speech to the DATI's Council of Agriculture, which set out his first priority to redefine the relationship between the IAOS and Department. As he tackled the 'serious controversy' he chose as his theme the unfairness of the annual allocation of £3,700 to the IAOS from public funds. While he understood that the IAOS promoted the 'genuine work of agricultural co-operation' in dairying and agricultural production he objected when co-operators 'go outside the farmer's business altogether, and actually try to turn farmers into shopkeepers'. The practice of creameries and other societies performing ad hoc retail services meant farmers got 'into competition with the ordinary shopkeepers', which Russell declared meant 'I, for one, will be no party to a penny of the Department's money going to promote co-operation of this kind'.[48] Russell proposed that the 'annual subsidy paid to the Society by the Department should not be continued'. The proposal passed with the grant eventually phased out.[49] The *Irish Homestead* report of the speech suggested they hoped to change Russell's mind on the matter in the near future: 'Mr Russell will learn the facts of the work of the IAOS later on, and we are sure he will prove a good friend as one misconception after another is cleared away.'[50]

Such hopes proved to be misplaced. The subsidy to the IAOS from the DATI ceased on 1 January 1909. Moreover the official connection between the bodies ceased when the DATI decided to end the arrangement whereby two of its officials attended the IAOS General and Executive Committees.[51] From this point onwards the IAOS moved to the margins of official agricultural policymaking and presented itself as an embattled movement under attack from powerful enemies at the DATI.

Sensing the hand of political forces behind the direction of this new agricultural policy Æ used the *Irish Homestead* to attack the Nationalist Party at Westminster. In particular, Æ accused John Dillon of a 'misrepresentation of facts' when he spoke of Plunkett and the co-operative movement in Parliament. Æ criticised Dillon's narrow focus on constitutional politics at the expense of social and economic issues:

> Without organisation in this sense Mr Dillon might finally have got his Parliament
> in College Green [Dublin] and found rural Ireland economically controlled and
> enslaved by bodies like the English Wholesale Society.

A co-operative political economy in practice offered an alternative conception of independence based on economic autonomy which Æ defined as 'Industrial Home Rule'.[52] The IAOS's work to counter trade bodies such as the CWS contributed more to the liberty of Irish farmers than any campaign for a Home Rule Parliament up to that point.

Some at the IAOS privately welcomed the separation of movement and state. Robert Anderson and Fr Finlay viewed the relationship's end as potentially positive. Anderson, who held deep reservations about collaboration between the voluntary and state sectors, 'could see no good in a State-controlled IAOS which would be virtually an outside branch of the Department which subsidised it'.[53] At the first IAOS conference after Plunkett's removal from the DATI, Finlay's vice-presidential address elucidated his optimism for the movement. Finlay believed that the combined efforts of the DATI and IAOS to develop agriculture brought about a 'paralysis' among co-operators. Reliance upon the DATI subsidy encouraged the belief

> that the work in which [co-operative activists] were engaged had been taken up by the State, they considered themselves absolved from vigorous activity in prosecuting it, and that was specially the case in a movement which, by its nature, was to be promoted chiefly by individuals whom it benefitted. They were now returning to the condition in which they must rely entirely upon themselves. They might have to face difficulties, but for himself he looked forward with confidence to the future. (Applause.)

Not all co-operators agreed with this assessment. HF Norman, an IAOS official and former *Homestead* editor disagreed with Finlay and argued that the relationship between the DATI and IAOS had proved beneficial for co-operators.[54] The extent to which the state's role in co-operation was desirable provided a longstanding source of controversy.

One immediate loss of prestige for the IAOS was its inability to use its acquired expertise to influence departmental investigations that looked into the economic conditions of Irish agriculture. Under Plunkett's leadership, DATI reports received significant input from a range of agricultural experts and included an advocate from the co-operative movement. One example was an investigation in 1903 into ways the Irish dairy industry might end the adulteration of butter while countering the threat to butter producers from the sale of cheap margarine labelled as butter. Plunkett chaired the investigative committee, which included Robert Anderson as the IAOS's representative alongside a range of public health officials, trade body representatives and politicians. The investigative committee cross-examined a number of experts from countries that included Holland, Denmark and the United States. The final report recommended the need for some form of control and regulation over produce and greater international co-operation between countries to achieve this goal.[55]

The DATI investigated the condition of the dairy industry once again in 1910. A major focus of this examination focused upon the various trade descriptions applied to different grades of Irish butter sold across the United Kingdom. This time the investigating committee included no IAOS representative.[56] The committee did cross-examine Robert Anderson, whose evidence drew upon his long experience at the largest trade organisation in the field of butter production. Anderson revisited some of his 1903 arguments that 'creamery butter remained too loosely defined' and greater legislative regulations were required as lower-quality butter made within households continued to be sold as creamery produce. Anderson suggested three clear proposals that the DATI could implement to improve the international reputation of Irish butter, but crucially, any effective scheme needed the co-operation of the IAOS as the largest corporate body in the industry. The proposals included repeated calls to encourage winter dairying alongside the introduction of cow testing facilities to improve the quality of cattle stocks. His final proposal was the 'formation of an "Irish Co-operative Creamery Control"' to establish and maintain a high level of excellence in butter production.[57] He ended his evidence on the hopeful note that he felt

> confident that the Department, so far from placing any obstacles in their way, will cheerfully and cordially co-operate with the co-operative creameries and with the IAOS in supplementing and seconding any useful and practical effort which may result from the greater manifestation of the spirit of self-reliance and self-help.[58]

The final report ignored Anderson's evidence. In a summary description of the people and organisations from which the committee received input, the co-operative movement appeared as an afterthought:

> Creamery proprietors and managers, owners of butter factories, merchants of Belfast, Dublin, and Limerick, farmers who make butter on their own farms, delegates of the Cork Butter Market trustees, of the Irish Butter Trade Association, of the Irish Creamery Managers' Association, and of the Irish Creameries Protection Society. We have also received evidence on the subjects of our inquiry from the Irish Agricultural Organisation Society.[59]

The only substantive mention made of co-operative creameries in a final report that looked at Irish dairying offered a jaundiced assessment of their work as 'extremely lax in the discharge of their duties'. Co-operative managers lacked the sufficient interest in 'such important matters as costs of production, cleanliness of the milk supply, prices realised for their produce, and other conditions upon which the success or failure of the creamery depends'.[60] Rather than view co-operative creameries as the major point for legislative reform the report betrayed an official attitude that these societies represented an impediment to progress.

At the local level the work of organisers continued to keep the co-operative movement functioning while personalities at the elite end of the dispute between the DATI and IAOS wrangled over funding. The co-operative business model continued to increase its appeal among the rural population during this period of apparent crisis. Between 1907 and 1914 the number of societies affiliated to the IAOS experienced some fluctuations but overall the trend was one of continued growth in terms of membership. At the point of the split with the DATI in 1907, 913 co-operative societies, with a total of 82,311 members, belonged to the IAOS. By the outbreak of the First World War, these figures had increased to 1,023 co-operative societies and membership figures reached 106,212 (table 3.1).

Organisers continued to work towards Plunkett's ideal of 'Better Business' by promoting educational improvement at the society level. Disassociation from

Table 3.1 Co-operative societies and members, 1907–14

Year	No. of societies (creameries, credit societies, etc.)	Membership
1907	913	82,311
1908	881	85,939
1909	835	91,661
1910	880	94,512
1911	934	97,318
1912	947	101,991
1913	985	104,702
1914	1,023	106,212

Source: IAOS, *Annual Reports, 1907–1914*.

the DATI limited this aspect of their work. Nevertheless, organisers continued to visit societies in order to diffuse new agrarian techniques to help farmers to remain competitive. For example, in December 1913, the IAOS organiser suggested to Abbeydorney Co-operative Society in County Kerry that they invite Thomas Wibberley, an eminent agrarian expert to address their farmers on the topic of 'continuous cropping, and the production of milk in Winter'.[61] Wibberley, an agricultural lecturer, had published pioneering work on farming methods and offered advice to farmers in the nearby districts of Ardfert and Lixnaw.

The IAOS organiser ensured the IAOS retained a key role in driving economic development in the countryside during this period. The organisational team's size reflected the stretched financial resources of the IAOS. In 1907 the IAOS Executive restructured its team of eight organisers and relied upon this small staff to communicate their views of the grass-roots membership back to Dublin. The IAOS assigned each individual to a geographical area (table 3.2).[62] The benefit of assigning organisers to specific regions meant they accumulated detailed local knowledge and provided a recognisable point of contact for societies. This gave the organiser important symbolic capital within their districts, which helped them to resolve local disputes and problems. In 1913 a visiting American Commission established to investigate agricultural co-operation overseas described the IAOS organisers as 'the hardest worked people in Ireland'. It also took an outsider's perspective to credit the IAOS with the provision of an invaluable service for farmers in spite of the controversies in which they became embroiled. Following a four-day visit to Ireland in July 1913, the Investigative Commission concluded that the movement had achieved 'good work, which the founders of the movement may well look on with pride, and those who gave it support may regard their money as well invested … The change of feeling in the country has been effected.'[63]

Table 3.2 Structure of organisational staff, 1907

Name	Responsibility
Mr C.C. Riddall	Counties Cork, Kerry, Limerick and Waterford
Mr P. Gregan	Counties Mayo, Leitrim, Roscommon, Longford, Westmeath and King's
Mr R. Noble	Counties Donegal (Flax Societies), Derry, Antrim, Down, Tyrone and Armagh
Mr M. Joy	Counties Louth, Meath, Dublin, Kildare, Carlow, Queen's, Kilkenny, Wicklow and Tipperary
Mr M.A. Lyons	Counties Galway and Clare
Mr J. Moore	Counties Cavan and Monaghan
Miss Reynolds	Counties Donegal, Sligo and Fermanagh
Mr M.J. Hickey	County Wexford

Source: IAOS, *Annual Report, 1908.*

Co-operation and the Development Commission

T.W. Russell's vice-presidency saw the DATI promote a rural political economy that aimed to roll back the influence of co-operative ideas. The discontinuation of the annual grant in 1909 placed immediate strain on the IAOS's resources. After this date IAOS remained financially vulnerable with its work 'sadly hampered by lack of funds'.[64] This loss of funding encouraged conservatism within the movement as priorities shifted from expanding the repertoire of co-operative activities to the maintenance of a healthy creamery sector. The importance of private donors to the continuation of the IAOS's work proved to be most crucial at this point. The IAOS appealed for higher contributions from its societies to meet this shortfall. However, the level of contributions failed to match expectations. In 1910 the funds raised amounted to £4,708. Of this total, £2,417 came from individual subscriptions. The total amount raised from the co-operative societies only amounted to £1,230.[65]

To compound matters further, Russell used his position as an ex-officio member on the CDB to reduce the limited financial assistance granted by that body to the IAOS. According to the CDB's Secretary, William Micks, Russell appointed a committee to review the use of public money to fund co-operative credit societies. During 1898 to 1910 the CDB lent £7,345 to co-operative banks which provided seed capital to farmers for small-scale developmental projects on the western seaboard. When the Committee reported 'in favour of recalling all loans made out of public money to the Banks', the CDB 'felt obliged' to recall these loans made to co-operative banks. All money was repaid with interest except for one sum of three shillings and one penny. Micks recalled that Russell 'felt very strongly on the subject and was provocative about these loans'. Russell seldom interfered with the administrative work of the CDB, which suggested his strength of feeling on the subject of co-operative credit. Micks described the episode as the 'only matter that caused unpleasant friction at the Board's meetings'. Despite pressure from Russell the CDB still managed to direct limited funding towards the co-operative movement. At the height of the IAOS's financial quarrel with the DATI, the CDB funds provided welcome funds to defray the travelling expenses of co-operative organisers.[66]

The financial woes of the IAOS looked set to end when David Lloyd George, the Liberal Chancellor of the Exchequer, announced the controversial 'People's Budget' in late 1909. This budget delivered a host of measures to fund new welfare reforms and included provisions to create a Development Commission. Established in May 1910, this body encouraged the development of British resources via scientific approaches to agriculture, including the 'promotion of co-operative marketing'. The emphasis of the Development Commission lay in 'promoting the country's rural and agricultural development'.[67] Plunkett successfully lobbied the government to insert a clause that allowed the Development Commission to fund agricultural co-operation.[68] The Commission aimed to fund innovative practices but looked to achieve this through the medium of existing centres of research and expertise.[69] The IAOS represented an ideal candidate for such development funds due to its fifteen years' experience in rural reform.

The IAOS immediately seized the opportunity and applied to the Development Commission for a new grant to replace the lost DATI subsidy. However, the devolution of agricultural powers to Ireland worked against the IAOS as the decision over the allocation of this new grant money resided with the DATI. The IAOS and its sister organisations, the Scottish Agricultural Organisation Society and the English Agricultural Organisation Society, applied for funding. The latter two received grants of £1,000 and £3,000 respectively. In Ireland the grant application needed to be submitted to the DATI for approval before it passed to the Development Commission. The IAOS submitted its funding application to the DATI in January 1911. Russell delayed the application process and that November refused to endorse the IAOS's claim for support. His reasoning remained the same as previous years. First, he cited the controversial and political nature of the IAOS, which became publicly associated with a hostile attitude towards the IPP. Second, he argued that 'certain trading interests in this country naturally objected to state aid being accorded to the formation of societies that were intended to enter into competition with them in the exercise of their legitimate trading operations'.[70]

In a series of letters published in *The Times* that December, Plunkett addressed what he termed a crisis in rural progress and argued that Russell's actions threatened the co-operative movement's attempts to build 'a new social economy'.[71] Æ made similar arguments in the *Irish Homestead*. While the English agricultural co-operative movement received the money applied for without difficulty, the IAOS struggled to survive. Æ launched an appeal for donations with the hope that 'the organised farmers of Ireland will take note of the difference of treatment of the IAOS in Ireland and the AOS in England'.[72] In 1911, the IAOS temporarily withheld payment of employees, who only received their wages following a donation of £1,800 by Horace Plunkett.[73] Robert Anderson believed that, without Plunkett's generosity at this juncture, the IAOS would have disbanded while its application to the Development Commission lay unprocessed.[74]

T.W. Russell's decision to block the IAOS application reflected his support for private traders, shopkeepers and butter merchants opposed to the IAOS's role in the rural economy. He gave a revealing interview to the *Co-operative News* while in Glasgow the following February. In the course of the interview Russell claimed that he held no prior opinion about the IAOS and its work before he became the leader of the DATI. However, when Russell assumed office he learned that an annual department grant of £3,700 to the movement provided a major source of controversy and he was aware that the 'Irish Nationalist party charged the agents of the IAOS with working against the Nationalist cause'. The traders of Ireland also 'objected to State money, part of which they as taxpayers had to contribute, being used to oppose them in business'. Having weighed up these arguments Russell concluded that the IAOS purposefully antagonised the Nationalist Party and he could no longer justify a state subsidy to fund such a movement. When asked to elaborate further on his refusal to support the IAOS's application to the Development Commission, Russell responded: 'because the traders object as taxpayers to State money being used to cut their throats'.[75]

The conflict with the DATI led to public declarations of support for the IAOS from a multitude of voices from outside the mainstream of Irish politics. Importantly, a younger generation that grew to maturity influenced by the ethos and creative energy unleashed by the cultural revival began to announce itself in favour of the co-operative ideal. In particular, this crisis for the IAOS encouraged declarations of support from seemingly disparate political quarters, but gathered together in one source – *The Irish Review*. This monthly nationalist journal showcased writing on the topics of Irish literature, science and politics, and existed for three years between 1911 and 1914. During its short life the journal exerted considerable influence upon the direction of Irish politics. It published work by writers, some of whom (including co-founder Thomas MacDonagh) became leading participants in the Easter Rising.[76] The *Review* offered a platform for nationalists whose opinions did not fit with the parliamentary orthodoxy. Instead, the journal gave 'expression to the intellectual movement in Ireland', which encompassed a broad range of people united in their interest in 'the application of Irish intelligence to the reconstruction of Irish life'. The first editorial stressed that 'science and economics will claim an increasing share of attention as our people progress towards the command of their resources'.[77] The *Irish*

Review aimed at an audience which anticipated some form of political autonomy against the backdrop of Home Rule negotiations, but which also wished to understand how an independent Irish society should be organised. It provided readers with a wide range of cultural and political topics to engage with, and debates about the co-operative movement's role in Irish society featured prominently. In social and economic subjects, particularly those related to agriculture, the editorial line supported co-operative methods to promote national development. Æ's "The Problem of Rural Life" appeared across its first six issues. The *Irish Review* acted as a useful guide to the issues concerning an emergent nationalist elite in the early twentieth century.

The cessation of state funding to the IAOS formed a dominant topic that preoccupied many contributions. James Hannay, a writer, clergyman and Gaelic League activist, more popularly known by his nom de plume, George Birmingham, rejected the parliamentary methods applied by the IPP in its pursuit of political freedom and viewed British liberalism as a hypocritical doctrine. Instead, his political philosophy led him to believe that the real national energy existed beyond the dry politicking at Westminster and arguing that 'the Gaelic League, the co-operative movement and Sinn Féin could bring about a true national revival based on individual self-reliance and free discussion'.[78] Birmingham attacked Russell's policy of 'non-controversial co-operation' in *The Irish Review*, which he characterised as a piece of disingenuous politicking. He argued that Russell knew 'perfectly well that there is no such thing as non-controversial co-operation. All co-operation amongst farmers must provoke the hostility of someone':

> Co-operative creameries excite the fury of the butter merchant. Egg societies enrage the gentlemen at present occupied in packing stale eggs in dirty straw. Even Raffeissen [*sic*] banks [credit societies] injure the business of the local trader whose customers are tied to him by their debts, and the publican-politician whom it suits to have a financial hold over the farmers. When Mr. [T.W.] Russell spoke of the non-controversial co-operation which he would organise, he meant either that he would organise no co-operation at all or else that he would organise co-operation in the teeth of the protests of the very class through whose influence the money was withheld from the IAOS.[79]

Russell's policy excluded the co-operative movement whenever possible, but Birmingham recognised the powerful implications of a co-operative intervention for the rural community.

These debates played out against a backdrop of tense political negotiations and a potential constitutional crisis that coloured the controversy. One astute analyst of the situation made a connection between how one's support for the co-operative movement over the DATI highlighted an attitude in favour of a new, socially enlightened variant of nationalism. 'An Ulster Imperialist's' assessment of the political situation outlined various positions regarding the Home Rule debate, alongside potential political developments if a Home Rule Bill failed or succeeded. The author argued that if the Bill failed, nationalist Ireland threatened to divide into two camps and identified attitudes to the co-operative movement as the major fault-line:

> The conflict between Nationalists of the Co-operative movement and Nationalists of the T.W. Russell party would probably split a new line of cleavage across the whole body of Irish politics, giving rise to a new party which would contain nearly all the constructive elements of Irish life … upon an agrarian policy, and becoming inevitably a Home Rule party in which gradually … the best of our citizens would be very much of one mind. In some way such as this, Ireland might, before the lapse of many years, arrive at a settlement of the Home Rule Question.[80]

This analysis of Irish nationalism proved insightful. For the anonymous 'Imperialist' the question of Home Rule and agrarian economics were intimately bound up with one another.

In the end, direct intervention came from Westminster. The Irish Chief Secretary, Augustine Birrell, personally placed the case of the IAOS before the Cabinet and cited his disapproval of Russell's actions.[81] The Development Commission granted the IAOS a sum of £2,000 in 1913 through the Chief Secretary's office. In subsequent years the Commission offered a generous annual grant of up to £4,000 per annum on the basis of £1 for every £1 subscribed by members. This measure incentivised societies to contribute to the IAOS and morale soared on account of the grant, which provided financial security and offered a seal of approval for the co-operative movement's work.[82]

The grant's conditions introduced important limitations upon the IAOS's activities. The Commission banned the IAOS from creating co-operative retail societies and narrowed the range that forms of co-operative organisation promoted by the IAOS could take and separated the junior retailing branch of the organisation from the larger, established productive branch. The link between co-operative societies and the Dublin-based IAOS was reformed. Previously, the IAOS offered assistance to all co-operative societies, but under new conditions 'contributory affiliation' became 'a condition of receiving advice and assistance from the Society'.[83] While this constrained various co-operative activities, the most politically important outcome of this decision lay in the Development Commission's decision to circumvent T.W. Russell's authority. This undermined the political autonomy of the DATI and occurred while political tensions in Ireland grew evermore volatile. The fact that Westminster moved to circumvent the devolved DATI to ensure funding reached the co-operative movement revealed how officialdom viewed the IAOS's work as providing an important economic function. It also showed that Westminster's patience with Irish political independence had limitations.

The high regard in which central government held the IAOS, and the importance it placed upon its developmental role in Irish rural society, saw the British administration override the fragile devolved governmental apparatus then in place. The new funding assured the IAOS of its immediate future and guaranteed its continued involvement in agrarian matters despite the opposition of the DATI.[84] *The Irish Homestead* welcomed the Commission's findings as a vindication of the co-operative movement's work, describing the financial aid as a measure that allowed it to 'carry on its agricultural programme in the future as in the past'.[85]

An important development also materialised in the support for the co-operative programme from a new generation of voices that came to maturity immersed in the Irish Revival. New ideas emerged from a wide range of culturally nationalist groups and organisations, among which the IAOS provided a fertile source. Stephen Gwynn, an IPP MP between 1906 and 1918, noted that a younger generation of Irish nationalists preferred ideas associated with Sinn Féin to those preached by his own party. Gwynn observed with the benefit of hindsight a decade later that although a relatively small sect before 1914, 'Sinn Féin, rather than Parliamentarianism, was the growing creed, and it based its claim on different grounds and had a different outlook'.[86] The Sinn Féin party increasingly became a politically heterogeneous home for individuals disenchanted with the IPP's brand of politics. This 'different outlook' defined the new nationalists who would be brought under the umbrella of the Sinn Féin party after 1916.

The IAOS maintained its organisational work in the face of institutional and political obstructions and, in the process, captured the attention of foreign observers interested in agricultural development. In a 1913 submission to an American Commission investigating the condition of agricultural co-operation across Europe, the IAOS made a great claim for its work as it embedded co-operation throughout the Irish countryside. On the eve of the First World War the IAOS looked upon its achievements with satisfaction, and anticipated the next phase of a co-operative revolution: 'The hardest part of [its work] is done. The change of feeling in the country has been effected. Rural Ireland is ready to be completely organised.'[87]

Notes

1 Æ's address, 'The Building up of a Rural Civilisation', given at the IAOS Annual Conference. The IAOS published a transcript in pamphlet form. IAOS, *Annual Report, 1909*, 38.
2 Paul Bew, *Ideology and the Irish Question: Ulster Unionism and Irish Nationalism, 1912–1916* (Oxford: Clarendon Press, 1994); Ronan Fanning, *Fatal Path: British Government and Irish Revolution 1910–1922* (London: Faber & Faber, 2013).
3 IAOS, *Annual Report, 1909*, 38.
4 Horace Plunkett, New York, to Fr T.A. Finlay, Dublin, December 1909, NLI, Ms 49, 803/44/2
5 Edward E. Lysaght, *Sir Horace Plunkett and his Place in the Irish Nation* (Dublin: Maunsel & Co., 1916), 17.
6 R.F. Foster, *Modern Ireland, 1600–1972* (London: Penguin, 1988), 431–493.
7 Lionel Smith-Gordon and Cruise O'Brien, *Co-operation in Denmark* (Manchester: Co-operative Union, 1919), 24.

8 Horace Plunkett, 'The Relations between Organized Self Help and State Aid in Ireland', *North American Review*, 67.503 (1898), 497–498 (p. 498).

9 David A. McCabe, 'The Recent Growth of Co-operation in Ireland', *Quarterly Journal of Economics*, 20.4 (1906), 547–574 (pp. 571–572).

10 IAOS, *Annual Report, 1896*, 6.

11 IAOS, *Annual Report, 1899*, 29.

12 Ciara Breathnach, *The Congested Districts Board of Ireland, 1891–1923: Poverty and Development in the West of Ireland* (Dublin: Four Courts Press, 2005).

13 IAOS, *Annual Report, 1895*, 5.

14 James Logan, *Ulster in the X-Rays: A Short Review of the Real Ulster, its People, Pursuits, Principles, Poetry, Dialect and Humour* (London: Arthur H. Stockwell, n.d.), 99.

15 Dermot Meleady, *Redmond: The Parnellite* (Cork: Cork University Press, 2008), 258–259.

16 Michael Clune, 'The Work and the Report of the Recess Committee, 1895–6', *Studies*, 71.281 (1982), 72–84; Carla King, 'The Recess Committee, 1895–6', *Studia Hibernica*, 30 (1998/1999), 21–46.

17 K. Theodore Hoppen, *Governing Hibernia: British Politicians and Ireland, 1800–1921* (Oxford: Oxford University Press, 2016), 274.

18 Andrew Gailey, *Ireland and the Death of Kindness: The Experience of Constructive Unionism 1890–1905* (Cork: Cork University Press, 1987), 3.

19 Mary E. Daly, *The First Department: A History of the Department of Agriculture* (Dublin: Institute of public Administration, 2002), 14.

20 Horace Plunkett, 'The Recess Committee and Remedial Legislation for Ireland', *Economic Journal*, 7.25 (1897), 131–136 (p. 134).

21 William P Coyne, 'Preface', in *Ireland: Industrial and Agricultural*, ed. by Department of Agriculture and Technical Instruction (Dublin: Brown and Nolan Limited, 1902), unpaginated.

22 'Surprise Butter Competition, 1905', *Irish Homestead*, 2 September 1905, 661.

23 Cited in R.A. Anderson, 'Agricultural Co-operation in Ireland', in *Ireland: Industrial and Agricultural*, ed. by Department of Agriculture and Technical Instruction (Dublin: Brown and Nolan Limited, 1902), 218–234 (pp. 233–234).

24 The social production of psychological instability remained a long-held view by many in Ireland. Both medical experts and lay people 'believed that generations of emigration had siphoned off the cream and left behind a "weaker" and "vulnerable" population'. Nancy Scheper-Hughes, *Saints, Scholars and Schizophrenics: Mental Illness in Rural Ireland*, 2nd edn (Berkeley: University of California Press, 2001), 34–35.

25 DATI, *Second Annual General Report of the Department, 1901–02* (Dublin: HMSO, 1902), 12.

26 IAOS Office Committee Meeting, 22 July 1902, Gore-Booth Papers, PRONI, D/4131/M/14.

27 IAOS, *Annual Report, 1904*, 164–175.

28 Copy of Lismore Rural District Council Resolution, 2 July 1902; 'Agricultural Co-operation', R.A. Anderson's Circular to Rural District Councils, 19 July 1902, Gore-Booth Papers, PRONI, D/4131/M/14.

29 'Irish Clergymen and Irish Civilisation', *Irish Homestead*, 7 October 1905, 733–734.

30 IAOS, *Home Rule in the Dairy* (Dublin: Irish Agricultural Organisation Society, 1903).

31 F.S.L. Lyons, *The Irish Parliamentary Party, 1890–1910* (London: Faber, 1951), 233; John Coolahan, *Irish Education: Its History and Structure* (Dublin: Institute of Public Administration, 1981), 92.

32 House of Commons Parliamentary Papers [HCPP] [Cd. 3572] *DATI Report of the Departmental Committee of Inquiry* (1907), 120.

33 HCPP [Cd. 3574], *DATI Minutes of Evidence Taken Before the Departmental Committee of Inquiry* (1907), 348–349.

34 IAOS, *Annual Report, 1906*, 85.

35 Cited in Anderson, 'Agricultural Co-operation', 234.

36 Marianne Elliott, *When God Took Sides: Religion and Identity in Ireland – Unfinished History* (Oxford: Oxford University Press, 2009), 200–211.

37 Hansard *HC Deb 28 November 1906 vol. 166 cc65–7,* http://hansard.millbanksystems.com/commons/1906/nov/28/subsidies-to-the-irish-agricultural#S4V0166P0_19061128_HOC_100 *[accessed 10 June 2016].*

38 Eunan O'Halpin, *The Decline of the Union: British Government in Ireland, 1892–1920* (Dublin: Gill & Macmillan, 1987), 69; Trevor West, *Horace Plunkett, Co-operation and Politics* (Gerrards Cross, Bucks.: Colin Smythe, 1986), 76–81.

39 James Loughlin, 'Russell, Sir Thomas Wallace', in *Dictionary of Irish Biography: From Earliest Times to the Year 2002, Volume 8*, ed. by James McGuire and James Quinn (Cambridge: Cambridge University Press, 2009), 665–666. On Russell's early career, see Loughlin, 'T.W. Russell, the Tenant Farmer Interest and Progressive Unionism in Ulster, 1886–1900', *Eire-Ireland*, 25.1 (1990), 44–63.

40 Nicholas Whyte, *Science, Colonialism and Ireland* (Cork: Cork University Press, 1999), 97–98.

41 IAOS, *Annual Report, 1906*, 85.

42 IAOS, *Annual Report, 1907*, 55–56.

43 IAOS, *Annual Report, 1907*, 57.

44 R.A. Anderson, *With Horace Plunkett in Ireland* (London: Macmillan and Co., 1935), 176.

45 'The Irish Co-operative Grant', *The Times*, 22 March 1913, 6.

46 F.S.L. Lyons, *Ireland Since the Famine* (London: Fontana Press, 1975), 215.

47 Anderson, *With Horace Plunkett*, 123; Líam Kennedy, 'Farmers, Traders and Agricultural Politics in Pre-Independence Ireland', in *Irish Peasants: Violence and Political Unrest, 1780–1914*, ed. by James S. Donnelly and Samuel Clark (Manchester: Manchester University Press, 1983), 339–373 (pp. 350–353).

48 T.W. Russell, 'The Vice-President's Address to the Council of Agriculture', *Department of Agriculture and Technical Instruction for Ireland*, 8.2 (1908), 209–226 (pp. 220–222).

49 DATI, *Seventh Annual Report of the Department, 1906–07* (Dublin: His Majesty's Stationery Office, 1908), 2.

50 'In Darkest Department', *Irish Homestead*, 23 November 1907, 926.

51 Department of Agriculture and Technical Instruction for Ireland, *Eighth Annual Report of the Department, 1907–08* (Dublin: His Majesty's Stationery Office, 1908), 35.

52 'Is Co-operation a Political Dodge?' *Irish Homestead*, 4 May 1907.

53 Anderson, *With Horace Plunkett*, 133.
54 IAOS, *Annual Report, 1907*, 55–6.
55 HCPP [Cd. 1749], *Committee on Butter Regulations, Final Report* (1903), 3.
56 HCPP [Cd. 5092], *Report of the Departmental Committee on the Irish Butter Industry* (1910), unpaginated minute appointing the committee.
57 HCPP [Cd. 5093], *Departmental Committee on the Irish Butter Industry, Minutes of Evidence, Appendices and Index* (1910), 475.
58 HCPP [Cd. 5093], *Departmental Committee*, 477.
59 HCPP [Cd. 5092], *Report of the Departmental Committee*, 2.
60 HCPP [Cd. 5092], *Report of the Departmental Committee*, 19.
61 C.C. Riddall to T. O'Donovan, Abbeydorney, 19 December 1913, NAI 1088/2/2.
62 IAOS, *Annual Report, 1907*, 15.
63 American Commission to Investigate Agricultural Credit and Cooperation, *Agricultural Cooperation and Rural Credit in Europe* (Washington: Government Printing Office, 1913), 888.
64 'The Irish Co-operative Grant', *The Times*, 22 March 1913, 6; IAOS, *Annual Report, 1911*, 22.
65 IAOS, *Annual Report, 1912*, 22
66 William L. Micks, *An Account of the Constitution, Administration and Dissolution of the Congested Districts Board for Ireland from 1891 to 1923* (Dublin: Eason & Son, Limited, 1925), 95–96.
67 Bruce K. Murray, *The People's Budget 1909/1910: Lloyd George and Liberal Politics* (Oxford: Oxford University Press, 1980), 146.
68 West, *Horace Plunkett*, 85.
69 Bentley Brinkerhoff Gilbert, 'David Lloyd George: Land, the Budget, and Social Reform', *American Historical Review*, 81.5 (1976), 1058–1066 (p. 1065); Robert Olby, 'Social Imperialism and State Support for Agricultural Research in Edwardian Britain', *Annals of Science*, 48.6 (1991), 509–526.
70 Daly, *First Department*, 43.
71 Horace Plunkett, *The Crisis in Irish Rural Progress: Being Three Letters Reprinted from The Times* (London: John Parkinson Bland, 1912), 1–3.
72 'The Position of the IAOS', *Irish Homestead*, 2 September 1911, 688–689.
73 West, *Horace Plunkett*, 86.
74 Anderson, *With Horace Plunkett*, 175.
75 'Irish Agricultural Organisation', *Co-operative News*, 17 February 1912, 188–189.
76 W.J. McCormack, *Dublin 1916: The French Connection* (Dublin: Gill & Macmillan, 2012), 74–96.
77 Editor, '[Untitled Introduction]', *The Irish Review* 1.1 (1911), 1–6 (p. 1).
78 Patrick Maume, 'Hannay, James Owen ("George A Birmingham")', in *Dictionary of Irish Biography: From Earliest Times to the Year 2002, Volume 4*, ed. by James McGuire and James Quinn (Cambridge: Cambridge University Press, 2009), 444–448 (p. 445).
79 George A. Birmingham, 'Politics in the Nude', *Irish Review*, 1.10 (1911), 469–476 (p. 471).
80 Ulster Imperialist, 'An Appreciation of the Situation', *Irish Review*, 2.13 (1912), 1–11 (p. 9).

81 Margaret Digby, *Horace Plunkett: An Anglo-American Irishman* (Oxford: Basil Blackwell, 1949), 146.
82 West, *Horace Plunkett*, 86.
83 HCPP [Cd. 6735], *Copy of Treasury Letter, dated 1st April, 1913, Respecting the Conditions on which a Grant will be made to the [Irish Agricultural Organisation] Society, from the Development Fund* (1913).
84 Patrick Bolger, *The Irish Co-operative Movement: Its History and Development* (Dublin: Institute of Public Administration, 1977), 105–106; Kennedy, 'Farmers, Traders and Agricultural Politics', 351–353.
85 'The IAOS and the Development Commission', *Irish Homestead*, 19 July 1913, 593–594.
86 Stephen Gwynn, *Ireland* (London: Ernest Benn, 1924), 97.
87 American Commission, *Agricultural Cooperation*, 888.

4

Co-operation and life during wartime

Following Horace Plunkett's departure from the Department of Agriculture and Technical Instruction (DATI) and until the end of the First World War, the Irish co-operative movement experienced a series of trials that threatened its programme for rural improvement. The Irish Agricultural Organisation Society (IAOS) contended with hostile agricultural policymakers and nationalist politicians, but the organisation also faced new challenges presented by the outbreak of the Great War in August 1914 and the demands of a wartime economy. At the end of the war the IAOS assessed where it stood at the end of that experience:

> The stability of the movement for which the IAOS stands has been subjected to a crucial test during the last five years. Its steady growth and remarkably rapid development in new directions – some of a far more ambitious character than any previously undertaken by the organised farmers – afford yet another proof of the superiority of co-operative organisation under conditions of stress. The societies have not only held together, but have also improved their buildings and equipment as well as their business methods, and have increased their output to an extent greater than during any other period.[1]

Throughout the war the IAOS acted as a centre of stability for tens of thousands of farmers and emerged with a newfound sense of confidence and purpose despite the trying circumstances it met during those years. However, at the same time Ireland emerged from the global conflict bitterly divided and on the precipice of violence and revolt.

When the co-operative movement moved into the twentieth century's second decade its prospects seemed mixed. The IAOS had established the co-operative society as a familiar institution throughout the countryside that placed the means of dairy production, distribution of goods to market and access to limited finance under the control of farmers. The IAOS also showed it aptitude to profoundly shape the agrarian economy through its displacement of the Co-operative Wholesale Society (CWS) as a major player in the dairy industry. Yet the decade also heralded serious problems. The immediate challenge that beset the IAOS concerned its relationship with the DATI. The change in departmental leadership meant a reorientation in Irish agricultural policy and a reduced role for co-operative voices in the formulation of agricultural policymaking. In peacetime, the IAOS and DATI sat uncomfortably alongside one another. The outbreak of the Great War compounded an already problematic relationship at a time when the Irish farmer's ability to meet the demands made by a wartime economy mattered more than ever.

The Great War drastically changed Ireland's political relationship with the rest of the United Kingdom. One major reason stemmed from developments that resulted from the Easter Rising in April 1916. This armed rebellion against British rule by a radical minority of Irish nationalists in Dublin changed the contours of the Irish Question and led to increased sympathy for the separatist cause.[2] The Sinn Féin party, founded in 1905, experienced a rapid growth in support after the armed uprising in Dublin. Sinn Féin benefited from an ability to position themselves as the heirs to the rebellion's legacy and as their demands for an Irish Republic gathered momentum they displaced the Irish Parliamentary Party (IPP) as the mainstream representatives of nationalist Ireland at the 1918 General Election.[3] Sinn Féin's electoral performance heralded the arrival of a new, separatist force in Irish nationalist politics that hastened a conflict between Irish Republicanism and the British state after the war. However, economic changes in Ireland following the war also played a part in changing the colour of nationalist opinion in Ireland. This chapter focuses on the ways in which this new generation of 'vivid faces', to use R.F. Foster's soubriquet for the young nationalists of the early twentieth century, used economic arguments and ideas associated with the co-operative movement to define a nationalist developmentalist strategy. Æ's economic ideas proved particularly influential in this intellectual shift.

During the war, the issue of a secure food supply was one of the political priorities facing the British government as it looked to secure military victory. Ireland emerged as an important part of the British war economy. As a country with a large agricultural sector, it was well-positioned to help ensure Great Britain received its required foodstuffs despite the German navy's efforts to disrupt imports. The Great War proved to be a relatively plentiful time for Irish farmers as the state guaranteed the prices of agricultural produce. Over the course of the conflict Irish agricultural produce doubled in value which, despite the rise in wage and price inflation, represented a bonanza for Irish farmers.[4] Patrick Kavanagh colourfully recalled the generous impact of the wartime price guarantees on the farmers' pocket. Kavanagh, who grew up in rural Monaghan during the war, recalled boyhood scenes whereby 'every Sunday coming home from Mass I heard all around me: "It's a great war for the farmer. Cattle up four pounds a head." "The German's a good soldier. Up the German."'[5]

Certainly the notion that 'the war brought floods of money into Ireland' was widely held and an impression lingered that 'agriculture had a golden time, and all the profits of agriculture went to the occupiers of the land'.[6] The distribution of profits reflected the amount of land a farmer held, with larger farmers drawing a greater benefit than smaller farmers and labourers. Agricultural prices were three times higher in 1920 than in 1913 and farmers with larger landholdings made more money, owing to their ability to exploit the prices paid for crops.[7] However, the picture of wartime economic prosperity painted by Kavanagh sits uneasily alongside the violent rejection of the British state that occurred in the war's immediate aftermath. This chapter attempts to understand how this discontent partly arrived out of the economic sphere by examining how the war effected the co-operative movement's position. An important factor in the promotion of disaffection came from Æ's intellectual positioning of co-operators in an increasingly hostile state system. He shaped the perceptions of nationalists that the war allowed Britain to impose a tyrannical economic arrangement on the Irish people.

The outbreak of the First World War overturned the prevalent political circumstances across Britain and Ireland. The domestic political context changed dramatically. The outbreak of a nationalist rebellion in Dublin during Easter 1916 shifted the tectonics of the 'Irish Question'. Members of the secretive underground organisation, the Irish Republican Brotherhood, alongside the socialist Irish Citizen's Army, directed a city-wide armed uprising against British rule. On 24 April 1916, its leaders announced the existence of an independent Irish Republic and the very public arrival of a nationalist opinion much advanced from the familiar demands for Home Rule. Suppressed within a week, and its leaders executed, the legacy of the Easter Rising exerted a radical change in mainstream nationalist opinion. F.S.L. Lyons famously described the Rising's principal political achievement as 'the point of departure ... for all subsequent Irish history'.[8] One IAOS leader was directly affected by the events. Robert Anderson, whose experience of those years mirrored 'that of many thousands of fathers', lost his son Alan on the Western Front in 1914. Anderson was wounded in the Rising as he fought as a member in the army's reserve volunteer force known as the 'Gorgeous Wrecks' due to their uniform's inscription of Georgius Rex.[9]

However, everyday experiences in rural communities remained largely unaffected in the immediate aftermath of the rebellion challenging perceptions of 1916 as a moment of sudden and radical change. The consequences of the rebellion took time to filter down to the rural community. When they did the effects would be brutal and violent, but in the summer of 1916 farmers remained more concerned about their ability to produce items such as butter, milk and livestock as they aimed to sell these goods at the best price upon the market.

The IAOS remained an institution in demand among members and its continued work amid moments of political change implied an element of continuity within the state of Ireland. Increased instances of state intervention that drastically shaped everyday life across Britain and Ireland dramatically affected the lives of rural people. Farming regulations, control orders and the repercussions of an economic blockade intensified demand for Irish foodstuffs across the United

Kingdom. However, such state interventions needed to pass through existing institutions. In Ireland this meant the demands placed on agriculture by an increasingly centralised government still occurred via farmers' businesses and institutions that predated the shift to a wartime economy. Co-operatives were central to the shift to a wartime economy. Fran Brearton has argued the war exerted a different impact upon Ireland, from that of England. In England, the war symbolised a break with the past and the destruction of pre-war institutions, but in Ireland the war 'played a part in a history whose main themes and "institutions" existed long before the Great War and continued long after it was over'.[10] The wartime experience of the co-operative movement supports this claim. The co-operative movement helped farmers to meet new expectations through its co-ordination of expertise and resources. Co-operators helped to ensure the necessary output of food and that their members shared in the rewards and achieved those things despite the fact that the DATI continued to marginalise the IAOS in official agrarian policy. Lionel Smith-Gordon, who worked in the IAOS's headquarters at Plunkett House, noted in 1917 that, 'the IAOS has been swallowed up in the vortex of war and is playing its important part in comparative obscurity'.[11] This obscurity defined its relationship with the state, but its work did not go unheeded by those who relied upon the IAOS.

The movement on trial

The outbreak of the First World War caused a seismic change within Irish society. Political debates around Home Rule became side-lined as the government intensified the war effort. In 1914, the IAOS executive issued a patriotic rallying cry which emphasised that the economic challenges of war could only be met with the aid of their movement:

> Without the co-operative movement, the scarcity of labour, consequent on the war, would probably result in a still further diminution of the acreage under tillage; with it the shortage of labour can be to a great extent counterbalanced by the more general use of labour saving machinery. *The movement is on its trial* [emphasis added].[12]

The challenge for Irish co-operators lay in the execution of their duties at a moment of international crisis. Horace Plunkett 'had from the first seen that food supplies would be one of the keys to victory, and he had been anxious for the IAOS to use its powers to increase food production in Ireland'.[13] In a presidential address to the IAOS in October 1915 Plunkett pointed out that in normal circumstances 'the man in the street, as the final authority in the mind of the politician is not inaptly called, does not bother his head about agriculture'. As long as this individual and the intelligent housewife can buy their groceries at a moderate price they are satisfied. However, war transformed this situation and

the man in the street has been alarmed by the new conditions of naval warfare. As he walks along with his head erect, a sort of periscope to his stomach, he sees on the newspaper posters the exploits of the submarine and, in the shop window, the prices of his food mounting up. It dawns upon him that those who devote themselves to growing food within the safe borders of these islands are fulfilling a useful purpose; and so the neglected industry comes in for an unusual share of public attention.[14]

Plunkett saw that the war represented a new test of co-operative principles. The war offered a test 'of the character and a capacity of the rural democracy' built by co-operators up to that date.[15] Moreover, the role played by the IAOS in spreading technological innovations through Ireland showed one important way it prepared the country to meet wartime demands.

The outbreak of the war led to a rapid increase in the output of agricultural produce in the British economy.[16] Food supply formed a major concern of British governance in wartime and Irish agriculture remained a central plank to Britain's economic performance. The IAOS pleaded with the DATI to co-ordinate their work for the sake of the war effort and to put 'an end to all friction between the official and voluntary agencies working for agricultural development in Ireland and insuring their harmonious co-operation'.[17] The DATI and IAOS initially presented a united front as they appealed to farmers' patriotism to utilise their resources to the greatest national advantage. The IAOS and DATI issued complementary public notices to farmers to conserve food and offered instructions on issues such as vegetable cultivation, crop rotation and directions to maximise production. J.R. Campbell, Assistant Secretary for Agriculture at the DATI, urged farmers to concentrate upon tillage farming and increased efforts to extend dairying in Ireland to cover winter months.[18]

The IAOS's ability to provide targeted support proved to be of immense value for farmers. The co-operative movement provided assistance to Irish farmers during the war as organisers helped to adapt the economic functions of societies where necessary. This mirrored similar experiences in other countries. For example, agricultural co-operatives in Russia helped peasants meet new demands as leading co-operators saw the war 'as an opportunity to create a more systematic programme of agronomic research and assistance'.[19] As early as 1911, Æ argued that the co-operative movement offered the means through which farmers could respond to pressures in a nimble fashion: 'the power to continuously adjust production to the needs of the market is one of the greatest advantages of association among farmers'.[20] Æ had not envisaged anything of the order entailed by a shift to a war economy, but adaptability to the needs of consumers and producers would be a hallmark of co-operative utility during wartime. For example, the IAOS disseminated information to large sections of the population. In August 1914 the IAOS issued every co-operative society with a supply of leaflets that offered farmers instructions 'as to how supplies of human and animal food may best be increased and conserved'.[21] The manager of Abbeydorney Co-operative Dairy Society requested copies of this pamphlet to share with its members. The IAOS immediately sent 200 copies of its 'War and the Food Supplies' pamphlet to Abbeydorney to advise the local farmers.[22] The IAOS maintained contact with a large number of farmers and remained aware of their requirements and anxieties.

In a sign that past grievances might be placed to one side, the DATI invited Horace Plunkett on to a departmental committee that considered the steps needed to increase Irish food production. In particular, the committee wanted to reverse the trend that saw the number of acres under tillage decrease in previous years and effect an increase in the amount of grain produced for consumption. Among its recommendations was a commitment to increase the area of land under tillage with an agreement to introduce some price controls such as a one-year regulation to set a minimum price for wheat and oats. Other commitments included new powers for the DATI to prevent the slaughter of breeding livestock and loans offered to farmers and fishermen to buy implements and machinery.[23] Alone among the committee members, Plunkett dissented from the majority's findings and refused to support the report. He grew frustrated about the lack of precise detail around such recommendations and worried about the absence of any proposal to utilise the existing co-operative network to achieve these aims. He proposed an amendment to the report which argued that any rise in food production depended upon 'at least as much voluntary effort as upon governmental action'. Plunkett argued that the IAOS had proved in the past that it could stimulate an increased level of food production as exemplified by the uptake of modern dairying in earlier years. 'Where farmers have used their co-operative organisation for the purpose of enabling them to adopt a more intense cultivation', Plunkett proposed in a resolution to the Departmental Committee, 'a remarkable increase in food production has already taken place'. He cited a number of expert witnesses to support this point including Thomas Wibberley, an agricultural instructor based at Queen's University, Belfast, and expert on continuous cropping.[24] Plunkett's amendment lost by eleven votes to four and the attempt to gain official approval of the IAOS's work failed. Instead, he submitted his Minority Report, in which he argued that an increase in food production required the adoption of the co-operative method. In submitting this report, Plunkett claimed to 'speak for tens of thousands of farmers, whose wishes and opinions I am in a position to know'.[25] Plunkett's minority report remained unheeded by the DATI.

The failure of the IAOS and DATI to reconcile differences and work harmoniously represented a lost opportunity. The IAOS Report for 1915 interpreted the rejection of Plunkett's amendment as an act of 'official discouragement' to co-operative work. The Department's attitude betrayed a determination to deal with farmers on an individual basis rather than through corporate entities like the co-operative society. A view that the war provided a cover for economic opponents to undermine the IAOS peppered the movement's discourse over the next few years. As the report summarised, 'the knowledge that the Department … is hostile to the IAOS must obviously have a disturbing, if not a paralysing effect upon the scattered working farmers throughout the country'.

In stark contrast to continental farmers the war showed up how the efforts of governmental and voluntary agencies lacked 'efficient economical co-ordination'.[26] As the workload of co-operative organisers increased due to the new stresses caused by wartime conditions the absence of state support grew apparent. The number of demands made on an organiser's time meant attendance to co-operative societies' requests often needed to wait for weeks. In an indication of the frustrations borne out of these demands Anderson confided to Charles Riddall that he abhorred the habit of societies to organise meetings for Sundays because 'quite apart from the indecency of it our organisers ought to have a rest at the week end'.[27] Notably, a failure to promote a standardised approach to increased levels of food production across the whole farming population harmed Irish producers in the longer term and contributed to the loss of goodwill from customers after the war.[28]

The IAOS expanded its knowledge base to enable societies to adapt to wartime conditions. The Co-operative Reference Library proved useful in this matter. The idea for a co-operative research centre came out of Horace Plunkett's annual visits to the United States. Plunkett established a fruitful working relationship with Charles McCarthy in Madison, Wisconsin. McCarthy, a young Irish-American social scientist and policy researcher, founded the first legislative reference library in the United States and saw the role of good policymaking as something that needed to be informed by thorough research and an understanding of the results provided by international experimentation.[29] Inspired by McCarthy, Plunkett conceived of a Country Life Institute to stimulate new innovations in Irish rural development. Plunkett anticipated that such an 'Irish-American contribution to rural progress' would aim

> to advance the well-being of the large and scattered agricultural population by bringing together information as to the progress of rural communities, by encouraging the scientific study and investigation of the conditions which contribute to their social and economic advancement, and by spreading knowledge and stimulating public opinion on the vital importance of a strong farming and rural community to the maintenance of the national life as a whole.[30]

Although several years elapsed before such an institution started up, Plunkett founded the Co-operative Reference Library following the receipt of a Carnegie Trust grant in 1914. The library aimed to become an international centre 'of information for practical workers and others interested in the development of agricultural and industrial co-operation'.[31]

The war interrupted this cosmopolitan work, but within Ireland the library published wartime studies, which investigated issues such as food supplies, the establishment of co-operative bakeries, and hygienic concerns around urban milk supply.[32] Between 1914 and 1918 the library's staff tried to synthesise as much international material as possible to inform future directions in co-operative farming. Francis Cruise O'Brien's work on co-operative mills and bakeries provided co-operators with information on how to extend productive capacities. Obtaining the required information proved difficult. The German co-operative bakeries O'Brien wished to examine proved inaccessible. However, the international contacts made through the Co-operative Reference Library meant he had access to a wide range of information.

O'Brien maintained a successful correspondence during the war with a milling society in southern France, which meant he 'obtained much valuable information, and from other sources I have been put into possession of important facts not hitherto published'.[33] Drawing upon such research, the IAOS encouraged the establishment of co-operative milling facilities, in order to increase the levels of food production and to increase and diversify the productive capacities of co-operative societies. Lionel Smith-Gordon, employed as the co-operative librarian, argued in 1914 that many of the economic difficulties instigated by the war 'could be solved by putting business on a co-operative basis'. The 'clash of interests' which caused friction during periods of emergency 'cannot arise when the interests of the retailing agency are identical with those of the consuming public'. A complete co-operative arrangement of the economy that encompassed production, distribution and retail offered one response to the demands placed on the population at the start of the war and suggested a hope that 'the present time is one which opens up tremendous possibilities for the co-operative movement'.[34]

Co-operative societies shored up their position in the economy through a diversification of their operations, which required a mighty co-ordinated effort from the IAOS. Robert Anderson recalled that 'Co-operation was called on to put forth efforts in directions as novel to its staff as they were to the reluctant farmers to whom they had to make appeal'.[35] Co-operative creameries proved ready to adapt to new demands, which in turn ensured members could share in any profits that derive from new methods of production. Co-operative creameries rapidly diversified in order to meet economic demands, and simultaneously expanded their utility to members. As early as 1915, 248 out of 344 co-operative creameries engaged in the trade of goods other than butter. This 'agricultural trade' encompassed a wide range of services, including the sale of agricultural inputs and the provision of credit.[36]

The members of Drumcliffe Co-operative Society decided to establish their own new co-operative mill in April 1916 after increased prices charged for bread led farmers to view such a move as beneficial. The establishment of such societies also incentivised the increase in tillage farming desired by the government. Josslyn Gore-Booth outlined in a speech to members that the committee of the society realised that 'it was the want of a mill with up-to-date machinery within reasonable distance which more than anything else was keeping the people from growing more grain'.[37] The establishment of new modes of production at the co-operative society showed how co-operative committees could nudge farmers towards new working practices that proved financially beneficial.

The IAOS played an important part in helping societies to instigate reforms in response to changed economic circumstances and it 'was called on to organise societies for milling, for curing bacon, for owning expensive machinery in common, to be lent out to members'.[38] For example, in January 1915 Abbeydorney Co-operative Society in County Kerry had 150 members, which included members of their auxiliary at Kilflynn. A hundred of these members directly supplied the central creamery and the remainder supplied the auxiliary. Organiser John O'Leary visited Abbeydorney and reported back to Robert Anderson on a well-managed society. All sewage and waste water was disposed of in a satisfactory manner; the grounds, building and machinery were maintained in good order; the quality of the milk supplied by members was 'clean and sweet' with all sour milk rejected; the creamery supplied loans to members on the condition that they continued to supply milk; and 'the books were examined compared and found in order'.[39] Later that month, Abbeydorney's manager wrote to Anderson to inform him that the members established flour mills in order to engage in bread production.[40]

For the year 1915–16, the society also benefited from a significant increase in the amount of milk supplied, from 109,180 gallons in July 1915 to 129,245 gallons in July 1916. This expanded milk supply came from an increased number of suppliers to the creamery who refused to subscribe as members with the membership stuck at 150 members; but an increase in the number of suppliers reached 190.[41] The war highlighted a recurrent free rider problem that dogged local co-operative societies. Co-operatives tended to rely on a committed core of co-operative farmers for their success, which in turn brought a wider economic benefit across the district in the guise of cheaper implements and higher prices paid for milk. A refusal to turn away milk supplied by non-members helped societies increase output in the short term. In the longer term this practice failed to convince non-member suppliers to join the co-operative, which meant a section of farmers remained free to use a rival creamery if they calculated the move paid better. Such arrangements exposed the limitations of the IAOS to convert the whole rural population to the benefits of co-operation.

Charles Riddall arrived at Abbeydorney on 6 August 1916 to address a meeting of local non-member suppliers to convince them to become full members. Riddall's timing proved unfortunate. He arrived at the town to find the meeting cancelled due to two funerals taking place in the area.[42] Anderson wrote to Riddall and expressed his annoyance with the priority granted to traditional customs by country people over what he regarded as the higher priority of the administration of the local society:

> It is most disappointing to have meetings rendered abortive in this way. The country people do not seem to value time in the slightest degree and they will spend a whole day over a funeral or rather over the part of the ceremony which has nothing to do with the internment and attend to nothing else.[43]

Whether the IAOS head office liked it or not, marking the passing of the dead still demanded people's attention.

Food production methods tailored to meet the changing wartime dietary needs of the British population required co-operative societies to erect new facilities and purchase new machinery. The purchase of new plant facilities came under the strict regulation of the new Minister of Munitions established after the severe shortage in shell production during 1915 caused a panic in the Liberal Government. As IAOS Secretary, Robert Anderson made representations to the minister on behalf of individual societies. Anderson presented the case for co-operative societies to be granted permission to purchase new engines and plant material in order 'to enable the Creamery to continue its business of manufacturing butter for which there is at present a special urgency in this country'.[44] Anderson highlighted in an article written to promote the achievements of the IAOS how new co-operative societies designed to purchase expensive machines that members could then hire emerged during the war. This placed 'small farmers in a position to command labour-saving implements which they could never have purchased individually' and meant some of 'the poorest neighbourhoods have increased their tillage by nearly a hundred per cent in a year as a direct result of this development'.[45]

Creameries also shifted from butter to cheese production in the final months of the war. They offered high prices for cheese as a way to meet the demand for protein required in British diets. Irish cheese production expanded hugely from 10,000 tons produced for export in 1914 to 286,000 tons by 1919.[46] An advertisement featured in the *Irish Homestead* framed the switch from butter to cheese production within a discourse that emphasised 'Economy, patriotism, health', three virtues that 'all call for a greater use of this valuable food'.[47] The IAOS's support to local societies once again proved to be a crucial factor in the establishment of new cheese-making facilities, with creamery inspections designed to aid the smooth and rapid transition to the new manufacturing process. Managers requested the IAOS's aid in order to equip creameries with the required machinery for cheese-making. Inter-creamery competition also incentivised the adoption of cheese-making across Munster. The manager at Newtownsandes Co-operative Society, Thomas de Lacy, decided to switch from butter to cheese production facilities when he noticed that other nearby creameries had already decided to do so. He wrote to Charles Riddall at Dublin to explain that he arrived at the decision as the society needed to keep up with other co-operatives because 'if they can do this we must follow suit or go under'.[48]

James Fant contributed to this infrastructural shift more than any other. Fant worked for the IAOS as a creamery expert but possessed special expertise as an engineer and architect. By 1914 Fant already proved his worth to the movement as he assisted societies when they required information about the type of plant machinery they required such as creamery separators, refrigeration devices and pasteurising equipment. In James Fant, the movement possessed a 'special creamery organiser with expert qualifications ... [whose] services are always in demand, and ... the IAOS could profitably employ at least four such organisers if it had the funds wherewith to do so'.[49]

Fant often supplied co-operative societies with engineering drawings and plans for their use in the upgrade and improvement of their buildings and capabilities. He offered help when societies had to decide what dairy technology they needed, and visited societies across the country as required.[50] At an IAOS Ulster District meeting held at Monaghan in February 1917, the region's co-operative movement celebrated its ongoing development during the war. Ballinode Co-operative Society represented a model of progress made by the movement as it boasted premises that 'has been remodelled and re-equipped, and there was a very considerable increase in supply during the year'. William de Vismes Kane, a leading member of the society singled out James Fant for praise, claiming that the people of Ballinode 'owed an eternal debt of gratitude' to the IAOS engineer for all the advice which 'enabled them to pull through a very great difficulty'.[51]

The shift towards new forms of production led the IAOS to celebrate their involvement in the Irish farmer's war record:

> The most notable of the developments attributable to the war is the widespread adoption of cheese-making in Munster, and to a less extent other parts of Ireland. Few creameries in Munster that have failed to engage in it have been able to meet the stress of competition.[52]

The IAOS's organisers offered the requisite support to meet the government's demands to meet the nutritional needs of consumers. Nevertheless, cheese production proved to be a temporary feature of Irish creamery production due to changes in the post-war economy, but also due to the low quality of the produce.[53] The demand for cheese was such that the state purchased any grade of produce for a guaranteed minimum price. As the war drew to a close the IAOS appealed to co-operative committees to 'examine their consciences' when it came to quality control of their cheeses.[54] By the 1920s creameries once again focused on the production of butter.

The IAOS's main purpose during the war was to assist local societies adapt to a wartime economy. For many farmers the local co-operative society helped

Table 4.1 Co-operative societies, 1914–18

Year	No. of societies (creameries, credit societies etc.)	Membership
1914	1,023	106,212
1915	991	102,591
1916	958	106,301
1917	947	113,640
1918	950	117,484

Source: IAOS, *Annual Reports, 1914–1918.*

to mediate their experience of this boom in Irish agriculture. The work of IAOS employees such as James Fant and Robert Anderson helped the local co-operative committees repurpose their buildings to create a new economic infrastructure suited to the wartime economy and ensured farmers continued to supply the goods required. Local co-operative societies provided the capacity for farmers to engage in a wider range of economic activities and experiment in ways they could not achieve if they tried to act alone. To illustrate this point Æ cited the example of a society in Kerry, which invested a £2,000 overdraft in new methods of production that benefited members, where

> grain was bought and the mill worked to the utmost extent possible, with the result that members were able to get feeding stuffs for cattle and pigs, and there has been more prosperity in the district than at any time in its history.[55]

Fixed prices played an important part in this prosperity, but Æ asserted that only the local co-operative society provided farmers with the tools and philosophy to attain their rightful share of available wealth.

By 1918, farmers understood that connection with a local co-operative society promoted their interests and improved their industry. Although the number of societies contracted slightly, the membership experienced a slight growth from 106,212 to 117,484 members (see table 4.1). One result of wartime prosperity saw co-operative societies increase their affiliation payments to the IAOS. Subscriptions jumped by 30 per cent between 1917 and 1918 in recognition of the assistance rendered by the organisation.[56] However, there remained significant competition for milk supplies from a resilient private sector that ensured a number of milk suppliers remained impervious to the charms of co-operative membership.

Co-operative credit and the war

The war exposed the frailty of the IAOS's credit societies as the provision of co-operative credit collapsed. Organisers viewed the promotion of co-operative credit societies since the 1890s as a crucial means through which small farmers might be immunised against usurious elements within the rural economy. The co-operative credit society was an association of borrowers who came together to provide each other with a collective guarantee and provided a source of funds in lieu of banks and moneylenders. Co-operative credit societies aimed to provide farmers with:

> the kind of credit which it is not worth the ordinary banker's while to give – in the first place, because it is asked for an inconvenient length of time – a time which may be altogether uncertain, and which will certainly be too long for occasional lending, and too short for permanent investment.[57]

The IAOS transplanted the Raiffeisen credit society pioneered in Germany to Ireland with the assistance of the British agricultural credit expert Henry Wolff. Raiffeisen co-operative banks were designed as small institutions that operated in limited geographical areas, such as the parish. The most important condition set by Raiffeisen societies for entry into a credit society related to the character of an individual. Someone applying to become a member of a credit society would only succeed if their peers considered them to be reliable and respectable.[58]

   In Ireland, the spread of co-operative credit societies proved to be one of the most remarkable phases in the early growth of the movement – at least on paper. The IAOS's role in these societies mirrored the assistance granted to creamery societies as they provided administrative help in the early stages and periodical inspections followed. The first co-operative credit society was founded in 1895. By 1911, 236 credit societies existed, but only 163 of these furnished annual returns to the IAOS.[59] The existence of 'skeleton' societies attested to the uneven development of the credit society movement and a reduced number of active societies. While the societies expected to draw upon local funds and savings over time, in the early years these societies were reliant on state loans passed through the DATI in order to add financial liquidity to the rural economy. An investigative committee estimated that in the first seventeen years of the co-operative credit movement a sum of £500,000 had been loaned to small and medium farmers 'a sum which, even allowing for mere renewals of loans, must have been productive of much benefit to many of the smaller agriculturists, especially in the poorer districts of the country'.[60]

   The institutional transplant of the German co-operative finance model failed to thrive in Ireland owing to several factors. First, pre-existent forms of rural credit offered too much competition and deprived the rural economy of individuals with a capacity to save. Second, the monitoring aspect of the German model, whereby peer oversight between members forced debtors to repay loans or face ostracism, never took root. This failure on behalf of members to strictly police the credit societies effectively meant that despite their existence on paper, in practice many credit societies failed to perform their primary function.[61]

Furthermore, the Raiffeisen model failed to make inroads into the Irish credit market on account of the better-suited and longer-established joint-stock banking institutions.[62]

The Great War exposed the precarious position of co-operative credit in Ireland. At the outbreak of the war the DATI and Congested Districts Board (CDB) withdrew the loan capital they lodged in the credit societies. This action led the IAOS to bemoan the fact that the withdrawal of these loans would 'have a marked effect on the future of the co-operative credit movement. In cases where but a small business is being done and a joint stock bank is not conveniently accessible or an overdraft obtainable, the business of the society may cease with the repayment of the Board's or the Department's loan'.[63] Such expectations were borne out over the next four years. The increased prosperity of farmers during the war masked the weakening of this section of the movement. In the more self-reliant credit societies whose books exhibited savings lodged by members business managed to continue. Between March 1918 and March 1919 thirty-nine co-operative societies were wound up, of which thirty-three were credit societies. The IAOS displayed a relaxed attitude to this decline of its credit section as the agricultural boom apparently rendered them unnecessary. Although a return to lower prices for agricultural produce seemed likely in the future the IAOS leadership concluded that:

> Of [the co-operative credit society's] utility in past years there is no doubt at all, but the rise in deposits (in many instances due to old borrowers, now comparatively well off, who wish to invest their gains in their societies) and the reduction in the number of loans granted prove that the urgency of the need for cheap credit has diminished.[64]

Co-operation under the wartime state

Æ emerged as the co-operative movement's most vocal advocate during the second half of the war as he argued for Irish economic self-sufficiency. Horace Plunkett was invited to chair the Irish Convention during 1917 in a failed attempt to find a solution to a political impasse that remained around the proposed implementation of Home Rule after the war.[65] This left Æ to shape the co-operative movement's response to quickly changing political and economic circumstances. For example, in the immediate aftermath of the Easter Rising, Æ used his position as *Irish Homestead* editor to address his 'unhappy country'. Despite the unrest caused by the rebellion and the new political uncertainties created in its wake, Æ retained a firm belief that the co-operative movement offered a cause for optimism and a possible avenue for a future consensus between political traditions on the island. 'Because our movement is already national … and because it alone seems capable of bringing the majority of Irish people into its ranks', he wrote, 'we hold that it is the best thing Ireland has at present, and in it is the promise and potency of a happy and prosperous Ireland to be found.'[66] A couple of weeks later, Æ offered another assessment for Irish economics in an uncertain world as he invoked the language of national self-sufficiency. He argued 'that national safety for the people in Ireland demands a complete change in economic policy here … we must aim at making Ireland self-supporting in respect of food and only sell the surplus'.[67] A change in economic policy soon arrived, but not one to Æ's liking.

Æ watched how the state in Ireland changed over the course of the war with horror. He viewed the attempt to reorganise the food supply and agriculture in particular, under a new regime of control regulations as an assault on the achievements made by the co-operative movement in previous years. The passage of the Corn Production Act in 1917 'marked a new departure in the agricultural policy of the United Kingdom' that directed farmers to adopt specific methods of agricultural production in pursuit of higher grain yields.[68] Food production campaigns during 1917–18 encouraged larger yields of vital food staples such as wheat, oats and potatoes. For example, the potato crop for Ireland grew by 27 per cent and annual corn production stood at 545,000 tons more than the respective pre-war figures.[69] As the war progressed the British government extended its involvement in the politics of food production and distribution. Æ fleshed out his vision of Irish economic self-sufficiency in response to what he viewed as a state structure designed to promote private trading interests. The war demonstrated the continued relevance of the IAOS as an important social actor at a local level, but its influence within official policymaking circles remained negligible. Accordingly, Æ developed a stringent critique of the state system in Ireland based upon regulations and food policies and called for greater autonomy in the aftermath of the war.

Æ's critical theorisation of the co-operative movement's relationship with the state intensified throughout the course of the First World War. Official food policy granted no recognition for the IAOS's war work nor did it prioritise the interests of Irish farmers. Already disillusioned with government departments after the trials with the DATI, and the Development Commission's funding struggles with the DATI, Æ's cynicism of state interference hardened during wartime. The IAOS wielded an important influence over rural Ireland's economic machinery, which it helped to build. However, any hope that food policies might recognise and supplement the work of the IAOS evaporated. Æ's reticence about state interference reflected the influence of anarchist thought upon the poet-economist's intellectual development. In particular, Prince Kropotkin provided a formative influence over the young Æ as he developed ideas about the promotion of mutual aid and the pursuit of co-operative organisation as a moral imperative. Æ's great ambition for the IAOS remained the creation of a co-operative citizenry in Ireland.[70] His frustration with increased intervention reflected a belief that the state should allow society to grow out of interactions between voluntary organisations. Regulations only impeded such flourishing.

In 1916, Æ published *The National Being*, in which he outlined his vision of an idealised Irish polity. This book attempted to flesh out the social and economic values best suited to the Irish nation. Æ's concern with the social and economic aspect of the 'Irish Question' marks out *The National Being*, along with Plunkett's *Ireland in the New Century*, as exceptional contributions to the literature of the Irish Revival. Like his contemporaries, Æ anticipated the implementation of some form of political independence for Ireland after the war and he therefore made his case for a version of Irish nationhood that included a major role for co-operative societies as centres of social and economic development. Æ wrote in an idiosyncratic style that incorporated his abiding interest in mysticism and he defined the state as 'a physical body prepared for the incarnation of the soul of the race. The body of the national soul may be spiritual or secular, aristocratic or democratic, civil or militarist.' Therefore the type of social arrangement that prevailed would fundamentally shape the character of the type of state to come. Æ viewed the state in Ireland as a manifestation of the country's governmental institutions, and wrote: 'if there is anything in the theory of Irish nationality, we will apply original principles as they are from time to time discovered to be fundamental in Irish character'.[71] The leadership offered by the IAOS as it worked to extend the co-operative principle helped Irish people rediscover one of these fundamental national virtues.

In Ireland, ideas about the state came entwined within discourses around contested claims for political independence, based on physical territory and notions of national identity. For Æ, the nation, and therefore the state, was the summation of the character of its people. Æ believed that the outline of a potential, future Irish state had not been delineated and remained unclear. Despite passionate discussions around self-government, Æ lamented the lack of intellectual effort devoted to the 'speculation over our own character or the nature of the civilization we wished to create for ourselves. Nations, rarely … start with a complete ideal.'[72] The IAOS represented an important agent in the state-building process as it took the rural subject as its starting point and through its interventions and organisational work strove to remake the Irish population. Over the previous quarter century, Æ argued, 'the co-operative principle has once more laid hold on the imagination of the Irish townsman and the Irish countryman'. The adoption of 'a policy which will enable it to manifest once more … will create an Irish civilization, which will fit our character as the glove fits the hand'.[73] With its potential to unite the town and country, co-operation also contained the potential to bind together the Irish nation and produce the type of state Æ believed possible. The IAOS's economic work to reform the farmer amounted to the same thing as defining the nature of the state.

An Irish form of national economics rested on the principles of co-operation. This belief held by Æ helped to define an emergent nationalist conception of an ideal economy in Ireland and the growth of wartime controls offered the opposite. Æ reflected a trend in a country such as India whereby an anti-imperialistic conception of a national economy emerged in response to attempts to integrate regional economies into a wider imperial order. The evolution of national economics in India had its origins in the late nineteenth century and challenged the political-economic imagination that underpinned Britain's attempt to establish an imperial economy. Importantly, an economic critique of British rule provided anti-colonial activists with a basis to discredit British rule.[74] The experience of wartime controls that hampered co-operative economics provided evidence of a similarly tyrannical economic arrangement ill-suited to Irish needs. Critics saw the imposition of wartime controls over food production as something that served British imperial interests over Irish ones.[75] For the co-operative movement's leaders, the state frequently obstructed co-operative businesses from achieving their full potential as indicated by their lack of involvement within the food policymaking process.

Irish anti-colonial intellectuals with an interest in outlining a national form of economics paid close attention to the work disseminated by Æ. The intellectual engagement by nationalists with co-operative ideas that started with the public dispute between the IAOS and DATI only intensified during the war. The publication of *The National Ideal* had a profound effect on the Sinn Féin intellectuals, Darrell Figgis and Aodh de Blácam. These two writers tried to conceptualise a social programme for a future Sinn Féin administration that drew heavily upon the economic arguments made by Æ. Figgis published his own study of Æ with the revealing subtitle *A Study of a Man and a Nation* in the same year *The National Being* appeared.[76] The next year Figgis published *The Gaelic State in the Past and the Future*, in which he argued that co-operative societies already provided evidence of an emergent Irish state.[77] Aodh de Blácam, echoed this position in *Towards the Republic*, which sought to express the social and political aims of a new Ireland and took for granted 'that the future of Ireland lies in Co-operation no observer of the times can doubt'. De Blácam praised 'the co-operative work of Mr. George Russell' which he placed alongside the work of the leaders of the 1916 Rising and Arthur Griffith, the founder of Sinn Féin.[78]

The process whereby ideas of Irish nationhood became associated with co-operative principles accelerated as long as the war continued. The British government's agricultural policy during the war fit into two broad stages. Until December 1916, the policy followed a broadly laissez-faire direction which allowed the co-operative movement to work relatively unimpeded. After 1917 a new coalition government under Prime Minister David Lloyd George saw a more interventionist approach to economic policy.[79] At first Æ hoped that the voluntary efforts co-ordinated by the IAOS might remain unimpeded by creeping state interference. Expecting 'the State or a State Department to undertake this [agricultural] work is to ask a body influenced and often controlled by powerful capitalists, and middle agencies which it should be the role of the … [IAOS] to eliminate'.[80] The war intensified this position, as the direction of government policy failed to meet the expectations of co-operators.

As the government intervened in food policy, the co-operative movement became frustrated and alienated from the overall policy consultation. In their survey of British co-operation, Fred Hall and William Watkins noted that 'it was in the protection of the consumer … that war-time collectivism was seen in its extremest [*sic*] forms'.[81] From the perspective of a producers' movement these interventions proved less welcome, which Æ aggressively critiqued as an attempt to stifle the co-operative political economy. The government established the Food Production Department in 1917 with power to organise agricultural production, labour and technology.[82] The same year's Corn Production Act gave the Department powers to direct resources towards intensified production and output in priority foods such as corn and potatoes.[83] In Ireland, the practical implementation of these new government regulations fell under the DATI, which introduced the measures that included compulsory tillage orders, minimum wage rates, guaranteed prices for grain and a temporary suspension of land purchase and redistribution. In an example of rare co-ordinated action between the IAOS and government, the *Irish Homestead* carried DATI circulars and appeals aimed at readers to respond to these demands. For example, one publicity campaign explained that the government order to increase tillage farming would not harm farmers who relied on livestock for their income and identified increased tillage as a way to stimulate milk production: 'More tillage means more men, more cattle, more work, more prosperity.'[84] The same edition's editorial complemented the official message and reminded readers that just as soldiers, doctors and consumers were called upon to do their part in the war effort 'it is no less the honour of farmers to produce food as plentifully as they can when the nation requires it of them'.[85]

The wartime state represented a new type of tyranny that undermined the co-operative movement's attempt to create a better society. Æ viewed this state 'with profound mistrust, because we dread its alliance with the meanest and most greedy elements in society, the profiteers and Gombeen men, the class who furnish political parties with funds and who are therefore in a position to affect the policy of State departments'. Under the cover of the war the conflict between co-operators and long-standing economic rivals became an increasingly intense struggle for influence and access to state-controlled resources. In article headed 'The Allies of the State', Æ attacked those who accepted this situation as 'people with the ideas of an infant school who suppose that the State or its officials are always nobly moved or inspired to act solely for the general good'. Rather greater scepticism was required as the 'State allies itself with the party which seems to it economically most powerful … and this leaning to the economically powerful, even when that power is based upon pure greed and ferocious profiteering, has been evident through all the years of the war'. Instead under the cover of war, a new compact was struck in which the

> State made a deal with the profiteers early in the war. It said to them … 'Go you and fleece the people. We will allow you to keep forty per cent of the extra plunder and we will take sixty per cent.' That is exactly what the legislation about excess profits means, that and nothing else. The State at present is the prime profiteer, the profiteer of the profiteers. That is why we fear the future with the State dominating every factor in national life.[86]

Increased state intervention that aimed to stimulate Irish food productivity largely ignored the presence of the co-operative movement. Lord Rhondda was appointed Food Controller in June 1917 and established local committees to engineer the equitable distribution of food, commandeer supplies when required and eventually introduce compulsory rationing. The imposition of controls over which co-operative farmers had no say provoked an angry response from Æ and he used the *Irish Homestead* to attack Rhondda's agricultural policy. Æ criticised the state's decision to use other 'bodies to undertake new organisation of food production':

> We see continual reference to urban councils, district councils, boards of guardians, traders and merchants who are to supervise, procure land, re-allot it, get seeds, fertilisers, implements, and generally to control all this work. We have not seen the slightest official recognition of the existence of farmers' associations and co-operative societies, of which there are well over one thousand in Ireland.[87]

By 1917, the toxic relationship between the two largest agricultural institutions in Ireland led Æ to accuse the DATI of regarding farmers 'as people of no importance in agriculture, their organisations as bodies which need not be considered'.[88] The DATI refused to acknowledge co-operators as an instrument through which to work and preferred to work with farmers as individuals rather than through corporate entities. According to Æ, the DATI mistrusted the IAOS whose 'gigantic business by voluntary associations of farmers is regarded as another instance of [the IAOS's] lack of intelligence because it was built up in disregard of the Department's advice'.[89]

The Ministry of Food's distance from Dublin heightened the sense that Westminster used this ministry to override the interests of Irish farmers. Lord Rhondda appointed Robert Anderson to the Irish section of the Food Control Committee, but the Cork man saw his time there as 'spent in more or less fruitless ferryings over the Irish Sea to attend meetings in London'.[90] Anderson resigned his position on the committee in December 1917 and the *Homestead* reported the move as one to be expected as 'self-respecting men cannot remain on a committee whose advice is ignored by those who appointed it'. A more useful policy, the article continued, 'would be to have had an Irish Ministry of Food with complete authority in Ireland to act in the interests of the Irish people. How such things can be arranged by a food controller in London we do not know'.[91]

The Ministry of Food and the role played by the Food Controller in setting prices paid to producers attracted Æ's opprobrium. His problem with the food prices set by Lord Rhondda pivoted on the price differentials that existed between Irish produce and comparable goods from other countries that included England. While Kavanagh noted the increased prosperity of farmers during the war, the notion of a satisfied agricultural population becomes more complicated when compared to agricultural producers elsewhere. In anticipation of imminent fixed prices for butter, Æ repeated a rumour that Irish butter would receive around 6*d*. per cwt. less than the same article from New Zealand. The problem with such regulation resided in the fact that Irish butter would be enshrined 'in a position of inferiority'. If the regulation passed without protest, Æ argued, then 'the market will have hammered into it the idea that Irish butter is in the view of the Government an article inferior in food value to Danish or New Zealand butter'. Furthermore, the effects of regulation would shape long-term impressions that 'will last long after the War'.[92]

In July 1917, Æ again wrote on the 'fixing of prices' in which he argued that 'hardly any social problem so thorny … as food prices' existed and objected to 'the fixing of prices against Irish and in favour of English, Colonial, and foreign interests'.[93] The sense of injustice filtered down to local co-operatives. Ballycanew Co-operative Society passed a resolution that September objecting to the fact that Irish farmers received less than half the guaranteed price of their English counterparts. The society strongly protested 'against the maximum price of Irish creamery butter fixed by the Food Controller' and demanded 'an immediate advance of 30*s*. per cwt., with a further advance to meet the increased cost of production during the winter months'.[94]

At the start of 1918, Æ characterised the government's policies as an effort 'to empty Ireland of its food supplies, to transfer all grain, meat, butter, bacon, etc., possible to the other side, and to leave Ireland largely dependent on the chances of imported food'.[95] By June he wrote: 'Irishmen are threatened not only by the submarines which lie around their coasts, but by the action of the economic machinery which has grown up in their country.'[96] The impact of regulation led one correspondent to the *Homestead* to write that 'it is now manifest to the Irish farmer that the Food Controller is out to make a Sinn Feiner of him … Every new order the Food Controller makes confirms the belief that the Irish farmer must depend upon himself and not trust his big brother across the channel.'[97] The Food Controller provided a bogeyman for those who drew up Sinn Féin's economic thinking. In 1920, Darrell Figgis cited the 'English Food Controller' whose preferential treatment of English over Irish farmers gave grounds for political independence. Food controls served the interests of English manufacturers and their introduction revealed that 'war was only an excuse for national avarice and imperial depredation'.[98]

Under Æ's wartime direction the *Homestead* argued that farmers needed to exercise greater economic autonomy as the most effective way to guard against state tyranny. The fear that wartime controls might continue indefinitely provided a source of concern. In the final months of the war, the co-operative movement again attempted to rally members around its founding principles. By this point, Æ urged farmers that 'if you want political attention create economic organisations. Control trade, and you will be recognised by the state.' If farmers allowed their 'business [to] be controlled by others than yourselves ... the state will listen to those who control your trade, not to you.'[99]

By the war's end the dividing line between economic and political independence grew indistinct, as all threads of the Irish question became entwined. The IAOS ended the war having provided stability after 'a crucial test during the last five years':

> Its steady growth and remarkably rapid development in new directions – some of a far more ambitious character than any previously undertaken by the organised farmers – afford yet another proof of the superiority of co-operative organisation under conditions of stress. The societies have not only held together, but have also improved their buildings and equipment as well as their business methods ... members, too, have come to realise what their movement means to them, what it has accomplished and what it may yet accomplish. Co-operation is now a reality to many to whom it had hitherto meant little more than a trade term.[100]

The movement's overall progress up to 1918 indicated that co-operative societies maintained their popularity. Farmers looked towards the IAOS as a familiar source of authority in a period of social and political uncertainty. The new types of trade taken up by co-operative societies showed that the war incentivised a greater diversity of co-operative activities. After 1918 the IAOS received greater legal freedom with regard to its organisational work, as a reward. The Development Commissioners recommended that restrictions placed on the IAOS's involvement in other forms of co-operation beyond production should be loosened and there should be an end to the DATI's policy of non-controversial co-operation. This coincided with T.W. Russell's retirement from public life in 1918, which suggested an opportunity for a new relationship between the IAOS and the DATI. The emergence of a new type of diverse co-operative society that engaged in both agricultural production and limited retail by the end of the war led Horace Plunkett to express hope that the movement might now 'make much more rapid progress than hitherto in extending the benefits of co-operation to those who need them most'.[101]

If the war represented a trial of co-operative organisation, then, according to its leaders, the Irish movement had passed. Whatever the ultimate political settlement for Ireland, the will to play a prominent role in shaping the economic arrangement of an Irish nation-state was central to co-operative thinking. The ability of the co-operative movement to influence a future Irish state developed in unexpected ways after 1918. The failure to find an accommodation with the DATI combined with growing alienation from the government, moved the co-operative movement into a position whereby it became a hostile critic of the state as it operated in Ireland. This pushed the movement into a closer accommodation with an unexpected force – radical nationalism.

Notes

1 IAOS, *Annual Report, 1919*, p. 5.
2 Charles Townshend, *Easter 1916: The Irish Rebellion* (London: Penguin, 2006).
3 Michael Laffan, *The Resurrection of Ireland: The Sinn Féin Party, 1916–1923* (Cambridge: Cambridge University Press, 1999), 164.
4 Diarmaid Ferriter, *The Transformation of Ireland, 1900–2000* (London: Profile Books, 2004), 172–173.
5 Patrick Kavanagh, *The Green Fool* (London: Penguin, 2001), 58.
6 Stephen Gwynn, *Ireland* (London: Ernest Benn, 1924), 73.
7 Jonathan Bell and Mervyn Watson, *A History of Irish Farming, 1750–1950* (Dublin: Four Courts Press, 2009), 247.
8 F.S.L. Lyons, *Ireland Since the Famine* (London: Fontana Press, 1975), 369.
9 R.A. Anderson, *With Horace Plunkett in Ireland* (London: Macmillan and Co.,1935), 192, 196–197.
10 Fran Brearton, *The Great War in Irish Poetry: WB Yeats to Michael Longley* (Oxford: Oxford University Press, 2000), 7.
11 Lionel Smith-Gordon, 'Agricultural Organisation in Ireland', *Economic Journal*, 27.107 (1917), 355–363 (p. 355).
12 IAOS, *Annual Report, 1914*, 7.
13 Margaret Digby, *Horace Plunkett: An Anglo-American Irishman* (Oxford: Basil Blackwell, 1935), 207.
14 IAOS, *Annual Report, 1915*, 42.
15 IAOS, *Annual Report, 1914*,7.
16 Alan S. Milward, *The Economic Effects of the Two World Wars on Britain* (London: Macmillan Press Ltd, 1972), 50.
17 IAOS, *Annual Report, 1915*, 5.
18 J.R. Campbell, 'The War and Irish Agriculture', *Department of Agriculture and Technical Instruction Journal*, 15.1 (1914), 10–19 (pp. 12–15); IAOS, *Annual Report, 1915*, 7.
19 Peter Gatrell, *Russia's First World War: A Social and Economic History* (Harlow: Pearson Longman, 2005), 46.
20 George W. Russell, 'The Problem of Rural Life', *Irish Review* 1.8 (1911), 365–372 (p. 368).
21 Lionel Smith-Gordon and Cruise O'Brien, *Ireland's Food in War Time* (Dublin: Co-operative Reference Library, 1914), 44.

22 T. O'Donovan, Abbeydorney to Anderson, Dublin 14 August 1914, and Anderson to O'Donovan, 15 August 1914, NAI 1088/2/2.

23 HCPP [Cd. 8016], *Department of Agriculture and Technical Instruction for Ireland. Report of the Departmental Committee on Food Production in Ireland* (1914–1916), 4–6.

24 Wibberley published a work on intensification of tillage farming in 1917. T. Wibberley, *Farming on Factory Lines: Continuous Cropping for the Large Farmer* (London: C. Arthur Pearson Ltd, 1917).

25 HCPP [Cd. 8016], *Report of the Departmental Committee on Food Production in Ireland* (1914–16), 11–12.

26 IAOS, *Annual Report, 1915*, 7–8.

27 R.A. Anderson to C.C. Riddall, 25 August 1916, NAI 1088/2/3.

28 James Meenan, *The Irish Economy Since 1922* (Liverpool: Liverpool University Press, 1970), 302–303.

29 Edward A. Fitzpatrick, *McCarthy of Wisconsin* (New York: Columbia University Press, 1944).

30 Horace Plunkett, *A Country Life Institute: A Suggested Irish-American Contribution to Rural Progress* (Dublin: Plunkett House, 1909), 25.

31 Lionel Smith-Gordon and Cruise O'Brien, *Co-operation in Ireland* (Manchester: Co-operative Union Limited, 1921), 26.

32 These reports included D. Houston, *The Milk Supply of Dublin: Report of a Bacteriological Investigation of the City of Dublin Milk Supply* (Dublin: The Co-operative Reference Library, 1918); Cruise O'Brien, *Co-operative Mills and Bakeries*, Series: Miscellaneous Publications No. 2 (Dublin: Co-operative Reference Library, 1918); Smith-Gordon and O'Brien, *Ireland's Food*.

33 O'Brien, *Co-operative Mills*, 1.

34 Smith-Gordon and O'Brien, *Ireland's Food*, 39.

35 Anderson, *With Horace Plunkett*, 194.

36 Patrick Bolger, *The Irish Co-operative Movement: Its History and Development* (Dublin: Institute of Public Administration, 1977), 208.

37 'A Commendable Enterprise', *Sligo Independent*, 29 April 1916; Notes for speech on Co-operative Mill for Drumcliffe by Josslyn Gore-Booth, undated, *c*.1916, PRONI, D4131/M/11A.

38 Anderson, *With Horace Plunkett*, 197.

39 John O'Leary, IAOS Creamery Organiser's Report for Abbeydorney, 7 January 1915, NAI 1088/2/3.

40 T. O'Donovan, Abbeydorney to R.A. Anderson, Dublin, 22 January 1915, NAI 1088/2/3.

41 J. O'Leary's Creamery Report, Abbeydorney, 11 September 1916, NAI 1088/2/3.

42 C.C. Riddall's Report on Visit [6 August 1916], 24 August 1916, NAI 1088/2/3.

43 Robert Anderson to C.C. Riddall, 25 August 1916, NAI 1088/2/3.

44 Robert Anderson to Director General of Munitions Supply, Westminster, 7 February 1917, NAI 1088/2/3.

45 R.A. Anderson, 'The IAOS and the Food Problem', *Studies*, 6.21 (1917), 8–14 (p. 11).

46 Mary E. Daly, *The First Department: A History of the Department of Agriculture* (Dublin: Institute of public Administration, 2002), 58–60.

47 'Irish Cheese' [advertisement], *Irish Homestead*, 17 August 1918, 553.

48 Thomas de Lacy, Newtownsandes to C.C. Riddall, Dublin, 27 February 1918, NAI 1088/751/6.

49 IAOS, *Annual Report, 1909*, 10.

50 For example see J Byrne, Ballymacelligott to James Fant, 31 July 1922, NAI/1088/70/1.

51 'Co-operative Conferences', *Anglo-Celt*, 3 February 1917, 10.

52 IAOS, *Annual Report, 1919*, 9.

53 Daly, *The First Department*.

54 IAOS, *Annual Report, 1919*, 9.

55 'Economic Independence', *Irish Homestead*, 15 June 1918, 397–398.

56 IAOS, *Annual Report, 1919*, 19.

57 Henry W. Wolff, *People's Banks: A Record of Social and Economic Success* (London: P.S. King and Son, 1896, 2nd edn [originally published 1893]), 68.

58 Anthony P. Quinn, *Credit Unions in Ireland* (Dublin: Oak Tree Press, 1994), 10–11.

59 HCPP [Cd. 7375], DATI, *Report of the Departmental Committee on Agricultural Credit in Ireland* (1914), 128.

60 HCPP [Cd. 7375], *Report … on Agricultural Credit in Ireland* (1914), 129–130.

61 Timothy Guinnane, 'A Failed Institutional Transplant: Raiffeisen's Credit Cooperatives in Ireland, 1894–1914', *Explorations in Economic History*, 31 (1994), 38–61.

62 Eoin McLaughlin, 'Competing Forms of Co-operation?: Land League, Land War and Co-operation in Ireland, 1879 to 1914', *Agricultural History Review*, 63.1 (2015), 81–112.

63 IAOS, *Annual Report, 1915*, 17.

64 IAOS, *Annual Report, 1919*, 13–14.

65 R.B. McDowell, *The Irish Convention, 1917–18* (London: Routledge & Kegan Paul, 1970).

66 'The Hope that Remains', *Irish Homestead*, 29 April, 6 and 13 1916, 285–286.

67 'Lessons from the War', *Irish Homestead*, 10 June 1916, 353–354.

68 Department of Agriculture and Technical Instruction for Ireland, *Eighteenth Annual General Report of the Department, 1917–18* (Dublin: His Majesty's Stationery Office 1919), 12.

69 Margaret L. Barnet, *British Food Policy during the First World War* (London: George Allen & Unwin, 1985), 193–208.

70 Nicholas Allen, *George Russell (Æ) and the New Ireland, 1905–30* (Dublin: Four Courts Press, 2003), 40–43.

71 George William Russell, *The National Being: Some Thoughts on an Irish Polity* (Dublin: Maunsel & Co., 1916), 2.

72 Russell, *The National Being*, 3.

73 Russell, *The National Being*, 125–126.

74 Manu Goswami, *Producing India: From Colonial Economy to National Space* (Chicago: University of Chicago Press, 2004), 279–280.

75 Ian Miller, *Reforming Food in Post-Famine Ireland: Medicine, Science and Improvement, 1845–1922* (Manchester: Manchester University Press, 2014), 192.

76 Darrell Figgis, *George W. Russell: A Study of a Man and a Nation* (New York: Dodd, Mead and Company, 1916).

77 Darrell Figgis, *The Gaelic State in the Past and Future or 'The Crown of the Nation'* (Dublin: Maunsel & Co. Ltd, 1917), 74.

78 Aodh de Blácam, *Towards the Republic: A Study of New Ireland's Social and Political Aims* (Dublin: T. Kiersey, 1918), 26, 119.

79 P.E. Dewey, *British Agriculture in the First World War* (London: Routledge, 1989), 23.

80 Russell, *The National Being*, 53.

81 F. Hall and W.P. Watkins, *Co-operation: A Survey of the History, Principles, and Organisation of the Co-operative Movement in Great Britain and Ireland* (Manchester: Co-operative Union, 1937), 197.

82 Dewey, *British Agriculture*, 91–93.

83 Daly, *The First Department*, 58–61.

84 'The Country's Food Supply, 1917' [advertisement], *Irish Homestead*, 10 February 1917, 97.

85 'Agriculture on its Trial', *Irish Homestead*, 10 February 1917, 85–86.

86 'The Allies of the State', *Irish Homestead*, 20 January 1917, 34–35.

87 'The New Guides for Agriculture', *Irish Homestead*, 13 January 1917, 17–18.

88 'The New Guides for Agriculture', *Irish Homestead*, 13 January 1917, 17–18.

89 'The New Guides for Agriculture', *Irish Homestead*, 13 January 1917, 17–18.

90 Anderson, *With Horace Plunkett*, 194.

91 'The Food Control Committee', *Irish Homestead*, 29 December 1917, 950–951.

92 'The Fixing of Prices' *Irish Homestead*, 24 March 1917, 205–206.

93 'The Fixing of Prices', *Irish Homestead*, 14 July 1917, 521–522.

94 'Among the Societies: Ballycanew C.A. & D.S.', *Irish Homestead*, 29 September 1917, 734.

95 'Killing Food Production', *Irish Homestead*, 19 January 1918, 34.

96 George Russell (Æ), 'The Self-Supporting Community', *Studies*, 7.26 (1918), 301–306 (p. 301).

97 Farmer, 'A Policy for Irish Farmers', *Irish Homestead*, 29 September 1917, 730.

98 Darrell Figgis, *The Economic Case for Independence* (Dublin: Maunsel & Co., 1920), vi.

99 'The State and Organisation', *Irish Homestead*, 20 July 1918, 477–478.

100 IAOS, *Annual Report, 1919*, 5.

101 IAOS, *Annual Report, 1919*, 38.

5

The co-operative movement and the War of Independence

On 21 January 1919 a meeting of twenty-seven Sinn Féin MPs at Dublin's Mansion House inaugurated Dáil Eireann. This opening of a newly constituted revolutionary Irish Parliament marked a new phase in nationalist claims for Irish self-rule. The 73 representatives from the Sinn Féin party elected at the December 1918 General Election made up the Dáil's membership, and in fulfilment of their promise to the electorate refused to take their seats at Westminster. The Irish Parliamentary Party (IPP) paid the political cost of Sinn Féin's electoral victory as the radical nationalist party reaped the benefit of growing support for a separatist political platform in the aftermath of the Easter Rising.[1] The Home Rule Act that passed in 1914 after a bitter, protracted negotiation process between the IPP, Ulster Unionists and the British government proved to be a distant memory in Ireland after the war. The decision taken to suspend the Home Rule legislation at the start of the war proved fatal to the implementation of the IPP's main political goal.[2] The establishment of Dáil Eireann by Sinn Féin killed the IPP's dream of Home Rule. Instead, a new generation demanded a more advanced form of political independence in the shape of an Irish Republic.

While Sinn Fein's rise appeared to mark a break in Irish political culture, the party's attempt to establish a new hegemonic agenda for Ireland drew on older traditions that included agrarian populism, revolutionary Fenianism and the urbane intellectualism of the party's founder, Arthur Griffith. Within this grand project, co-operative thought helped to shape the new variant of mainstream nationalism and formed a vital part of Sinn Féin's political economy after the war.

This Irish alternative to Westminster immediately looked to implement its own legislative platform. At the first meeting the revolutionary assembly outlined its social and economic priorities in its Democratic Programme at its first sitting, which stated that 'it shall be the duty of the Republic to adopt all measures necessary for the recreation and invigoration of our Industries, and to ensure their being developed on the most beneficial and progressive co-operative lines'.[3] The stimulation of the Irish economy along co-operative lines represented one important aspect of this aspirational programme for government. Thirty years after the establishment of the first society, co-operatives were a familiar presence in the countryside and attained the status as an important symbol of rural modernity. The ideas and arguments promoted by Plunkett and Æ played a crucial role in nurturing sympathy for co-operative ideas among Sinn Féin's intellectual wing. What began as a contentious and controversial intervention into the Irish economy became a normalised institution that shaped everyday rural life. Their presence still provoked rancour in some quarters, but by the end of the war, the co-operative movement provided a source of economic ideas for those who demanded a radical change in how their country was governed.

The Dáil's attempts to promote limited governmental programmes represented a real, subversive attempt to create a counter-state.[4] The assembly represented a potent symbol of popular resistance against British power in Ireland and acted as 'a source of legitimacy for fighting men in the guerrilla war that followed'.[5] Although the new legislative assembly proposed to represent the whole island of Ireland, Ulster Unionists unsurprisingly declined the invitation to sit in Dublin. To counteract the Dáil's influence, Westminster passed the 1920 Government of Ireland Act, which provided for two parliaments in Ireland – one each in Belfast and Dublin. This established the partition of Ireland in principle as the six north-eastern counties became Northern Ireland. Technically the other twenty-six counties constituted an entity called Southern Ireland, but this iteration of an Irish polity emerged stillborn as the contestation of Ireland's political future intensified.[6]

The co-operative movement experienced at first hand the violence which characterised the revolutionary years between the end of the Great War and the establishment of the Irish Free State in 1922. To what extent a revolution occurred in Ireland remains an open question in the historiography. For example, Michael Laffan argues that the Irish revolution took 'nationalist, political and military forms' but made no attempt to instigate radical social change.[7] However, this notion of what constituted the nationalist form requires greater definition. Important works examining social change at a local level highlight how social and economic questions affected Irish life in this period with the issues of land ownership and agrarian violence suggesting that questions of property and status helped to fuel the political upheaval.[8] Fergus Campbell convincingly argued that the revolutionary impulses found in Sinn Féin provided continuity with the land agitations of the late nineteenth and early twentieth centuries.[9] Sinn Féin drew support from these rural grievances that constituted dissatisfaction with the status quo. The apparent embrace of co-operative ideals by Sinn Féin provided an opportunity for the IAOS's co-operative principles to become part of the discussion about what a future Irish state might look like.

The IAOS came through the war with rediscovered confidence and cause for optimism. Co-operative societies continued to organise working practices in the countryside, and farmers derived financial benefit from their membership. The movement stood on the threshold of new opportunities as membership numbers reached a high watermark at this time. The establishment of a new general-purpose society that carried out a more diverse trade provided a cause for some cheer among the movement's leaders. The fact that Dáil Eireann's Democratic Programme made a commitment to Irish industrial development also offered an opportunity to advance the IAOS's influence over a potential government in waiting. Concerted efforts to bring about measurements that promoted economic development despite the Dáil's limited resources did take place. In relation to agricultural development, the co-operative movement offered a ready-made instrument through which the rural policies might be carried out. From the vantage point of the IAOS, the shift in the political landscape raised the possibility of advancing attempts to construct a Co-operative Commonwealth. However, any prospects of a peaceful transition into the next phase of a more co-operative economy soon dissipated. The Irish War of Independence saw the country collapse into a violent guerrilla conflict fought between the Irish Republican Army (IRA) and British security forces, which lasted from 1919 to 1921. Co-operative creameries suffered greatly in the conflict as they found themselves targeted by Crown forces in reprisals aimed at local communities in the wake of IRA activities.

This chapter is divided into three sections. The first examines how the co-operative movement exerted a significant intellectual influence within the Sinn Féin movement. Despite the co-operative movement's official non-political status, radical nationalists appropriated their language of rural construction as another aspect of an Irish nation-building project. The readily accessible reservoir of co-operative ideas aligned to one of Ireland's largest mass-membership organisations offered a generation of would-be legislators a source of policy ideas for the future. This potential utility guaranteed the IAOS a role to play within whatever iteration of an Irish nation-state came out of the conflict. The second section examines the co-operative movement's own developmental trajectory as it started to experiment with new types of co-operative businesses in the immediate aftermath of the Great War. The timing of such experimentation proved fatal as violence stunted the movement's ability to diversify – a factor that helped to contain co-operative energies firmly within the dairying sector. The chapter ends with an exploration of the movement's experience of violence during the War of Independence. The resilience of the movement built up over previous decades left the co-operative movement well positioned to endure state-sponsored attacks. Such experiences ensured that co-operative societies became increasingly nationalised as tools for economic development because of victimisation by Crown forces. It also allowed the IAOS to position itself as a national institution for social and economic development on the eve of independence.

Co-operation, nationalism and labour

Co-operation and Sinn Féin

Ireland caught the interest of a new wave of foreign investigators and journalists keen to understand the dynamics of political change after the Great War and the co-operative movement stood out among the motley forces at work. In part, the reason for this attention stemmed from Æ, whose reputation as a literary man of letters and an economic thinker lent him an international stature. Æ's was a familiar name outside Ireland, and his house provided a first port of call for intrepid investigators who wanted to grasp the dynamics of a changing Irish Question. One of this number, Ruth Russell, worked as a journalist with the *Chicago Tribune* and published an account of her visit entitled *What's the Matter with Ireland?* As Russell travelled across an Ireland descending into violence and unrest, she concluded that the Irish Question turned on the social and economic problems she encountered on her travels. The cause of unrest resided in the fact that Ireland was poor: 'poor to ignorance, poor to starvation, poor to insanity and death. And that the cause of her poverty is her exploitation by the world capitalist next door to her.'

Russell's grand tour brought her into contact with political and social activists who provided answers to her questions about the unsettled state of the country. In urban areas she met with labourers who argued that a Workers' Republic provided the only means to end poverty. Her forays into the countryside revealed that in the 'villages and country places where the co-operative movement is growing strong, there are those who believe that the new republic must be a co-operative commonwealth'.[10]

Ruth Russell visited Æ's home during one of his regular Sunday soirées where intellectuals gathered to discuss a number of topics that ranged across politics, the arts and economics. Russell observed first-hand the high regard in which the visitors held Æ who she described as 'the north star of Ireland' and someone 'who gives ear to all sincere radicals, Sinn Féiners and "Reds"'. The opportunity to talk with Æ in his home 'goes far ... towards easing the strain on the taut nerves of the Sinn Féin intellectuals who attend them'. Importantly, the geniality of Æ provided him with frequent opportunities to impress his views on 'the peaceful revolution of co-operation' on those at the heart of the Sinn Féin project.[11]

Russell devoted a chapter of her book to the co-operative movement and encountered a movement that promoted rural development and encouraged a spirit of self-reliance among its members. Speaking to Russell just before violence broke out, Æ optimistically assessed the contemporary situation as one where 'Ireland can and is developing her own industries through co-operation'. However, Æ viewed British government in Ireland as an impediment to this development and undermined farmers' efforts to improve the agricultural sector through their own efforts. He supported 'the building of a co-operative commonwealth on co-operative societies', but felt English rule prevented this outcome because its imperial lens proved too large to see the importance of government at the village level.

> She [Ireland] is developing [industries] without aid from England and in the face of opposition in Ireland. England, you see, is used to dealing with problems of empire – with nations and great metropolises. When we bring her plans that mean life or death to just villages, the matter is too small to discuss. She is bored.[12]

Ireland needed a governmental template that prioritised the rural village, which Æ believed was the backbone of the nation. The recent years of wartime economic management emphasised the veracity of this view for Æ, which he passed on to interested observers such as Russell.

At this time, Æ directed Russell, to visit one of the new types of society in Dungloe, County Donegal. Æ directed Russell there to understand

> the poverty of the Irish countryside, of the extent that the poverty is due to the gombeen men ... and of the ability of the co-operative society to develop and create industry even in such a locality.[13]

There Russell met with the local co-operative activist named Patrick Gallagher.[14] Gallagher had moved from Donegal to Scotland in 1899 where he saw the economic benefits provided to people there by the presence of co-operative stores. Gallagher returned to Donegal in 1902 determined to establish a similar co-operative society which opened as Templecrone Co-operative Society in 1906. Templecrone stood out against the backdrop of the IAOS's societies and it shared similarities with the retail societies promoted by the Co-operative Wholesale Society (CWS). It started as a small store to make collective purchases of manure for local farmers, but gradually expanded to serve the requirements of the local population. Gallagher recounted the impact of Templecrone Co-operative Society as one that freed the local population from indebtedness to local traders and shopkeepers by loosening their financial hold upon locals: 'Thank God the slave mind is gone. If it is in any other part of Ireland today, it is not in the Rosses.'[15]

Ruth Russell encountered a thriving society involved in many aspects of local life, which encouraged 'the hints of growing industry'. This reflected the local influence of the United Irishwomen. These included a bacon-curing plant, the co-operative production and sale of eggs, the rental of modern farm machinery to members, a bakery, orchard, beehives and a woollen mill, which employed local women who no longer planned to emigrate to America or Scotland 'as their older sisters had had to plan'. The society's managers intended to develop other local industries such as fishing and local transportation. Besides offering affordable provisions, the society provided locals with a space for social interaction. The co-operative hall held dances, lectures and other entertainments. Furthermore, the society pioneered a concern for the social welfare of members, employing a nurse 'to care for the mothers at child-birth … the first nurse who ever came to work in Donegal'.[16] Russell concluded that Templecrone Co-operative Society successfully prevented the economic exploitation of local inhabitants by reducing the influence of local traders and shopkeepers.

Irish co-operation demanded the attention of foreign visitors. The movement's work enthused Ibrahim Rashad, an Egyptian nationalist who published his travelogue *An Egyptian in Ireland* in 1920. Having studied economics and lived in England, Rashad wanted Egypt to attain 'her political emancipation, her economic freedom [and] her social uplifting'. Rashad travelled to Ireland as part of the responsibility of every 'intellectual among the rising generation in every country, especially in those countries which circumstances have placed in a backward position, to investigate and to make known those movements in other lands from which their own people may learn'. Like Ruth Russell before him, Rashad visited Æ, who the young Egyptian cited as a chief intellectual influence: 'His views of ideals and realities … fill the young and ardent with the desire to do great things. His inspiring influence on the rising generation cannot be exaggerated.' Æ gave Rashad an informal education on Ireland and co-operation. As a result, Rashad grew enthused by the possibilities for national revival offered by co-operative principles as practised by the Irish:

> Here the spirit of association and power of organisation seemed to have full play in many of the ways of life. As applied to political and social questions they appeared to be as effective as when applied to economics. I now discovered that my enthusiasm for the Co-operative Movement was to lead me further than the desire merely to improve the economic position of my people. It was to show me what the power of organisation and force of associated effort can do in every department.[17]

Rashad observed what he viewed as one of the Irish co-operative movement's most powerful attributes, which was that once the principle of economic autonomy was practised widely then the desire for political autonomy naturally grew. Rashad recognised something denied by Horace Plunkett at the IAOS's inception – namely that the establishment of a co-operative society represented an inherently political act. Rashad left Ireland convinced that co-operation offered a means to attain social, economic and political independence as he wed principles of mutualism and co-operative economic organisation to the assertion of a nationalist identity.

Within Irish nationalist circles, the connections with the co-operative movement grew more pronounced. Æ's influence over Sinn Féin intellectuals grew throughout the early twentieth century. His prolific output through books and journalism meant he provided constant commentary upon unfolding political events from a co-operative perspective. In particular, his 1916 treatise, *The National Being*, provided an important intellectual touchstone for Sinn Féin intellectuals such as Darrell Figgis, Aodh de Blacam and Patrick Little. The first two individuals published a series of books and articles that argued in favour of Sinn Féin policies, while Little edited the Sinn Féin newspaper, *New Ireland*. All displayed this book's influence within their own writing.[18] The language of co-operation employed by these writers granted a social and economic coherence to the vision of a future independent Irish nation-state they aimed to create.

Darrell Figgis's contribution to the intellectual development of the Sinn Féin project bore the imprimatur of co-operative idealism. Figgis, a regular visitor to Æ's house, spent several stints in prison on account of his political activities. He published nationalist propaganda and enjoyed close access to Sinn Féin leaders, becoming a trusted confidant to Arthur Griffith, the Vice-President of Dáil Eireann. After independence, he played a key role in writing the Irish Free State's first constitution.[19] Figgis argued in 1916 that Æ's economic and social philosophy provided an ideal foundation for an Irish nation-state as it offered 'a distinct nationality with its own conception of civilization; and [Æ] would house that nationality in a distinct State worthy of the praise of noble men'.[20] A year later Figgis identified the co-operative society as the means through which Irish farmers had already started to build this modern state. Although Figgis believed that Ireland existed already as a nation, it had yet to graduate to the rank of 'a Sovereign State'. Figgis argued that farmers seized upon the co-operative ideology as a means to recapture a sense of an old statehood that existed in an idealised Gaelic past. These farmers 'turned their co-operative societies into rural communities that were a re-birth in modern conditions of their old stateships'.[21] According to Figgis, the conditions for a return to a Gaelic state arrangement already existed in those rural communities engaged in co-operative activity. Rural co-operatives provided a glimpse into the independent Irish nation-state yet to come.

Aodh de Blacam, another Sinn Féin publicist, also drew heavily from Æ's well and later described the artist as someone who 'developed a plan for a co-operative commonwealth that amounted to a draft constitution'.[22] In de Blacam's own work written during the years before Irish independence, he argued that Sinn Féin reflected the mood of the nation, which he primarily defined as rural.[23] This reification of the rural represents an important motif of the separatist nationalist élite, who were largely from an urban, middle-class professional background.[24] Between 1918 and 1921 de Blacam published several books in which he argued for a national policy to promote and protect the agricultural mode of life.[25] De Blacam's view that 'the future of Ireland lies in Co-operation no observer of the times can doubt', revealed a conviction such principles could resolve the Irish Question. He understood that the co-operative movement's influence over rural life resulted from its long-term, gradual extension throughout the country. However, its continued success relied upon an ability to attract support from a new generation: 'Co-operation … had to be preached, as in the wilderness, for the space of a generation, but today every young man of intelligence

… accepts co-operation as the progressive policy.'[26] De Blacam echoed the arguments made by Figgis when he asserted that 'every Irish social thinker envisages the Gaelic polity as a rural polity'. This definition of Gaelic was important as it equated rurality with a more authentic type of Irish society that had been lost. De Blacam argued that Irish people regarded the 'great industrial cities of Britain or America … as horrible perversions of the natural order'. He conceded that the 'Irish objection of urban concentration is factitious', but continued, 'when all allowances are made it is deep-rooted in the Irish mind'.[27]

The adoption of co-operative values set Sinn Féin apart from the constitutional nationalists. Whereas the IPP treated the co-operative movement with outward hostility, Sinn Féin embraced its ideas. Just as the IPP represented an older generation and the past, Sinn Féin exuded a youthful, modern appeal as they positioned themselves as the political movement of an Irish future. It was the *young* farmer who walked 'the progressive path'. The archetypal Sinn Féin supporter read 'modern Irish literature, and finds every one of the intellectual leaders of the country preaching co-operation [and] sees no one defending the cause of the old regime of traders who grew rich on selling bad seeds and inferior manures'.[28] The years of *Homestead* editorials and IAOS rhetoric, in which the co-operator stood in opposition to an economic system rigged by traders and gombeen men, found its way into nationalist critiques of social conditions. Links between the spread of co-operation and wider cultural development echoed the objectives that animated the cultural revivalists in the 1890s.[29] De Blacam highlighted the co-operative movement's attempts to enrich cultural life as further evidence of their role as a force for national regeneration. For example, Enniscorthy Co-operative Society displayed its modern credentials when it established a cinema for the local community. In this way, co-operation provided a mechanism which contained 'the possibility of Irishising the people's amusements', and in the near future societies could become 'the most effective patrons of Irish music, Irish drama and Irish talent that [the public] have ever enjoyed'.[30]

Any commitment to co-operative principles among leading Sinn Féin individuals is likely to have varied in its levels of enthusiasm. Nevertheless, an appropriation of the language of co-operation emerged as a trope that peppered Sinn Féin commentary on social and economic matters. At times, this commitment went beyond the pages of political treatises. In June 1919, Sinn Féin ordered all local party branches to 'promote the organisation of Co-operative Societies to deal with neglected resources and industries'.[31] Michael Collins, one of the Republican leaders and the Dáil's Finance Minister, advocated that industrial development in Ireland needed to occur on 'on co-operative lines rather than on the old commercial capitalistic lines'.[32] The Dáil showed some support for co-operative principles and institutions in pursuit of their counter-state through some of the reforms they proposed to pass as legislation. As such these attempts to pass remedial legislation suggested a degree of practical commitment to co-operative principles beyond the pages of intellectual treatises, which arguably helped to manifest Arthur Griffith's aim that Sinn Féin display a 'spirit of self-reliance'.[33]

Æ cautiously welcomed these nationalist overtures in April 1919. On one level, he applauded this interest in co-operative ideals, which seemed 'to have many voluntary propagandists, for we find Irish papers on all sides reporting speeches in which the future Ireland is spoken of as a Co-operative Commonwealth'. However, he questioned the sincerity of these 'new propagandists of the Co-operative State whose advent in the field of co-operative effort we welcome'. Æ challenged the new advocates to 'define more clearly the kind of social order they are working for, and the steps by which they propose to attain what they desire'.[34]

The next month, the Dáil provided Æ with some policy evidence. Ernest Blythe, the Dáil's Director of Trade and Commerce, argued for the organisation of the Irish economy along co-operative lines, stating that this provided 'the only feasible method of combating foreign trusts and combines'.[35] Blythe had worked at the Department of Agriculture and Technical Instruction (DATI) during Horace Plunkett's time as Vice-President when co-operative principles informed official agricultural policy.[36] Under Blythe's direction, a pragmatic working relationship between the IAOS and Dáil Eireann emerged. On 6 May 1919, Sinn Féin's executive urged all party branches to support the establishment of co-operative societies and the Dáil formed a commission to study 'the whole question of co-operation in Ireland'. The commission's committee included prominent IAOS figures such as Æ, Fr O'Flanagan, Edward Lysaght (the latter two members of the National Committee) alongside the Dáil's Director for Agriculture, Robert Barton. By August, Arthur Griffith had produced a pamphlet urging that co-operative organisation be applied to matters of trade and distribution and President of the Dáil, Eamon de Valera, communicated from America that he 'endorsed the idea of the Co-operative Commonwealth'.[37] Later that year the Dáil grew more involved in the IAOS's day-to-day operations as Robert Barton was co-opted onto its governing committee.[38] Two years later, Ernest Blythe joined Barton on that committee, which provided Sinn Féin with an insight into the administration and structure of the movement.[39] This formalised a working relationship between an insurgent government and the premier agency of rural expertise, which provided the basis for a long-term relationship.

Arthur Mitchell argued that Sinn Féin's commitment to co-operatives declined within months. Instead, the party concentrated its attention and resources upon local elections in 1920 as it looked to build on its successes as an efficient electoral machine.[40] Electoral successes remained the immediate priority for Sinn Féin, but between 1919 and 1921 members of the Dáil still aimed to demonstrate that they represented a serious government and social issues received due care and attention. For example, the question around land ownership remained contentious. The 1903 Wyndham Land Act legislated for the break-up of estates and the transfer of land to the tenant farmers.[41] Perceived as a legislative solution to previous decades of agrarian unrest the persistence of land ownership and distribution as a controversial issue continued to reverberate.[42]

In December 1919, a Dáil committee investigated the possibility of creating a central co-operative bank. This resulted in the foundation of the National Land Bank as a way to provide credit to farmers in order to continue the extension of land ownership among farmers. The National Land Bank, or Banc na Talmhan, was registered under the provisions of the 'Industrial and Provident Societies Acts as a co-operative institution' and aimed to ensure the circulation of Irish money remained within Ireland and 'establish a financial centre for their interests'.[43] At a later date, Ernest Blythe would describe the rationale behind its foundation as a means to prevent 'the national struggle from being turned into a land war'.[44] However, the co-operative structure applied to this banking institution demonstrated a serious level of commitment to the pursuit of co-operative principles beyond idle talk.

The Dáil appointed Lionel Smith-Gordon as the bank's managing director. Born in England and educated at Eton and Oxford,[45] Smith-Gordon worked at the University of Toronto until 1912. He later recalled that around that time he 'became very much interested in the co-operative movement in Ireland. I went there and soon became a revolutionist.'[46] Smith-Gordon moved to Ireland in 1914 where he worked at the Co-operative Reference Library in Plunkett House and championed the role of co-operatives in Irish and European economic development. Smith-Gordon fitted the criteria required as bank manager by virtue of being 'a gentleman who has considerable experience in connexion with agricultural banking operations'.[47] His intellectual development mirrored that followed by other Irish nationalists as he became attracted to the philosophy of Sinn Féin through his work for the co-operative movement.

Lionel Smith-Gordon's appointment at the National Land Bank brought him into close orbit with Sinn Féin officials and his advocacy of co-operative principles became shot through with political separatism. Critics of Sinn Féin singled out Smith-Gordon for attack. In September 1921, playwright and Ulster unionist, St John Ervine, launched a scathing attack upon Sinn Féin in *The Times*. Ervine's criticisms rested on his ability to demonstrate his impeccable Ulster credentials by tracing his ancestry back for at least 300 years. That record granted Ervine 'some claim to the title of Irish'. In contrast, Ervine accused key members of Sinn Féin as unable to make a claim to genuine Irishness. Ervine identified Eamon de Valera, the Dáil's President, as 'a citizen of the United States, born in New York of a Spanish father and an Irish mother'; Arthur Griffith was 'a Welshman, who, like Medea, is "sullen-eyed and full of hate"'; and Erskine Childers, 'the most extreme adviser of Sinn Féin', was in the end, 'a very gallant Englishman'. Ervine then asserted that 'one of the ablest officials the Sinn Féiners possess in their non-political activities is an Englishman, Mr Smith-Gordon'.[48] Smith-Gordon viewed himself as a patriotic Irishman at this stage and took umbrage with Ervine's portrait, which provoked a strong defence against the accusation of 'Englishness'. 'Honoured by being mentioned among the *dramatis personae* of Mr Ervine's Wonderland', Smith-Gordon rubbished the claim that he was 'an official possessed by Sinn Féin'. Instead, he defined his occupation as a means to 'serve my country as a manager of a registered company'. He stressed: 'I am not an Englishman, by blood, temperament, domicile, citizenship, or outlook', and claimed that, 'I try to atone for an alien upbringing by living in and for my country.'[49]

As manager, Lionel Smith-Gordon helped to embed the co-operative society as a developmental instrument among Irish policymakers and laid out the scope of this ambition in 1921 when he claimed 'we have to arrive at quite a new point of view – the attitude that a bank is a national institution with a national objective'.[50] The bank's charter asserted that, 'The National Land Bank is an Irish institution founded to assist in the rebuilding of Ireland's prosperity, the restoration of her population and the securing of her economic independence'.[51] The bank's work was of 'an experimental nature'. Its primary objective was to provide mortgages to co-operative societies made up of landless farmers who could then purchase property.[52] The way in which banking policy might achieve a national objective was through a mass land purchase scheme. From the outset, Smith-Gordon looked beyond this initial objective of land purchase and looked to position the National Land Bank as a means through which a more co-operative economy might be realised – one in which a national bank provided the finances to extend the co-operative movement from a producer movement to one in which a co-operative retail sector might flourish.[53] He argued:

> The ideal is to create co-operative communities of men who will work in harmony with one another and help one another to get the highest possible yield out of the land, to standardise the produce, to brighten the life of the countryside, and to do away with the existing class distinctions and feelings of bitterness which arise from unequal distribution of wealth and opportunity.[54]

The National Land Bank was founded with a nominal share capital of £406,000.[55] It received an initial £203,000 investment from the Dáil and by June 1921, the bank had loaned out £315,000. Most of this money funded land purchases, but several loans funded other industries such as fisheries. Importantly, all capital flowed through co-operative societies utilised as instruments of nationalist development.[56] The bank only achieved limited success. During the War of Independence, Crown forces frequently raided branches and hostility from established banks frustrated any attempt to diversify into commercial banking. After independence, the establishment of an Irish Land Commission superseded the functions of the bank as land distribution policies became centralised.[57]

However, the National Land Bank offered a brief but potent symbol of a national economic policy based on co-operative principles. It also showed that Sinn Féin representatives proved willing to work with co-operators in order to achieve its policy objectives.

Co-operation and Labour

Co-operative principles also found a receptive audience within the Irish labour movement. With its collectivist political economy, trade unionists and labour activists advocated co-operative ideas with somewhat different emphases to the principle espoused by the IAOS. James Connolly served as the intellectual figurehead of the labour movement in the early twentieth century. Connolly's execution, as one of the leaders of the 1916 Easter Rising, deprived the labour movement of its most dynamic leader. Prior to that, he had engaged with co-operative ideas in his writings on Irish labour history. He concluded the Co-operative Commonwealth represented an appropriate form of social organisation for Ireland. However, Connolly's conception of a Co-operative Commonwealth differed from that advanced by the IAOS. From organised labour's perspective a focus on the consumer instead of the producer better served working-class aspirations. If a more satisfactory form of co-operation were to take root in Ireland, rural and urban co-operators needed 'to find a common basis in order that one might support and reinforce the other'.[58] Connolly identified the failure to achieve this objective as an inherent flaw in the IAOS's vision. Instead, in line with some of the syndicalist views that circulated around the Irish labour movement before the war, Connolly advocated an industrial strategy that placed the interests of all workers under the leadership of one single trade union. This offered the most effective way of achieving a 'Social Administration of the Co-operative Commonwealth in the future'.[59] Fr Finlay of the IAOS vociferously disagreed with Connolly's conception of co-operative organisation, which he viewed as a worrying tendency towards a more materialistic form of political activism and a threat to the IAOS's pre-eminence in the field of organising.[60]

During the Dublin Lockout – a major industrial dispute that occurred between August 1913 and January 1914, involving about 20,000 workers – the Manchester-based CWS provided an important source of material and moral support for strikers and their families. The first shipload of food supplies sent by the CWS, with the support of the Trades Union Congress, to support families in dire need of assistance arrived in Dublin on 27 September 1913. The SS *Hare* delivered much needed food to over 18,000 people who been supplied with food tickets by local trade union societies, and the CWS's correspondent reported that as 'every package bore the letters "CWS" … the whole of Dublin is discussing the growing power of this people's organisation'.[61] Supply-laden ships continued to cross the Irish Sea to Dublin until the end of the strike in which almost 1.8 million loaves of bread were distributed along with other staples such as margarine, clothing, tea and sugar.[62] The consumer-oriented version of the Co-operative Commonwealth, represented by the urban CWS movement, resonated within the trade union movement more than the rural producers' movement. Trade unionists continued to promote this consumerist model in the years after Connolly's death.[63]

Potential for a fruitful relationship between labour and rural co-operators existed by the end of the war. In the wake of the Russian Revolution, the confidence of international labour movements increased. In Ireland, the Russian Revolution galvanised the labour and co-operative movements and contributed to demands for social change. In February 1918 the leader of the Irish Labour Party, Tom Johnson, reflected upon the implications of the Russian Revolution in an article entitled, 'If the Bolsheviks Came to Ireland'. Johnson found an Irish equivalent to the Russian soviets in

> the trades councils, *the agricultural co-operative societies*, and ... the local groups of the Irish Republican Army. An Irish counterpart of the Russian revolution would mean that these three sections, co-operating, would take control of the industrial, agricultural and social activities of the nation.[64] (Emphasis added)

Such rhetoric provided no reassurance to a British government alive to the threat that militant Irish workers posed to its authority, but also raised the spectre of revolutionary potentialities attached to co-operative societies.

Æ echoed Johnson and welcomed revolutionary developments in Russia. Writing in the *Irish Homestead*, he argued that the Russian Revolution represented a vindication of co-operative principles. In the revolution's immediate aftermath in November 1917, Æ wished that

> revolutionaries in Ireland were afflicted with something of the Russian madness and realised, as the Russians do, that economic institutions are at least as of much importance as political institutions ... A co-operative society is an economic republic.[65]

In March 1919, such a positive appraisal of the Russian social order remained part of Æ's worldview. In an article entitled, 'All Co-operators Now!' he presented Russia as a potential model for a future Irish state:

> We are not advocating compulsory co-operation in Ireland, but we find it impossible to be indignant with a State which carries the co-operative idea so far as the Russian Republic has done... there is only one country in the world where all distribution is on co-operative lines, and, personally, we hope that system will never be upset, whoever may come or go as leaders of the Russian people.[66]

Æ's enthusiasm for the revolution did not survive 1920 when the Bolsheviks nationalised the co-operative movement there.[67] However, in 1919 his admiration led him to consider how co-operative organisation and labour's interests might be more comprehensively addressed under the IAOS.

In January 1919, the leaders of the Irish Labour Party contributed to the Dáil's Democratic Programme. The party stepped aside to provide Sinn Féin with a clear run, but still looked to influence policies within the Dáil. In an earlier draft of the document, Tom Johnson indicated the labour movement's interest in co-operative societies in a sentence:

> It shall be the purpose of the government to encourage the organisation of people into trade unions and co-operative societies with a view to the control and administration of industries by the workers engaged in the industries.[68]

Ultimately, the labour movement and IAOS diverged on how best to achieve this end. The largest and most militant trade union in Ireland was the Irish Transport and General Workers' Union (ITGWU). Founded by Liverpool-born trade union activist, James Larkin, in 1908, the union possessed 14,500 members in 1916. By 1919, these figures grew to 101,917.[69] The labour movement's radicalism manifested during 1917–23 through a variety of tactics, such as strikes and workplace takeovers. Terms such as 'Workers' Republic', 'industrial unionism' and 'co-operative commonwealth' peppered the labour movement's rhetoric. The ITGWU advocated a revolutionary syndicalist ideology that encouraged the creation of a working-class political movement under its leadership.

During 1918–20 the ITGWU expanded into the countryside as it recruited heavily among agricultural labourers.[70] As such, a rural labour militancy emerged from the ITGWU's 'efforts to develop a working-class counter-culture, through co-operatives, May Day parades, aeríochtaí [festivals], and labour newspapers'.[71] In County Kerry, labour organisations turned to co-operative principles to secure the economic interests of their members. In November 1918, the *Irish Homestead* reported the establishment of a workers' co-operative store in Tralee. The enthusiasm shown by workers for the new venture in a town where 'local opposition usually barred the way' appeared to highlight a great change that occurred under the cover of the war – the 'capitalist fear of organised labour'.[72] The following January, the ITGWU established another co-operative store in the market town of Listowel 'for the benefit of the workers'.[73] Located in County Kerry's most urbanised areas, these co-operative stores reflected the ITGWU's desire to use co-operative methods to benefit local working-class consumers and highlighted an appetite for a new type of retail in the area.

This incursion into the IAOS's heartlands led to an uneasy relationship with organised labour. By May 1919, antagonisms between rural co-operators and the trade union movement emerged. Æ hoped that workers would continue to establish co-operative societies, but suggested that trade unions and the IAOS should co-ordinate their efforts. He wondered if:

> trade union leaders would communicate with the [IAOS], so that investigation may be made, and it may be seen whether labour would be better advantaged by coming in with farmers in starting a single strong society catering for both.[74]

This incorporation never occurred as rural labourers looked to the ITGWU for leadership. However, the challenge offered by the labour movement concentrated the minds of the IAOS's leaders about how the movement might break into the area of rural consumption.

New explorations in co-operation

The IAOS's position by the end of the war appeared mixed, but cause for optimism existed among co-operators as 1919 dawned. Wartime saw an increase in agricultural income and farmers rallied around the IAOS with a generosity not previously seen. Dues and subscription for 1920 amounted to almost £9,000, or roughly two-thirds of IAOS's total income for that year.[75] In 1920, membership for the movement reached a peak of 157,766.[76] These figures reflected a greater affluence among farmers, but also suggested that a greater number of rural inhabitants recognised that co-operative societies offered one way to acquire cheap agricultural implements at a time of rising living costs. The war led to an overall increase in the co-operative movement's trade turnover by 21.7 per cent in 1919 compared to 1914. Dairying remained the IAOS's most important sector, but throughout the war creameries increased turnover by only 3 per cent (see table 5.1). Although an unspectacular level of growth, this figure showed the resilience of co-operative creameries to hold their position at a time of declining milk supplies. Farmers in the dairying heartlands of Munster, where more than half of Irish milk production occurred, remained reliant upon the creamery as a source of income.[77]

Outside dairying, the co-operative credit movement collapsed during the war as activity contracted by 256 per cent. This collapse proved indicative of the IAOS's neglect of co-operative credit after 1914, itself partly a result of wartime affluence. In other areas, flax societies increased trade by 721 per cent, but this

Table 5.1 Financial position of IAOS in 1919

Type of society	Turnover for 1919 (£)	1919 turnover in 1914 prices (£)	turnover for 1914 (£)	Increase %
Dairy society	7,047,079	2,818,856	2,731,628	3
Agricultural societies	1,279,471	511,788	197,146	160
Poultry societies	246,599	98,639	65,487	51
Credit societies	33,834	13,533	52,926	−256
Misc. societies	696,649	278,659	187,826	48
Flax societies	47,791	19,116	2,328	721
Federations	1,807,160	722,864	429,383	68
Total turnover for movement	**11,158,583**	**4,463,433**	**3,666,724**	**21.7**

Source: IAOS, *Annual Report, 1920*.

accounted for less than 0.5 per cent of the IAOS's total business. Poultry societies expanded trade by 50 per cent, while trading federations increased turnover by 68 per cent. Both sectors remained a minor part of the co-operative movement's total business. The IAOS's overall financial position improved during the war but the movement remained reliant upon an annual subsidy from the Development Commissioners.[78] A pressing immediate concern stemmed from the fall in wartime dairy production. The compulsory shift towards greater tillage farming during the war occurred in an abrupt manner with a detrimental effect on the level of Irish dairy output. Lionel Smith-Gordon claimed that the situation deteriorated further due to 'the slaughter and export of milch cows, which, in spite of official denials, have been brought about by war conditions and by blunders incidental thereto'.[79]

A new, and potentially fruitful, set of relations between the IAOS and DATI beckoned in 1919. T.W. Russell retired from the DATI in late 1918 and Hugh Barrie, an Ulster Unionist MP, replaced him as Vice-President until November 1921.[80] However, from the outset, Barrie's time in office was beset by poor health and he made less impact in office than either of his predecessors. T.P. Gill, Secretary of the DATI, carried out many of Barrie's public duties.[81] A more benign relationship beckoned between the two agencies of rural development as IAOS officials once again began to acquire positions upon investigative committees established by the DATI. In late 1919, Robert Anderson and Harold Barbour represented the IAOS on the committee appointed to examine the causes behind the declining Irish milk supply.[82] As the largest operator of creameries, the co-operative movement provided an important service to the state in Ireland, as it proved able to efficiently collect and analyse data that related to the dairy industry. The committee drew heavily on evidence provided by creameries, which offered a window onto the intricacies of the economy in the dairy plains of Ireland. A sample taken from six creameries in Counties Limerick and Kerry showed how milk yields declined drastically by 16 per cent during a period that covered the implementation of wartime controls (table 5.2).

A weakened dairy industry offered serious cause for concern to the IAOS as its reputation and strength derived from its creamery sector. As the economy adjusted to post-war conditions, the rivalry between private and co-operative creameries re-emerged. The rates paid to milk suppliers varied across districts and depended upon the concentration of creameries. The fierceness of the rivalry

Table 5.2 Declining milk supply to six creameries in counties Limerick and Kerry

Year	1916	1917	1918
Milk supply (gallons)	4,067,000	3,840,000	3,420,000

Source: HCPP (Cmd. 808).

between co-operative and proprietary creameries played out most persistently in the south-western region of the country where conditions proved most suitable for dairy farming.[83] Co-operative society committees accused privately operated rivals of unscrupulous price-fixing. In August 1919, co-operative societies in Kerry held a conference which broached the subject of co-ordinating their work in an effort at

> combating the methods of Proprietary Creameries in paying artificial prices for milk in districts where Cooperative Societies exist while paying much lower prices per gallon in districts where they are no Cooperative Societies.[84]

In 1919, a legal challenge to the way in which co-operative creameries organised their milk supply threatened to unravel the IAOS network. Private creameries looked to weaken the co-operative movement's hold over the dairy industry through a legal challenge against the binding rule. In 1908, the IAOS introduced a controversial binding rule, which tied members into a permanent relationship with their co-operative society, and forbade them from supplying milk to any other creamery. If a member refused to supply good milk to their society, the committee penalised that member at the rate of one shilling per cow for each day milk was withheld.[85] This echoed the Danish system which bound farmers to the co-operative society for a period of up to seven to ten years and operated with successful results.[86] Unlike Denmark, the binding rule in Ireland continued indefinitely. Members took several legal cases against co-operative societies on the grounds that the rule unfairly tied them into a contract with the co-operative.[87] In 1919, the most significant legal action taken against Ballymacelligott Co-operative Society by Richard McEllistrim saw private rivals successfully overturn this binding rule.

Ballymacelligott in County Kerry was home to a thriving co-operative society that expanded its operations during the war. In 1912, the society possessed two creameries with an annual turnover of £8,000. By November 1920, it operated four creameries with a turnover of £58,500. In 1916, the committee called a special meeting of members and adopted the binding rule. The society later used the regulation to penalise a member, Richard McEllistrim, because he supplied milk to a creamery run by J.M. Slattery and Sons. However, the roots of this legal conflict partly lay in the fact that local kinship networks helped to govern the local economic distribution of milk supplies. According to Ballymacelligott's manager, John Byrne:

> The non-Co-operative Society … got … McEllistrim (whose sons they had employed as managers in their concern) to bring an action against this society to declare the rules invalid as in restraint of trade.[88]

Slattery and Sons wanted to entice the milk suppliers who frequented the co-operative creamery to their own premises and McEllistrim's decision to break the binding rule served their purpose. Aided by Slattery, McEllistrim brought his case to trial, which reached the House of Lords in early 1919.

The IAOS recognised the threat posed by this legal action and promised to pay for Ballymacelligott Society's defence. Although a local affair, the case became a test of the national movement's ability to withstand an assault on its position by the private sector. The outcome of the case held the potential to undermine the industry's future development. A majority decision found in favour of McEllistrim on the grounds that the binding rule imposed 'restrictions further than were reasonably necessary for the protection of the society, the rules were unenforceable as being in unreasonable restraint of trade'. The only dissenter, Lord Parmoor, argued that the contract between a co-operative society and its members possessed a 'distinctive character' whereby 'business can be instituted and carried on in a co-operative basis'.[89] Parmoor's words offered little comfort. The IAOS suffered a heavy financial loss of £3,850 and appealed to members in their newspaper for financial help as they fought the case 'in the interests of the movement' against 'a powerful and well-organised trade combination'[90] (see figure 5.1). The creamery business remained the IAOS's largest asset, but its position appeared much more vulnerable after the McEllistrim verdict.

The general purpose society

Despite the mixed outlook facing the dairy sector after 1919, in the field of co-operative retail and distribution the IAOS held great hopes that a breakthrough might occur after the war. The increased cost of living associated with the war brought the issue of rural consumption into focus. Co-operative agricultural societies allowed farmers to jointly purchase goods and machinery at wholesale prices and therefore cheaper than from traders. The IAOS viewed agricultural societies as necessary for the diffusion of new agricultural machinery, but growth in this sector proved disappointing before 1914.[91] In 1897, the Irish Agricultural Wholesale Society (IAWS) was founded as a trading federation to carry a range of retail and wholesale work for other co-operative societies. Individual agricultural societies could subscribe to the IAWS in order to provide the trade body with substantial capital that allowed the larger body to pass on significant savings to members through the mass purchase of seeds, fertilisers and machinery. Importantly, as a separate organisation the IAWS could help agricultural co-operative societies develop a limited retail business after the Development Commissioners prevented the IAOS from performing this function.[92] Therefore, the fact that all types of co-operative societies could federate to the IAWS allowed producer co-operatives to expand their businesses during the war. The number of co-operatives that affiliated to the IAWS increased from 188 in 1914 to 379 by the end of 1918.[93]

Agricultural co-operative societies increased economic output by 160 per cent during the war as they diversified their services (see table 5.1). The more expansive activity conducted by agricultural societies during the war 'brought

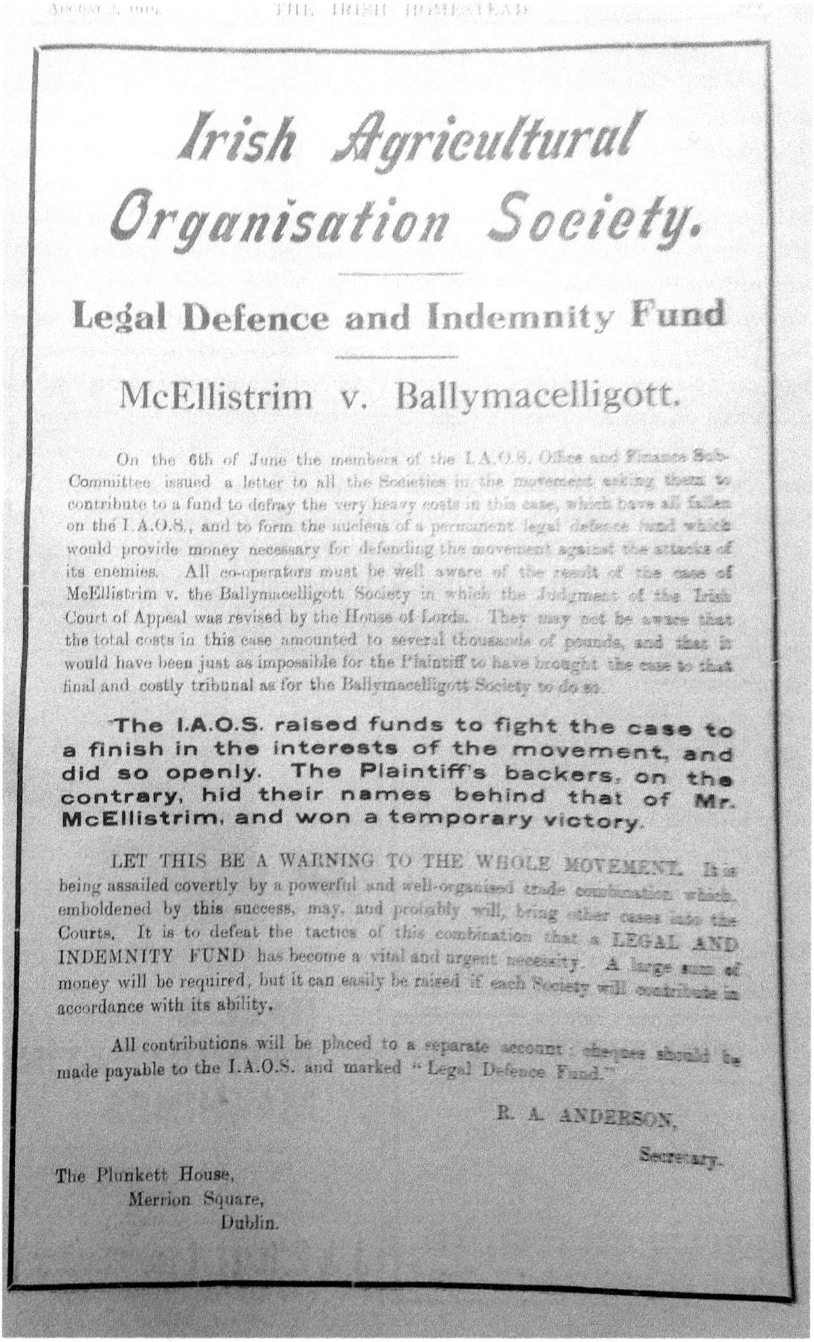

August 5, 1905.   THE IRISH HOMESTEAD

Irish Agricultural Organisation Society.

Legal Defence and Indemnity Fund

McEllistrim v. Ballymacelligott.

On the 6th of June the members of the I.A.O.S. Office and Finance Sub-Committee issued a letter to all the Societies in the movement asking them to contribute to a fund to defray the very heavy costs in this case, which have all fallen on the I.A.O.S., and to form the nucleus of a permanent legal defence fund which would provide money necessary for defending the movement against the attacks of its enemies. All co-operators must be well aware of the result of the case of McEllistrim v. the Ballymacelligott Society in which the Judgment of the Irish Court of Appeal was revised by the House of Lords. They may not be aware that the total costs in this case amounted to several thousands of pounds, and that it would have been just as impossible for the Plaintiff to have brought the case to that final and costly tribunal as for the Ballymacelligott Society to do so.

The I.A.O.S. raised funds to fight the case to a finish in the interests of the movement, and did so openly. The Plaintiff's backers, on the contrary, hid their names behind that of Mr. McEllistrim, and won a temporary victory.

LET THIS BE A WARNING TO THE WHOLE MOVEMENT. It is being assailed covertly by a powerful and well-organised trade combination which, emboldened by this success, may, and probably will, bring other cases into the Courts. It is to defeat the tactics of this combination that a LEGAL AND INDEMNITY FUND has become a vital and urgent necessity. A large sum of money will be required, but it can easily be raised if each Society will contribute in accordance with its ability.

All contributions will be placed to a separate account; cheques should be made payable to the I.A.O.S. and marked "Legal Defence Fund."

R. A. ANDERSON,

Secretary.

The Plunkett House,
    Merrion Square,
        Dublin.

Figure 5.1 Advert for Ballymacelligott Legal Indemnity Fund

home to farmers the necessity of complete control over their industry, and to agricultural labourers the vital importance of procuring the necessities of life on terms commensurate with their wages'. By 1920, 271 agricultural co-operative societies existed and the IAOS wanted these to become more diversified societies that expanded the co-operative principle into a whole new range of services for the rural consumer.[94] The IAOS referred to these new agricultural societies as 'general purpose societies'.[95] The development of agrarian distribution represented one way in which the IAOS attempted to bring the apparent divergent interests of Irish producers and consumers closer together. By 1920, the IAOS optimistically claimed that 'the distributive movement has begun to capture rural Ireland'. The IAOS attributed this development to the spontaneous initiative of farmers and labourers and claimed the establishment of new agricultural societies proved 'the fixed decision of the people to "self-determine" their own economic destiny'. This recasting of the 'old "agricultural society"' emerged when it was 'difficult to forecast the economic future of the country at such a time of stress and uncertainty'. The general purpose society represented the IAOS's attempt to link 'the success of farming … with the spread both of agricultural and distributive co-operation'.[96]

The Catholic clergy within the IAOS viewed the general purpose society as a way to bridge the interests of consumers and producers. Fr Michael O'Flanagan supported the co-operative movement as a force for social, economic and moral progress. A lifelong advocate of agricultural co-operation and with a reputation as a Republican priest, O'Flanagan became a vice-president of the IAOS in 1919 and vice-president of Sinn Féin in 1920. As an advocate of Catholic social teachings, O'Flanagan saw economic co-operation as an effective way to resolve class conflicts between capital and labour and a means to treat each member of society with dignity and respect. In a pamphlet simply called *Co-operation*, O'Flanagan argued that all private companies failed to achieve this objective because they were organisations bound together through 'money, or capital'. The co-operative organisation sought 'a different and higher bond. Instead of a money link co-operation seeks to substitute a human link. Instead of building with the pound as unit, co-operation builds with the man as unit'. For O'Flanagan, co-operatives restored human dignity to economics through their mutual business organisation: 'the Co-operative Society has members where the Joint Stock Company has shareholders'.[97]

A tension at the heart of the co-operative movement in Ireland related to the fact that it helped to bring class tensions about in a new guise that crudely pitted urban and rural citizens against one another. Fr O'Flanagan welcomed the introduction of the general purpose society because he wanted the IAOS to branch out into retail services. He argued that although co-operative retail had been attempted in Ireland, these efforts were conducted under great pressure. However, such a service was required because more than any other sector he believed that the 'great advantage of co-operative shopkeeping is that it is a very simple way of teaching people the rudiments of co-operation'.[98] Fr O'Flanagan believed if Irish co-operation could incorporate those consumers into the movement missed by the spread of creameries then the economic interests of farmers and labourers might be harmonised.

An example of pioneering work in this direction occurred in Rathmore, County Kerry. Rathmore's farmers established a general purpose society at the start of 1919, which combined a creamery and shop representing

> one of the newer type of creameries which it is believed will be the general type in the future. It was organised with the object of undertaking the manufacture of dairy products and the supply of all the requirements of its members.[99]

The Great War saw an evolution away from single-function societies. In the immediate aftermath, the wider co-operative movement anticipated the establishment of more societies like Rathmore, which represented a significant leap forward in the extension of the IAOS throughout the economy. The IAOS hoped that 'the general purpose type of society of which Rathmore is an example, promises much more success'.[100]

The movement celebrated Rathmore Co-operative Society's establishment with fanfare. A ballad written by the Bard of Rathmore and published in the *Irish Homestead* conflated Home Rule with the economic liberation of co-operation and equated farmers' control over their industry through the co-operative as a victory over landlords and exploitative dealers.

> Home Rule is coming to Erin's shore,
> And home industry to sweet Rathmore,
> The Farmers' Factory will shortly crown,
> Our handsome rising Blackwater town …
> The landlords reigned, but their day did come,
> So the proud fat dealers today are dumb,
> For the farmer rises now with a smile,
> Who forces bread from his native soil.
> Sure we all have shade from the farmers' wing,
> He feeds the tramp, and he feeds the King,
> He steers the ship, and he runs the train,
> And he wins the battle fought on the plain …
> So no more we'll pay for our goods too high,
> But the best of stuff at low prices buy,
> Down with high prices for evermore,
> And up the farmers, and up Rathmore.[101]

It also pre-empted the application of Home Rule. The ballad identified the farmer as the foundation stone of the Irish nation and emphasised that agriculture underpinned the whole social structure.

Rathmore Co-operative Society registered for business on 6 May 1919 and led one local inhabitant to describe the enterprise as 'the shopping and social centre of east Kerry and part of West Cork'.[102] Charles Riddall assured the IAOS that the society's prospects looked good. The society operated a creamery, but its main objective saw it 'engage very largely in a general store trade'. The society attracted support from 'all members without distinction [who] are extremely keen'. Rathmore remained untouched by the co-operative movement up to this point, but its varied business operations offered the potential to attract local members. The area was covered in small farms and most of the butter made in the district was produced within the home. The society's establishment encouraged the adoption of modern dairy techniques by opening a creamery, but also appealed to conservative inhabitants by selling local homemade butter through the co-operative store. The management hoped that the prices paid for creamery butter would encourage the conversion of local agriculturalists into modern co-operative dairy farmers. Before it opened, the society acquired 70 members who bought 1,000 shares.[103] This expanded to 208 members by July. Despite Riddall's early optimism, opposition soon emerged. Another organiser reported at the end of July that the creamery competed for local milk with the Lakelands Dairy Company, while because the society operated a shop, 'the local shop-keepers are offering all the opposition they can to the project'.[104]

The establishment of Rathmore Co-operative Society once more revealed the importance of IAOS organisers. Charles Riddall provided advice on hiring employees and a manager, and placed the IAOS's official accountancy services at Rathmore's disposal.[105] James Fant offered his services during the construction of the society's premises. However, the committee sometimes ignored his advice, which led Fant to describe Rathmore's building progress as 'slow and disappoint-ing'.[106] The appointment of a new manager in August 1920 saw increased col-laboration between the society and the IAOS. With someone in place to act as a fixed point of contact Fant helped with the acquisition of new creamery machinery and offered precise instructions for its installation.[107] At the start of 1921, Rathmore's creamery finally opened alongside the shop trade already ongoing.

The IAOS believed the general purpose societies provided an opportunity to capture new members and epitomised the movement's 'most representative type of institution'. The general-purpose society like that at Rathmore, sought to create a union of interest 'not merely between persons of varying political and religious beliefs, but between farmer and labourer, producer and consumer, countryman and townsman'. A period of renewed, popular enthusiasm about co-operation beckoned. At the IAOS annual conference in 1920, delegates com-mended the Dáil's enthusiasm for co-operation and welcomed the fact that a cross-section of 'political opinion in Ireland … accepted the co-operative movement as a recognised … element in national welfare'.[108] However, these new developments occurred against a backdrop of violence and unrest. At the very point that a new phase of co-operation looked set to occur, co-operative societies found themselves targets of state-sponsored violence and the site of political and social tensions that derailed this progress.

The Irish co-operative movement and the Irish War of Independence

Frantz Fanon described decolonisation as 'always a violent phenomenon' and this captures something of the Irish experience during 1920 and 1921.[109] Confrontations between the IRA and Crown forces, made up of the Royal Irish Constabulary, Auxiliaries and the Black and Tans,[110] took place with increased intensity as the government applied a military deterrent as part of its security policy.[111] Guerrilla warfare, raids on private property, martial law, industrial strike action and the spread of terror dominated news stories about Ireland from 1919 until the announcement of a truce in July 1921.[112] Pat 'the Cope' Gallagher, President of Templecrone Co-operative Society, recalled that 'the Black and Tans were worse than savages let loose. They were murdering, ravishing and burning.'[113] Much of the violence occurred in rural areas with a particular concentration in the south-west and the centre of the dairying industry.[114] Violence disrupted social and economic life throughout the country and co-operatives found themselves on the receiving end of state violence in the most serious threat to the movement yet.

The decision to target co-operatives formed a central component of British government's security policy. During 1920 and the first half of 1921, co-operative societies across the country were attacked by Crown forces. By 1 January 1921, 42 co-operative societies suffered severe damage to premises, and in some cases complete destruction. Robert Anderson claimed that each creamery destroyed put 800 farmers out of business.[115] Violence placed severe strain on the movement, with local societies forced to close and national resources stretched to breaking point. Security forces responded to IRA provocation through attacks on co-operative societies as a way to punish a community. The British government's recruitment of ex-servicemen as police auxiliaries provided the main perpetrators of violence. Attacks on co-operatives occurred as an act of reprisal after an IRA attack in an area, but also reflected a lack of discipline among this new police force.[116] In the short term, violence disrupted the working lives of farmers in the area, but in the longer term the economic capacities of co-operative societies experienced irreversible setbacks.

Throughout 1920 and 1921 IAOS staff received regular updates about assaults on co-operative societies. One such incident was carried out by a party of men on the night of 23 October 1920. The men travelled to the creamery in a police vehicle and stopped at a house in the townland of Ballydonoghue where they assaulted two young men and 'bobbed the hair of two girls'. When they arrived at the creamery 'they burned down a large part of the Co-operative Creamery, destroying machinery, a large quantity of cheese, and £1,000 worth of butter'.

Estimated damage to the society stood between £10,000 and £12,000.[117] Several days later another attack occurred less than six miles away at Abbeydorney Co-operative Society carried out by '3 lorries of armed men, some wearing khaki, and the majority [Royal Irish Constabulary] uniforms'. These men set fire to the creamery, caused £2,000 of damage, and looted stocks of butter and cheese.[118]

The result of these attacks placed affected co-operative societies on the brink of collapse and the IAOS provided a vital source of support. Organisers responded to calls for assistance from co-operative committees, which helped to reaffirm and strengthen the connection between individual societies and the national body. For example, Rattoo Co-operative Society based in a district of good dairy land in north Kerry let its IAOS affiliation expire during the war and ceased payment of the subscription fee. Charles Riddall informed Dublin in late 1919 that 'there is no bothering about this Society [Rattoo] for the present. No doubt they will return to the fold as so many other Societies have done.'[119] In November 1920, as news of attacks upon neighbouring societies filtered through, the IAOS leadership wired Rattoo Co-operative Society to ascertain news concerning its position. Rattoo replied: 'this creamery is not interfered with so far, & we are now hopeful it will escape for the present'.[120] Rattoo remained unharmed, but the IAOS's work in this period convinced the committee to renew its affiliation. In particular, the society's committee appreciated the publicity work carried out by Plunkett and Æ on behalf of the movement, and pledged a special subscription of 'funds for carrying on the campaign in Great Britain against the destruction of Societies'.[121] Rattoo Co-operative Society received the assurance of support from organisers if an attack occurred in return.

Violence aimed at co-operatives undermined British legitimacy in Ireland and forced the IAOS to abandon any pretence of a non-political position with regard to the government's policy. Horace Plunkett instigated a publicity campaign across Britain in which he highlighted the repressive tactics for a British audience. In September 1920, he wrote to *The Times* in protest against reprisals carried out against creameries. In an appeal to readers, Plunkett stated that he 'would not drag the Irish Agricultural Cooperative Movement into the Anglo-Irish controversy at its acutest stage without compelling reasons'. However, the network of trust built up disintegrated overnight as farmers refused to deal with co-operative businesses 'because they believe that these are specially marked out as objects of reprisal by the guardians of the law'.[122] The attacks damaged more than bricks and mortar; they wrecked the bond between farmers and their societies that had been hard won over previous years.

David Lloyd George, the Prime Minister, responded to Plunkett's intervention when he delivered a speech at Carnarvon, Wales, on 9 October 1920. The speech formed a defence of the government's Irish policy and overseas news agencies covered its content. He rejected demands to grant Ireland dominion-status Home Rule, which would have included Irish political control over their own military and naval bases. Furthermore, Lloyd George defended the violent behaviour of the police and military to suppress rebellious activity in Ireland. The main targets of Lloyd George's speech were critics from within his Liberal Party, but he aimed specific jibes at Horace Plunkett. Lloyd George ridiculed Plunkett's attempt to represent any serious opinion on the Irish Question and he joked that 'Sir Horace Plunkett ... cannot even speak for his creameries'.[123] Despite this attempt to deflect attention on to Plunket's political credibility, the plight of the Irish co-operatives remained newsworthy and continued to embarrass Lloyd George's Coalition Government.

Æ also pursued a publicity campaign aimed at the British public.[124] In 1920, he published *A Plea for Justice*, which called for a public inquiry into the attacks by '[t]he armed forces of the Crown ... [who] burned down factories, creameries, mills stores, barns and private-dwelling houses'. Æ understood the rationale behind these attacks as a punitive response calculated to lead 'to the wrecking of any enterprise in the neighbourhood the destruction of which would inflict widespread injury and hurt the interests of the greatest number of people'.[125] The publicity campaign attracted influential support within Britain and drew attention to grim realities in Ireland. In particular, the *Manchester Guardian* reported on the breakdown of law and order in the Irish countryside. Headlines such as 'The Burning of Irish Creameries', 'Outrages in Co. Kerry' and 'Blow to the Co-operative Movement: Farmers Punished for Work of IRA' characterised that paper's reportage of the Irish situation.[126]

This effect of such publicity work encouraged criticism of the government from a non-Irish perspective. The British Labour Party sent an investigative commission to Ireland in November 1920 to consider the case for Irish freedom and its concern over the 'degradation which the British people are now suffering in consequence of the policy of repression and coercion which has been carried out in its name'.[127] The Commission visited areas affected by violence in order to interview witnesses and provide an alternative narrative of the effects of British policy in Ireland than that offered by Lloyd George's government. As part of this fact-finding mission the Commission interviewed Robert Anderson, Æ and Paul Gregan of the IAOS, along with managers of victimised co-operative creameries 'who gave evidence on the economic hardships created by the wrecking of the machinery, plant, and buildings'.[128]

The British Labour Party criticised the government's policy in Ireland as counterproductive. The IRA's success resided in the fact it enjoyed popular support within communities and the actions taken by Crown forces exacerbated a volatile situation. The subsequent report confirmed the arguments of Plunkett and Æ that British security forces targeted civilian businesses in response to local guerrilla activity. These attacks aimed to 'cause the maximum economic and industrial loss to an Irish countryside or city' and that these 'reprisals have been *scientifically* carried out' (emphasis added). The policing tactics of the Crown force represented not so much a spontaneous reaction to local violence, but a calculated attempt to subdue the local population. Moreover, the Labour Commission argued that the IRA ultimately benefited from the military reprisal policy as the 'destruction of creameries and manufactories only serves to stimulate recruiting by increasing the number of desperate men'.[129] The destruction of co-operative businesses increased the unpopularity of the British state in Ireland and weakened the moral case for the government's Irish policy.

British co-operators also rallied to the IAOS's support in a sign that relations between the two movements had improved. Frequent articles in the *Co-operative News*, which reflected the official views of the movement in Britain, reported on the Irish situation and focused on outrages committed against Irish co-operators by Crown forces. The newspaper provided readers with detail on Plunkett's interventions and questioned the 'sanity' of the British Government that embarked upon a campaign to destroy the Irish movement. In a strong front page editorial, the *Co-operative News'* special correspondent called for an end to attacks on Irish creameries and stated firmly, 'if the Government is going to make war on co-operative establishments in any part of the British Isles, co-operative societies in the British Isles must accept the challenge and declare war upon the Government'.[130]

Not all readers shared this sentiment. The publication of a controversial cartoon that depicted a British soldier wielding a bayonet and fiery torch as he rampaged towards an Irish home provoked a backlash from some readers. The cartoon was a reprint from the *Catholic Herald* entitled 'Those Creameries' (see figure 5.2). The character of a young boy named Young Erin asked: 'Does he ever stop?' The boy's mother replies: 'Didn't he stop for two minutes on Armistice Day?' A series of letters appeared in the next edition which protested against the 'gross representation of the British soldier' that adorned the front page of the paper. Despite the criticism, the editors maintained that the government continued to prevent people from learning the truth about the conduct of the police and army in Ireland. In that context the publication of the cartoon was an attempt to portray the 'feelings of the innocent victims of the present regime of force in Ireland'.[131]

Alongside the attempts to bring the Irish Question back into the focus of British media attention, the IAOS's organisers continued to place themselves in danger on many occasions. On 12 May 1921, the Chairman of Rathmore Co-operative Society notified Plunkett House of an attack by Crown forces that destroyed the society's shop and machinery four days before the scheduled opening of a new creamery.[132] The attack occurred at a crucial point in the society's development and threatened to derail the co-operative project within the area. The IAOS despatched Nicholas O'Brien, who arrived 'after much inconvenience

Figure 5.2 'Those Creameries'

and personal risk'. Taxis refused to transport him to the district and he arrived a day later than scheduled on 31 May 1921. O'Brien's timing proved fortunate. He reported that on 30 May, the entire village 'was cleared out about 2 o'clock [a.m.] ... and had some other experiences also'. On visiting the society he noted that the 'building was completely destroyed, nothing but the walls stand and they too have suffered probably from bombs. The stocks in store were completely burned out.' O'Brien advised Rathmore's management to continue the store trade 'in an implement shed at the rear of the main building'.[133]

Fear undermined local solidarity around the co-operative society. The violent attacks upon co-operatives spread anxiety throughout the local population and trade suffered as a result. Thomas de Lacy, the manager of Rathmore Co-operative Society complained to James Fant that store business declined after the attack because 'the people are afraid to come in'. Local employment generated by the new society was also undermined. The committee implemented a cut in the manager's salary and released his assistant from employment.[134] Widespread awareness of the fact that armed forces targeted co-operatives damaged the business of societies such as Rathmore. Local inhabitants refrained from utilising the co-operative store and the creamery remained closed during this time. Rathmore staggered into the 1920s struggling to re-summon the initial enthusiasm of local members lost to alternative shops and productive centres. Once considered the IAOS's flagship society, Rathmore's rapid decline told a depressing story for co-operators who wished to usher in a new phase of economic experimentation in distributive and retail services.

It was not only fledgling societies such as Rathmore that suffered permanent injury – so too did long-established co-operatives. Some, such as Ballymacelligott Co-operative Society, even experienced fatalities as staff and suppliers got caught up in the violence. On the morning of 12 November 1920, security forces attacked one of the creameries attached to Ballymacelligott Co-operative Society and, as a result, two men were killed and two others injured. According to witness statements, a lorry carrying police and military arrived at Ballydwyer creamery and as they jumped from the lorry some of the employees fled from the scene. A member of the local IRA brigade, Thomas McEllistrim, recalled that members of the Ballymacelligott Active Service Unit happened to be close to the creamery and as they 'made a dash for escape ... fire was opened on them immediately by Tans and RIC'.[135] Another witness claimed that the people fired upon were 'suppliers and employees' to the creamery although one of the injured men, Jack McEllistrim, was an IRA volunteer.[136] The two men who died were John McMahon, a farmer and member of the committee who had brought corn to the society's mill to be ground into flour, and Patrick Herlihy, employed as the dairyman at the creamery. The official version of events presented to the House of Commons by the Chief Secretary of Ireland, Sir Hamar Greenwood, claimed that 'about seventy armed men' fired at a party of journalists and their police escort from the local creamery. This 'act of war' justified the reprisal. The British Labour Party who sent representatives to investigate the story disputed this account as a 'caricature of what actually happened'. Their commission's inquiries into the Ballymacelligott attack instead concluded that no shots were fired from the creamery and 'none of the men who were killed or wounded were carrying arms … [and] no arms or ammunition of any kind were found in the creamery'. The next afternoon a party of men approached the creamery from Castleisland and set fire to the premises. The perpetrators appeared not to be the military and those people who tried to rescue butter from the premises 'were prevented from doing do by the person who appears to have been in charge of the party.[137] After the commission's visit to Ballymacelligott, Crown forces raided the house of the creamery manager and killed another two men found there. The Labour Commission described the whole incident 'as discreditable to the Government as any of the occurrences for which the Government or its agents have been responsible'. It concluded that no basis existed for the attack and called for an independent inquiry.[138]

Rumours circulated that collusion between private creamery owners and the military encouraged the attacks on co-operatives. Robert Anderson discussed the events of Ballymacelligott with James Fant which he described 'as a result of a dead set made upon it by Crown forces, at the instance, to some extent I believe at least, of local creamery proprietors'.[139] A sworn witness statement provided by Ballymacelligott's manager, John Byrne, linked the attacks to recent court cases with Richard McEllistrim. Byrne accused agents of Slattery's creameries of spreading:

> false and malicious reports concerning me and members of the Co-operative Society with a view to undermine the loyalty of the members [and] … to set the forces of the Crown against the Staff and members of the Committee of the Co-operative Society. I regret to say and I charge that these false and malicious reports have been accepted and acted upon by the forces of the Crown. I was arrested in 1916 and interned for 3 months without charge or trial. The trade and business of the Society suffered as a consequence.

The attacks of 12 and 13 November halted production at the society and resulted in the development whereby 'a number of the members have gone over to the Non-Co-operative concern'.[140] This concern in question was J.M. Slattery and Sons, which showed that local rivalries remained a live issue in the area. Competition between private and co-operative creameries intensified once again under the cover of violence, which provided the movement's rivals with opportunities to capitalise. Suggestions of collaboration between private creamery owners and security forces arose out of this situation and created an impression that the War of Independence provided cover for private creameries to extend their own interests.

In February 1921, the *Manchester Guardian* described the effect of British policy as heralding 'the economic decay of Ireland':

> the burning of creameries, the destruction of farmsteads ... the withdrawal of labour from the land, through imprisonment or outlawery, the stoppage of co-operative organisation are steadily depreciating the productivity of Irish agriculture.[141]

Later that year crown forces modified their reprisal tactics to close down businesses instead of carrying out attacks. The cost of closures and interruptions proved high and placed financial stress upon a society's resources. The solicitor who represented Ardfert Co-operative Society detailed the outrage at his client's premises in an account prepared for the Kerry County Council office in pursuit of a compensation claim a year later:

> On March the 21st 1921 at Ardfert Crown Forces surrounded the Creamery and ordered the Staff to go out. The Staff were detained for a week in a 'round up' and when they returned, butter to the value of £625.10.0 was stolen, cream to the value of £200 had gone waste as had also the Cream in two Auxiliary Creameries to the value of £800. Wages for week £14, Consequential loss £1,200, Llyod's [sic] Insurance, Riot and Civil Commotion £300, Mare shot dead and consequential loss £97.0.0 – Claim: £3236.10.0.[142]

The differential treatment of co-operative and proprietary creameries by the military led to a further deterioration in the relations between the two sectors. The *Manchester Guardian* reported that 'a number of creameries in the South of Ireland have been closed by order of the military'. These tactics rendered stocks held at co-operative societies 'useless for the time being, and the effect of the order ... is to harm the country people as much as possible'.[143] Once again, the military's orders disproportionately affected the co-operative sector. The military closed down a creamery at Kilflynn operated by Abbeydorney Co-operative Society while local private creameries continued to trade. Abbeydorney's manager wrote to his brother after the creamery's closure, 'the funny thing is that Slattery's Creamery, which is within a stone throw of ours, was not closed at all, with the result, that a large number of our suppliers have gone to them'.[144] A few nights later, the military ordered Slattery's creamery to close temporarily, but they reopened once again on 9 June. In stark contrast, Abbeydorney Co-operative Society's Kilflynn premises remained shut. Nevertheless, the society's membership decided to reopen without permission 'and let the military do what they wished'. The result of this decision saw their machinery sabotaged by unidentified raiders after only one day of trading.[145] Nicholas O'Brien sent his assessment of these events to Robert Anderson:

> It is regrettable [sic] that local friction should cause any further trouble, but I fear that the interests of proprietary creamery owners in Co. Kerry have

been the cause of much damage to co-operative property. Of course there has been no definite proof of this, but there is a strong feeling that this is the case, as proprietors have not suffered near as much as co-operatively owned creameries …
I hope that when matters settle, if they ever do, we may be able to remedy much of this ill feeling by making an effort to wipe out proprietary opposition.[146]

Organisers who worked in areas where attacks occurred suspected collaboration between private creamery owners and Crown forces. In a handwritten note attached to the report, James Fant commented on O'Brien's analysis, writing that the 'feeling expressed above is well founded and people in Tralee and district are fully aware of the reasons for the "glove" treatment accorded to certain proprietary creameries'.[147] What is clear is that reprisal tactics rekindled socio-economic tensions between co-operative and private creameries that had remained dormant during the First World War.

The truce, July–December 1921

British security forces continued to apply their reprisal policy with increased desperation until the announcement of the truce on 11 July 1921. The Truce came as a relief for a population wearied by conflict and violence. The prospect of resolution led to a cessation in the fighting between Republicans and Crown forces, but uncertainty about what might happen next led to a period of political confusion. The negotiation of the Anglo-Irish Treaty between the British government and a Sinn Féin delegation led by Arthur Griffith and Michael Collins dominated the news that autumn and winter. The agreement signed on 6 December 1921 culminated in the establishment of the Irish Free State made up of the 26 southern counties of Ireland in 1922. The British sovereign remained the head of state and six north-eastern counties remained a separate Northern Ireland. Republicans in the Sinn Fein movement split over whether they viewed approval of the Treaty as an acceptable compromise or a betrayal of national aspirations.[148]

Before that and during the uncertain months of late 1921, the Truce period provided respite for struggling co-operative societies as attention turned to the immediate work of reconstruction. The co-operative movement's recovery depended upon the loyalty of local members combined with the guidance of the IAOS. Larger and long-established co-operative creameries demonstrated their resilience during these months. Ballymacelligott Society, which lost its central creamery, directed milk supplies to auxiliary creameries based in the neighbouring villages of Gortatlea and Polatty. Ownership of auxiliary creameries allowed larger co-operative creameries to recover more quickly as they were able to restart tentative production. The manager's fear that members would switch their allegiances to rivals proved inaccurate. John Jones, Ballymacelligott Society's president, informed

Robert Anderson that the 'loyalty of the Society's members is to be commended through all the harassing ... their determination not to be beaten down was inspiring'. Jones thanked the IAOS for their support during the months that followed the attack in November 1920 and added its work 'will not be forgotten by the people of Ballymacelligott for many a day'.[149]

The publicity generated around the co-operative attacks elicited sympathy for Ireland overseas. In America, fundraising efforts got under way with the establishment of a loan fund to aid the affected co-operative societies. The American Committee for Relief in Ireland was organised in New York after a report by a delegation of the American Society of Friends sent to Ireland in February 1921. The delegation investigated 'economic distress in Ireland, [and] ... has not been equalled in scope by any other investigative body, either Irish, British, American, or of any other nationality'. An estimated 25,000 families required relief and due to the 'crippling of the co-operative creameries in Ireland, 15,000 farmers ... are suffering severe loss and are faced with even more deeply serious distress in the immediate future'.[150] A special creamery expert travelled with the travelling party to 'give special attention to the destroyed creameries ... [and help] rehabilitate an essential industry'.[151] The Irish White Cross emerged out of the delegation's report. Based in Ireland and managed by the Dublin Quaker, James G. Douglas, the White Cross was 'an Irish organisation, independent of any religious and political body ... [that administered] funds either for immediate relief or for reconstruction'.[152] The White Cross provided the loan capital required to rebuild creameries and replace broken machinery. Injured co-operatives sought this loan capital to restart business as soon as possible and the IAOS lobbied on their behalf.[153] For example, the IAOS secured a White Cross loan worth £2,500 to stabilise Ballymacelligott Co-operative Society and with little pressure to repay 'any of the White Cross money until it is quite convenient for the society to repay it'.[154]

Less well-established societies experienced painful reconstructions and lost their positions in the community. In Rathmore, economic opponents frustrated the recovery of the co-operative society. When the White Cross launched a fundraising drive in the area, they met with local opposition when its people learned the funds would help replenish the local co-operative. For example, the application to the White Cross by the Rathmore Co-operative Society reignited dormant tensions. The manager of Rathmore Co-operative Society, Thomas de Lacy, wrote to Charles Riddall explaining: 'there is ... bitter opposition to the Coop here, as a matter of fact two Traders who collected the village for White Cross have refused to hand up the subscriptions when they heard [the] Creamery had applied for loan'.[155]

The IAOS placed great emphasis upon the reconstruction of Rathmore Co-operative Society. In August, James Fant visited the village and reported that the society required urgent financial aid. The reconstruction of the society would be a crucial step in the reinvigoration of the area and:

> would form the centre of a local industry much needed in the locality to aid and develop dairying and allied agricultural industries – the only source of income [for] hundreds of small farms and others in this district where much of this land is reclaimed bog and mountain land ... Knowing the efforts that these people have made to establish their creamery the amount of local free labour by horse and man that has been given and their efforts to help themselves I would specially request the fullest application for financial aid to give them a fresh start.[156]

The priority in the society's reconstruction was given to the creamery business as dairying offered the most likely source of income for farmers.

A society like Rathmore faced another problem different to that affecting a creamery society like Ballymacelligott. The attack upon the shop meant a loss of stock and capital and the longer it remained closed the more local enthusiasm for the new society decreased. Initially, the store business suffered because locals feared being caught up in further reprisals. Weekly turnover at the shop was £300, before the attack in May 1921. By October, this figure dropped to £120 and outstanding debts due from members totalled £1,100.[157] In Nicholas O'Brien's assessment, 'the store trade has fallen away considerably and I believe that unless something is done ... the store business will dwindle away altogether'.[158] By the end of 1921, the local population appeared to have returned to other shops to purchase their goods once again. Rathmore Co-operative Society limped through the next decade harried by problems before it passed into the receivership of a semi-state body, the Dairy Disposal Company (DDC), in 1930. By 1936, a DDC employee recommended the dissolution of Rathmore Co-operative Society, describing it and others like it as, 'to all intents and purposes failures'.[159] The general purpose society receded on the list of IAOS priorities as it looked to rebuild its creameries and capture the attention of an incoming Irish administration. The IAOS focused again upon the interests of the producer and the efforts to harmonise these interests with the consumer declined.

Over the course of the next few years, the task of stabilising and rebuilding co-operative societies preoccupied IAOS employees. Their recovery faced further challenges as the post-war period slid into a global recession, resulting in a depressed market for agricultural produce. National economic success depended on the ability of co-operative societies to maintain production in underdeveloped districts to effect change. In districts like Rathmore, where traditional and inefficient methods of production persisted and agricultural holdings were poor, co-operative institutions encouraged economic improvement and revitalised living conditions. However, opposition to co-operative societies in the form of private creameries and traders reasserted their position in the rural economy during 1919–21. The access granted to charitable loan capital enabled co-operatives to meet these challenges.

As Ireland prepared for independence, the movement reflected upon a period in which severe damage was inflicted on co-operative property and the lives of members and employees were threatened. The experience of those years immediately after the war meant that:

> The whole rural population in several districts had to carry on life under conditions that were … discouraging and frequently full of risk both to themselves and to their industry.[160]

Despite the violence, the movement emerged from its darkest period yet and the IAOS could assert that 'no stronger proof of the inherent vitality of the movement has ever been recorded'.[161] Nevertheless, violence exacted a heavy price. The survival of the movement through a moment of violent crisis reflected an adherence to co-operative organisation among the rural population. Many, although not all, people in rural areas rallied to the support of these societies ensuring they remained key players in national development. As political independence arrived, the co-operative movement looked to ensure that aspects of a Co-operative Commonwealth underpinned the new Irish Free State.

Notes

1 R.F. Foster, *Modern Ireland, 1600–1972* (London: Penguin, 1989), 495; J.J. Lee, *Ireland, 1912–1985: Politics and Society* (Cambridge: Cambridge University Press, 1989), 40.

2 Ronan Fanning, *Fatal Path: British Government and Irish Revolution, 1910–1922* (London: Faber & Faber, 2013).

3 Dáil Éireann, 'Democratic Programme of Dáil Éireann', *Parliamentary Debates*, Volume 1, 21 January 1919, http://oireachtasdebates.oireachtas.ie/debates%20authoring/debateswebpack.nsf/takes/dail19190121000016l [accessed 17 September 2017].

4 Arthur Mitchell, *Revolutionary Government in Ireland: Dáil Éireann, 1919–1922* (Dublin: Gill & Macmillan, 1995), 43.

5 Brian Farrell, *The Founding of Dáil Éireann: Parliament and Nation Building* (Dublin: Gill & Macmillan, 1971), 80.

6 David Fitzpatrick, *The Two Irelands, 1912–1939* (Oxford: Oxford University Press, 1998).

7 Michael Laffan, *The Resurrection of Ireland: The Sinn Féin Party, 1916–1923* (Cambridge: Cambridge University Press, 1999), 315. Also Joost Augusteijn (ed.), *The Irish Revolution, 1913–1923* (Houndmills, Basingstoke: Palgrave, 2002); John M. Regan and Mike Cronin, 'Introduction: Ireland and the Politics of Independence, 1922–49: New Perspectives and Re-considerations', in *Ireland: The Politics of Independence, 1922–49*, ed. by Mike Cronin and John M. Regan (Basingstoke: Macmillan, 2000), 1–12.

8 David Fitzpatrick, *Politics and Irish Life, 1913–1921: Provincial Experience of War and Revolution* (Dublin: Gill & Macmillan, 1977); Emmet O'Connor, *Syndicalism in Ireland, 1917–1923* (Cork: Cork University Press, 1988).

9 Fergus Campbell, *Land and Revolution: Nationalist Politics in the West of Ireland, 1891–1921* (Oxford: Oxford University Press, 2005).

10 Ruth Russell, *What's the Matter with Ireland?* (New York: The Devin-Adair Co., 1920), 13–14.

11 Russell, *What's the Matter*, 102.

12 Russell, *What's the Matter*, 107.

13 Russell, *What's the Matter*, 107–109.

14 Trevor West, 'Gallagher, Patrick', in *Oxford Dictionary of National Biography*, www.oxforddnb.com/view/article/65846?docPos=2 [accessed 14 August 2013].

15 Patrick Gallagher (Paddy the Cope), *My Story*, rev. edn (Dungloe: Templecrone Co-operative Society, n.d.), 173.

16 Russell, *What's the Matter*, 115–123.

17 Ibrahim Rashad, *An Egyptian in Ireland* (n.a.: privately printed, 1920), 2–3.

18 Mitchell, *Revolutionary Government*, 45.

19 William Murphy, 'Figgis, Darrell', in *Dictionary of Irish Biography: From Earliest Times to the Year 2002, Volume 3*, ed. by James McGuire and James Quinn (Cambridge: Cambridge University Press, 2009), 775–777.

20 Darrell Figgis, *George W. Russell: A Study of a Man and a Nation* (New York: Dodd, Mead and Company, 1916), 134.

21 Darrell Figgis, *The Gaelic State in the Past and Future or 'The Crown of the Nation'* (Dublin: Maunsel & Co. Ltd, 1917), 53.

22 Aodh de Blacam, 'Æ as I Knew Him', *Irish Monthly*, 63.747 (1935), 606–613.

23 Diarmaid Ferriter, *The Transformation of Ireland, 1900–2000* (London: Profile Books, 2005), 195.

24 Tom Garvin, *The Evolution of Irish Nationalist Politics* (Dublin: Gill & Macmillan, 1981), 100–113; Tom Garvin, *Nationalist Revolutionaries in Ireland, 1858–1928* (Oxford: Oxford University Press, 1987), 33–56.

25 Aodh de Blacam, *Towards the Republic: A Study of New Ireland's Social and Political Aims* (Dublin: T. Kiersey, 1918); Aodh de Blacam, *What Sinn Féin Stands For: The Irish Republican Movement: Its History, Aims and Ideals Examined as to Their Significance to the World* (Dublin: Mellifont Press Limited, 1921).

26 De Blacam, *Towards the Republic*, 26–27.

27 De Blacam, *What Sinn Féin Stands For*, 151.

28 De Blacam, *Towards the Republic*, 27–28.

29 P.J. Mathews, *Revival: The Abbey Theatre, Sinn Féin, the Gaelic League and the Co-operative Movement* (Cork: Cork University Press, 2003), 31.

30 De Blacam, *Towards the Republic*, 27–28.

31 Sinn Féin, Letter to Various Cumanns on Prospects of Co-operative Societies in Ireland (Dublin: Sinn Féin, 1919).

32 Michael Collins, *The Path to Freedom* (Dublin: Talbot Press, 1922), 133.

33 Arthur Griffith, *The Resurrection of Hungary: A Parallel for Ireland with Appendices on Pitt's Policy and Sinn Féin*, 3rd edn (Dublin: Whelan and Son, 1918), 141.

34 'The Co-operative Commonwealth', *Irish Homestead*, 12 April 1919, 251.

35 Blythe quoted in, Mitchell, *Revolutionary Government*, 47.

36 Patrick Buckley, 'Blythe, Ernest (de Blaghd, Earnán)', in *Dictionary of Irish Biography: From Earliest Times to the Year 2002, Volume 1*, ed. by James McGuire and James Quinn (Cambridge: Cambridge University Press, 2009), 616–624 (p. 616).

37 Mitchell, *Revolutionary Government*, 47–48.

38 IAOS, *Annual Report, 1919*, 2–3.

39 IAOS, *Annual Report, 1921*, 2–3.

40 Mitchell, *Revolutionary Government*, 48–49.

41 Barbara Lewis Solow, *The Land Question and the Irish Economy* (Cambridge Mass.: Harvard University Press, 1971),192–193; Michael Wheatley, *Nationalism and the Irish Party: Provincial Ireland, 1910–1916* (Oxford: Oxford University Press, 2004), chapter 2.

42 Fergus Campbell and Kevin O'Shiel, 'The Last Land War? Kevin O'Shiel's Memoir of the Irish Revolution (1916–1921)', *Archivium Hibernicum*, 57 (2003), 155–200 (pp. 172–173).

43 E.J. Riordan, *Modern Irish Trade and Industry* (New York: E.P. Dutton and Company, 1920), 259.

44 Ernest Blythe, 'National Land Bank', *Dáil Eireann Debates*, Volume 16.21, 20 July 1926, http://oireachtasdebates.oireachtas.ie/debates%20authoring/debateswebpack.nsf/takes/dail1926072000039?opendocument. [accessed 8 June 2018].

45 'Sir Lionel Smith-Gordon', *The Times*, 9 December 1976, 16.

46 'Titled Englishman, Dublin Banker, Spends Week Here', *The Evening Independent* [St Petersburg, Florida], 14 January 1924.

47 Riordan, *Trade and Industry*, 260.

48 St. John Ervine, 'Ulster and Sinn Féin' *The Times*, 7 September 1921, 6.

49 Lionel Smith-Gordon, 'Nationality and Sinn Féin', *The Times*, 12 September 1921, 9.

50 L. Smith-Gordon, *The Place of Banking in the National Programme* (Dublin: Cumann Léigheacht an Phobail, 1921), 12.

51 'The National Land Bank: Its Constitution and its Aims' (*c*.1921), 4, NLI P2282.

52 IAOS, *Annual Report, 1921*, 23–24.

53 Smith-Gordon, *The Place of Banking*, 8–9.

54 Lionel Smith-Gordon, cited in Mitchell, *Revolutionary Government*, 89.

55 'Free State Banking Policy', *The Times,* 22 July 1926, 21.

56 Mary E. Daly, *The First Department: A History of the Department of Agriculture* (Dublin: Institute of Public Administration, 2002), 68–70; Mitchell, *Revolutionary Government*, 86–92.

57 Peggy Quinn, Des Aylmer, Donal Cantwell and Louis O'Connell, *An Irish Banking Revolution* (Dublin: Bank of Ireland, 1995), 16–22.

58 James Connolly, *Labour in Ireland: Labour in Irish History; The Re-conquest of Ireland* (Dublin: Maunsel & Roberts Ltd, 1922), 320–321.

59 Connolly, *Labour in Ireland*, 327–328.

60 Thomas J Morrissey, *Thomas A. Finlay, SJ, 1848–1940: Educationalist, Editor, Social Reformer* (Dublin: Four Courts Press, 2004), 108–109.

61 'Relief of the Starving', *Co-operative News*, 4 October 1913, 1302–1304.

62 'Close of the Dublin Relief Fund', *Co-operative News*, 28 February 1914, 260.

63 Keith Harding, 'The "Co-operative Commonwealth": Ireland, Larkin and the *Daily Herald*', in *New Views of Co-operation*, ed. by Stephen Yeo (London: Routledge, 1988), 88–107 (pp. 88–89).

64 Cited in Fitzpatrick, *Politics and Irish Life*, 210.

65 'Village Republics', *Irish Homestead*, 17 November 1917, 839.

66 'All Co-operators Now!', *Irish Homestead*, 29 March 1919, 204.

67 Henry Summerfield, *That Myriad-Minded Man: A Biography of George William Russell 'Æ' 1867–1935* (Gerrards Cross, Bucks.: Colin Smythe, 1975), 191–192.

68 Cited in Ferriter, *The Transformation of Ireland*, 196.

69 ITGWU Return to Registrar of Friendly Societies 1917–25, NLI Ms. 27,034.

70 Dan Bradley, *Farm Labourers: Irish Struggle, 1900–1976* (Belfast: Athol Books, 1988), 43–55.

71 Emmet O'Connor, *A Labour History of Ireland, 1824–2000*, 2nd edn (Dublin: University College Dublin Press, 2011), 106–107.

72 'Co-operation in Tralee', *Irish Homestead*, 30 November 1918, 792.

73 'Listowel Co-operative Store', *Irish Homestead*, 25 January 1919, 59.

74 'Warding Off Antagonism', *Irish Homestead*, 3 May 1919, 311.

75 Joseph Knapp, *An Appraisement of Agricultural Co-operation in Ireland* (Dublin: Stationery Office, 1964), 25.

76 IAOS, *Annual Report, 1921*, 7.

77 Bolger, *The Irish Co-operative Movement*, 210.

78 IAOS, *Annual Report, 1920*, 7.

79 Lionel Smith-Gordon, *The Irish Milk Supply* (Dublin: Co-operative Reference Library, 1919), 17.

80 'Mr H.T. Barrie Resigns', *The Observer*, 20 November 1921, 14.

81 T.P. Gill, 'Address to the Council of Agriculture', *Department of Agriculture and Technical Instruction Journal*, 20.1 (1919), 12–19.

82 HCPP [Cmd. 808] Department of Agriculture and Technical Instruction for Ireland, *Report of the Departmental Committee on the Decline of Dairying in Ireland* (1920), 4.

83 IAOS, *Annual Report, 1919*, 11.

84 T. O'Donovan, Abbeydorney, to R.A. Anderson, Dublin, 27 August 1919, NAI 1088/2/4.

85 IAOS, *Annual Report, 1908*, 7.

86 Ingrid Henriksen, Morten Hviid and Paul R. Sharp, 'Law and Peace: Contracts and the Success of the Danish Dairy Cooperatives', *Journal of Economic History*, 72.1 (2012), 197–224.

87 Ingrid Henriksen, Eoin McLaughlin, and Paul Sharp, 'Contracts and Co-operation: the Relative Failure of the Irish Dairy Industry in the Late Nineteenth Century Reconsidered', *European Review of Economic History*, 19 (2015), 412–431.

88 John Byrne's Affidavit Concerning Events Surrounding the Burning of the Society, 9 April 1921, NAI 1088/70/1.

89 '*McEllistrim* v *Ballymacelligott* Co-operative Agricultural and Dairy Society Limited [1918–19] All E R Rep Ext 1294', in *Lexis Library*, www.lexisnexis.com/uk/legal/

results/enhdocview.do?docLinkInd=true&ersKey=23_T18046105861&format=GNB
FULL&startDocNo=0&resultsUrlKey=0_T18046105862&backKey=20_T1804610
5863&csi=279847&docNo=1&scrollToPosition=0 [accessed 29 August 2013]. Also
see M.J. Trebilcock, *The Common Law of Restraint of Trade: A Legal and Economic
Analysis* (London: Carswell, Sweet & Maxwell, 1986), 324.

90 'Private Interests and the Co-operative Movement', *Irish Homestead*, 2 August 1919,
570–571; Patrick Bolger, *The Irish Co-operative Movement: Its History and Development*
(Dublin: Institute of Public Administration, 1977), 205–206.

91 IAOS, *Annual Report, 1908*, 9–10.

92 Lionel Smith-Gordon and Laurence C Staples, *Rural Reconstruction in Ireland:
A Record of Co-operative Organisation* (London: P.S. King and Co., 1917),
141–147.

93 L.P. Byrne, *Twenty-One Years of the IAWS, 1897–1918* (Dublin: IAWS, 1919),
78–80.

94 IAOS, *Annual Report, 1919*, 12.

95 IAOS, *Annual Report, 1920*, 16.

96 IAOS, *Annual Report, 1920*, 16–17.

97 Rev. M O'Flanagan, *Co-operation* (Dublin: Cumann Léigheacht an Phobail,
1922), 2.

98 O'Flanagan, *Co-operation*, 9.

99 IAOS, *Annual Report, 1920*, 10–11.

100 IAOS, *Annual Report, 1920*, 11.

101 Bard of Rathmore, 'Farmer's Factory in Rathmore', *Irish Homestead*, 10 May 1919,
339–340.

102 R.A. Anderson, Dublin, to John O'Leary, Rathmore, 6 May 1919, NAI 1088/798/1;
Jeremiah Murphy, *When Youth was Mine: A Memoir of Kerry, 1902–1925* (Dublin:
Mentor Press, 1998), 40.

103 C.C. Riddall, Limerick, to Anderson, Dublin, 3 May 1919, NAI 1088/798/1.

104 J.H. McKee, Rathmore, to R.A. Anderson, Dublin, 26 July 1919, NAI 1088/798/1.

105 C.C. Riddall, Limerick, to John O'Leary, Rathmore, 31 January 1920, NAI
1088/798/1.

106 James Fant's Report re Attendance at Rathmore Committee Meeting, 13 September
1920, NAI 1088/798/2.

107 Correspondence between Fant and de Lacy, Rathmore, 3 September 1920, 27
November 1920, 28 November 1920 and 18 December 1920, NAI 1088/798/2.

108 IAOS, *Annual Report, 1920*, 17.

109 Frantz Fanon, *The Wretched of the Earth* (London: Penguin, 2001), 27.

110 Ex-servicemen referred to as such on account of the colour of their uniforms.

111 Colm Campbell, *Emergency Law in Ireland, 1918–1925* (Oxford: Clarendon Press,
1994), 21.

112 Julia Eichenberg, 'The Dark Side of Independence: Paramilitary Violence in Ireland
and Poland After the First World War', *Contemporary European History*, 19.3 (2010),
231–248.

113 Gallagher, *My Story*, 154.

114 Peter Hart, *The IRA at War, 1916–1923* (Oxford: Oxford University Press, 2003),
34–37.

115 Daly, *First Department*, 78.
116 Peter Hart, *The IRA and its Enemies: Violence and Community in Cork, 1916–1923* (Oxford: Oxford University Press, 1998), 81–82.
117 'The Burning of Irish Creameries', *Manchester Guardian*, 30 October 1920, 11.
118 'Terrorism in Kerry', *The Kerryman*, 30 October 1920.
119 C.C. Riddall to R.A. Anderson, Dublin, 6 October 1919, NAI 1088/800/2.
120 William O'Connell, Rattoo to R.A. Anderson, 4 November 1920, NAI 1088/800/2.
121 W.P. Clifford, Limerick, to William O'Connell, Rattoo, 19 March 1921, NAI 1088/800/2.
122 Horace Plunkett, 'Irish Creameries', *The Times*, 7 September 1920, 6.
123 'To Pacify Ireland by Stern Methods, Says Lloyd George', *New York Times*, 10 October 1920.
124 Æ, 'Irish Creameries', *The Times*, 23 August 1920, 6.
125 Æ, *A Plea for Justice: Being a Demand for a Public Enquiry into the Attacks upon the Co-operative Societies in Ireland* (Dublin: *Irish Homestead*, 1920), 2.
126 *Manchester Guardian*, 30 October 1920, 12 November 1920 and 27 May 1921.
127 Labour Party, *Report of the Labour Commission*, 1.
128 'Labour Mission's Peace Effort', *Manchester Guardian*, 3 December 1920, 10.
129 Labour Party, *Report of the Labour Commission*, 7–8. This point is also made by Francis Costello, *The Irish Revolution and its Aftermath, 1916–1923* (Dublin: Irish Academic Press, 2003), 83.
130 'Diabolical Attack Upon Co-operation', *Co-operative News*, 28 August 1920.
131 'Those Creameries', *Co-operative News*, 27 November 1920, 9.
132 James Daly, Rathmore, to R.A. Anderson, 12 May 1921, NAI 1088/798/3.
133 N.W. O'Brien, Report of Visit to Rathmore, 1 June 1921, NAI 1088/798/3.
134 Thomas de Lacy to James Fant, 2 July 1921 and 5 July 1921, NAI 1088/798/3.
135 Bureau of Military History, Thomas McEllistrim Witness Statement, 0882.
136 Bureau of Military History, Bessie Cahill Witness Statement, 1143.
137 Labour Party [Great Britain], *Report of the Labour Commission to Ireland* (London: Caledonian Press, 1921), 44–45.
138 Labour Party, *Report of the Labour Commission*, 51.
139 R.A. Anderson to Fant, 1 July 1921, NAI 1088/70/1.
140 John Byrne's Affidavit, 9 April 1921, NAI 1088/70/1.
141 'Ireland's Economic Decay', *Manchester Guardian*, 8 February 1921, 6.
142 John O'Connell, Tralee to Manager, Ardfert Co-operative Society, Ardfert, 19 April 1922, KLHA, O'Connell Papers.
143 'Creameries Closed by Military as a Punishment to Farmers', *Manchester Guardian*, 27 May 1921, 7.
144 T. O'Donovan, Abbeydorney, to Irish Co-operative Agency Society, Limerick, 24 March 1921, NAI 1088/2/4.
145 T. O'Donovan to R.A. Anderson, 15 June 1921, NAI 1088/2/4.
146 Nicholas O'Brien to R.A. Anderson, 22 June 1921, NAI 1088/2/4.
147 Nicholas O'Brien to R.A. Anderson, 22 June 1921 [handwritten addition by James Fant, 30 June 1921], NAI 1088/2/4.

148 Alvin Jackson, *Ireland, 1798–1998: Politics and War* (Oxford: Blackwell Publishers Ltd., 1999), 257; Lee, *Ireland, 1912–1985*, 47. For an account of the Anglo-Irish Treaty negotiations, see The Earl of Longford, Frank Pakenham, *Peace by Ordeal: An Account, From First-Hand Sources, of the Negotiation and Signature of the Anglo-Irish Treaty 1921* (London: Jonathan Cape, 1935).

149 John Jones, Ballymacelligott, to R.A. Anderson, Dublin, 3 July 1921, NAI 1088/70/1.

150 James G. Douglas, *Memoirs of Senator James G. Douglas: Concerned Citizen*, ed. by J. Anthony Gaughan (Dublin: University College Dublin Press, 1998), 138–140.

151 'American Relief for Irish Distress', *Manchester Guardian*, 11 February 1921, 9.

152 'Rebuilding Destroyed Irish Industries', *Manchester Guardian*, 13 May 1921, 9.

153 Bolger, *The Irish Co-operative Movement*, 212.

154 R.A. Anderson to James Fant, 1 July 1921, NAI 1088/70/1.

155 Thomas de Lacy to C.C. Riddall, 19 July 1921, NAI 1088/798/3.

156 James Fant's Report, 2 August 1921, NAI 1088/798/3.

157 N.W. O'Brien's Report, 18 October 1921, NAI 1088/798/3.

158 N.W. O'Brien's Report, 28 October 1921, NAI 1088/798/3.

159 Secretary of Dairy Disposal Company to Secretary of the IAOS, 9 March 1936, NAI 1088/798/7.

160 IAOS, *Annual Report, 1921*, 5.

161 IAOS, *Annual Report, 1921*, 5.

6

A co-operative commonwealth in the Free State?

On 7 January 1922 Dáil Eireann narrowly accepted the Anglo-Irish Treaty that led to the establishment of the Irish Free State.[1] During the contentious and bitter debates held in Dublin, former friends and allies disagreed over whether to accept or reject the Treaty. The co-operative movement's leaders emphatically supported those who urged its acceptance, which indicated a desire to secure a close accommodation with the incoming government. Æ urged the Irish people to support the Treaty or risk plunging Ireland back into 'scenes of bloodshed far beyond anything known for centuries'. He argued that acceptance of the controversial Treaty would bring Ireland closer to that 'solemn moment when full responsibility for our own civilisation and social order will be flung upon the shoulders of the Irish people'.[2] The new state, in turn, would have to recognise the co-operative movement's important efforts to bring the idea of the Irish nation into a practical reality. Looking forward Æ asserted that:

> The principles [the IAOS] has advocated have overflowed from the agricultural sphere into the national being ... we think the farmers who have enriched the movement by their varied application of the co-operative principle have reason to be proud of its effect on the thought of their country.[3]

That March, Horace Plunkett delivered a speech directed towards the incoming administration as much as the movement. He highlighted that as Irish people embarked upon the hard work of state building the IAOS already performed an 'immense amount of essential public work which no Government could undertake, but without which ... no Government could economically and efficiently develop agriculture'. Plunkett seized the opportunity to repeat his old mantra that any incoming Irish government needed to adopt the principle of 'better farming, better business, better living'.[4] The IAOS looked to position co-operative societies at the centre of any plans for national development.

This chapter examines how co-operative expertise shaped an Irish plan for agricultural improvement and rural development. Little recognition of the influence that Irish co-operation held over an emergent independent political culture exists. Basil Chubb's influential work on Irish government identified 'the British influence

[as] the most important in determining the pattern of much of Irish political thought and practice' and classified Irish agriculture as 'wholly geared to British needs'.[5] Garret Fitzgerald, Irish Taoiseach in the 1980s, articulated a similar view when he described the effect of British policy upon Irish development throughout the nineteenth and twentieth centuries as 'a form of exploitation of the Irish small farm structure … an exploitation which had been carried forward into the first half of the post-independence period'. Not until Ireland became an enthusiastic supporter of the European Community in the 1970s did this dependency start to recede.[6] The impact of nationalism, Catholicism and anti-intellectualism also counted as defining characteristics of government in Ireland.[7] However, co-operative ideas, developed through systematic economic experimentation aligned to a network of societies, also defined Irish social and political life.

Co-operation shaped nationalist thinking as it provided an economic framework to imagine what an independent Irish state might achieve. The attainment of independence within the harsh political and economic realities of the 1920s saw the emergence of a style of pragmatic governance at odds with some of the utopian thinking that characterised nationalism.[8] As argued elsewhere, from 1922 the Irish people 'became victims of their own aspirations' as post-independence governments failed to build the 'Gaelic Jerusalem'.[9] This long anticlimactic epilogue to the independence struggle accords with Clifford Geertz's view that the aftermath of independence is often a deflating experience.[10] Despite inauspicious beginnings, serious efforts to construct the Irish state did take place. This chapter begins with an outline of the postcolonial moment in Ireland in order to locate the co-operative movement against a backdrop of political, economic and military uncertainties that shaped public policy. Attention turns to examine how the movement played a central role in the creation and implementation of economic policy in the Free State. The chapter focuses on how the co-operative movement asserted itself in the southern jurisdiction. Partition of Ireland also saw a partition of the movement and the Ulster Agricultural Organisation Society (UAOS) represented the northern societies after 1922. However, the UAOS proved to be a less influential organisation in governmental terms, partly owing to the presence of a strong urban, industrial sector in Northern Ireland. Agriculture remained the main engine of economic development in the Free State, which provided greater scope for the IAOS to exert influence. The deliberations of the Commission on Agriculture are analysed to highlight how agricultural priorities for the new government emerged out of a two-year consultation between policymakers, economists and agricultural experts. The Commission's report, published in 1924, set out a governmental template with important implications for socio-economic development. The governmental strategies that arose from the final report show how co-operative ideas formed a key thread in the formulation of Irish rule as the movement once again acted as an instrument of the state in a way reminiscent of Plunkett's attempt to co-ordinate the IAOS and DATI.

An examination of the work undertaken by co-operators at a national and local level helps to redefine a historical understanding of the state in Ireland. The historical anthropologist, Akhil Gupta, in his work on states and development, focuses upon how:

> large-scale structures, epochal events, major policies, and 'important' people … failed to illuminate the quotidian practices of bureaucrats that tell us about the effects of the state upon the everyday lives of rural people.[11]

Applying this insight to Ireland reveals how a popular understanding of the state formed at the point of the local co-operative society for rural inhabitants. Dairy farmers attended their creameries on a daily basis to supply milk and relied upon it as a source of income. The government created the Dairy Disposal Company (DDC) in 1927 as a means through which a congested creamery sector might be rationalised and reorganised. The establishment of this semi-state body helped to ensure the existence of the co-operative movement and establish it as the primary actor in the dairying industry. The decision to create the DDC also showed how the co-operative society formed the primary institution through which the future of agricultural policymaking was imagined in the early decades of independence.[12] Another occurrence in the 1920s was a revitalisation of co-operative credit societies which insulated farmers against the most destructive effects of economic depression. In the south-western dairying heartland credit societies helped farmers mitigate the worst effects of an epidemic outbreak that depleted cattle stocks. Many of the reforms that emanated from the Commission on Agriculture's Report provide evidence of a renegotiation of the relationship between the state and the IAOS. Applying Gupta's insight to post-independence rural Ireland shows that the state was constructed, and simultaneously revealed itself, at the site of the co-operative society. The frequent and mundane interactions that occurred at creameries and credit societies proved as relevant to the lives of many people as the debates about the controversial decision to adopt the Treaty.

The main analysis of the co-operative movement's part in the state-building process ends in 1932 with the electoral defeat of the first Cumann na nGaedheal government and an end to the Irish Free State's first decade of independence. The co-operative movement became an integral part of Irish political culture and an effective part of the state infrastructure throughout the first half of the twentieth century. More importantly the IAOS's modernisation project pursued since the late nineteenth century remained relevant in a context after independence. Co-operative organisations formed an important institution within the new state.

The challenge of independence

The IAOS approached the new phase in Irish political upheaval with prag-matism and abandoned any utopian pretensions as it stated, 'the co-operative will remain a hope of the future rather than a gradually realised economic device or an immediately practicable ideal'.[13] This sentiment summarised the movement's position after the War of Independence, but also reflected a general political moment in which the Irish Free State faced an array of challenges. Sinn Féin split into pro-Treaty and anti-Treaty factions, with the former rebranded as Cumann na nGaedheal in 1923 and which formed the first government of the Free State.[14] A huge amount of activity characterised this government's decade in power as it sought to establish the parameters of sovereignty.[15] Foreign policy emerged as an immediate priority as the Irish Government worked to renegotiate its relations with Britain and the Commonwealth in order to extend its autonomy, work alongside other states and partake in the new forum for international relations, the League of Nations.[16]

The question of partition also preoccupied the Irish Government. At the end of 1920 the Government of Ireland Act established a six-county Northern Ireland. The establishment of a Boundary Commission as a concession offered to nationalists in the Anglo-Irish Treaty provided a possibility to renegotiate the border between Northern Ireland and the Irish Free State. A leak in the press about the Commission's work caused a public controversy and the Northern and Southern legislatures ratified the provisional border in 1925.[17] On the home front, the government's objectives centred upon defence of the state from internal dissent, establishing a rule of law, trade policy, reducing national expenditure and developing agriculture.[18] Despite a pessimistic economic and political context, the Irish Government benefited to a certain extent from one long-standing feature of Irish life – the resumption of systemic emigration after 1922 which decreased pressure upon resources.[19]

The IAOS looked to exert its influence over the area of agricultural development. In 1923, the organisation stated that Irish agriculture remained

> one of the few stable elements in the changing world through which we have recently passed, and though its position to-day is crucial, no ultimate fears of its recovery can be entertained ... Co-operative principles and practice in relation to that industry are sound.[20]

The Irish Free State was an agricultural nation – a fact emphasised after partition with the retention of urban industries in Northern Ireland. Patrick Hogan, Minister for Agriculture, accentuated this point when he noted: 'national development in Ireland ... is synonymous with agricultural development'.[21] The 1926 Census provided statistical support for such attitudes, showing that 53 per cent of the population engaged in agricultural occupations. By realising agriculture's untapped potential, no reason existed, 'why this country cannot in time have a largely increased population with an improved standard of living'.[22] In 1924, agriculture, food and drink accounted for 98 per cent of national exports with 86 per cent of this output bound for the United Kingdom.[23] The Free State remained integrated within the British economy where most of its agricultural exports ended up. By its long-term efforts to organise agriculture in Ireland the IAOS made a strong case for its relevance to Cumann na nGaedheal's plans. However, the utilisation of the co-operative movement might serve another government purpose. If the government used the IAOS to deliver rural policy, then the co-operative movement might achieve the dual objective of prioritising agriculture while limiting public expenditure.

The Irish Free State emerged onto the world stage in the middle of an agrarian depression. The Secretary of the Department of Agriculture and Technical Instruction (DATI) until 1921, T.P. Gill, summarised the fragility of Irish agriculture within the international trade structures after the First World War: '[t]he universal war has shaken and broken the economic fabric of the world, and, this being an era of interdependence, Irish agriculture is closely affected.'[24] The slump in prices that occurred in 1920–21 affected agriculture and left farmers exposed in a rural economy where sources of agricultural credit remained limited. Farmers found the 1920s a tough economic climate as the agricultural price index declined between 1920 and 1931.[25] Throughout the 1920s falling prices, depleted soil productivity caused by tillage without sufficient fertilisers during the war, crop and animal diseases, and poor harvests meant farmers faced economic hardship.[26]

As Minister of Agriculture, one of Patrick Hogan's priorities centred on the improvement of Ireland's export capabilities. Britain remained the primary buyer of agricultural goods and therefore Hogan wanted to ensure Ireland remained competitive in an overcrowded marketplace.[27] According to the economist George O'Brien, a one-time employee of Horace Plunkett, Hogan's policy 'did not involve any breach of continuity in the tradition of Irish farming'.[28] Hogan reinforced established patterns as he aimed to improve the quality of inputs (bulls, milk, etc.) and outputs (butter, eggs, bacon).[29] Cormac Ó Gráda argues that from the 1920s 'the increasing role of governmental and government-supported agencies was probably a benign influence'. The Department of Agriculture (as the DATI was renamed in 1922) and IAOS produced statistical data that detailed economic activity throughout Ireland. These agencies encouraged an improvement in the quality of outputs and alerted farmers to new techniques. In short, investment made to these bodies 'was not money wasted in the pre-1925 period'.[30]

Any debate about whether Irish national development pursued an agricultural or industrial policy immediately resolved in favour of the former.[31] The next significant move made by the government was to decide upon a free trade policy as opposed to protectionism. Joseph Johnston, an agricultural economist involved with the co-operative movement at various stages of his career, wrote in favour of the pursuit of a free trade policy in January 1923 after an assessment of Ireland's economic capacity. The lack of viable industry meant Johnston believed that 'agriculture will remain our staple industry. It will remain the broad foundation on which all other industrial developments will be solidly and securely built.' For Johnston, the proper economic function of government lay in the creation of an improved transport infrastructure to help manage distribution costs, and interventions to raise the standard of education. He further argued that any proposed improvement relied upon the efforts of farmers themselves, both as individuals and through co-operation.[32] The death of Arthur Griffith in August 1922 deprived the new administration of its first leader, but also the main champion of economic protectionism. The government's Fiscal Inquiry Committee recommended the continuation of a free trade policy and the Department of Finance supported these findings.[33] Throughout the 1920s, the Irish economy remained 'an open one' attached to a free trade orthodoxy, which served the interests of agriculture.[34]

The partition of Ireland also affected the question of economic development and the co-operative movement's role in it. Northern Ireland contained the most industrialised section of the island, which allowed the Free State's policymakers to make the case for agricultural development as a natural way to maximise their national comparative advantage. After 1922, the Free State Government demanded that the IAOS divide itself into two separate organisations to reflect the new geo-political reality. Patrick Hogan advocated this change to prevent 'the effect of releasing, for expenditure in the Northern Area, money subscribed in the Southern Area'.[35] In Northern Ireland, James Gordon wrote to Captain Petherick at the Ministry of Finance to explain 'there is no doubt that co-operation is essential to combinations of farmers', but if the Northern Irish Government provided a direct grant to the IAOS that would raise 'a very serious question – one which raises to mind a very serious political problem'.[36] The two centres of co-operative activity belonged to the south-western and north-eastern regions where dairying formed a popular mode of farming and a frequent leakage of funding for co-operatives between the two jurisdictions appeared to be a likely occurrence.

On 31 August 1922, the IAOS formally divided into two organisations. The body responsible for co-operative development in Northern Ireland was recon-stituted as the UAOS.[37] With the loss of the north-eastern centre, the IAOS's numerical strength decreased. In 1922, the IAOS possessed 1,102 co-operative societies, but the loss of its north-eastern societies saw this figure drop to 608.[38] The IAOS accepted this economic rationalisation and the partition of the movement passed with little fanfare. The south-west emerged as a crucial region in plans for economic improvement as the engine of the Free State's butter production. Four-fifths of the total employment in dairying and bacon curing was concentrated in the south-western province of Munster.[39]

The co-operative movement and civil war

Military conflict provided a stern challenge for the Irish Free State Government in 1922. The capture of Dublin's Four Courts by Republican forces opposed to the Treaty in April 1922 challenged the legitimacy of the new state. The government responded in June by using the newly established National Army to crush the occupation.[40] As a result, the Irish Civil War broke out in June and lasted until a ceasefire in May 1923. The Anglo-Irish Treaty was the nominal issue at stake, but Pro-Treatyites believed that irredentist republicans went further and called 'into question the proper basis of the social and political order in Irish society'.[41] A vicious guerrilla warfare campaign took place between former comrades in the IRA and the most intense fighting occurred in counties Kerry, Cork and Limerick.[42] The Civil War lasted for around a year but the legacy and memory of the war affected the political culture for decades.[43] Conservative estimates on the loss of life place it at 800 National Army deaths, with almost certainly a higher figure for Republicans. No records exist for the numbers of civilian dead.[44] The financial cost of civil war offered a major concern for a new administration intent on deficit reduction. Damage to infrastructure cost over £30 million with compensation and defence remaining high recipients of government expenditure.[45]

The Irish Civil War affected the co-operative movement on a national and local level. The most prominent individual affected was Horace Plunkett who was appointed to the Senate (the upper chamber of the new Irish parliament) by the President of the Executive and leader of the government, William Cosgrave. The honour recognised Plunkett's efforts in furthering the interests of Ireland throughout his career. Irish Republicans targeted the homes of these senators and in January 1923, Plunkett's home in Dublin was destroyed in an arson attack. Heartbroken, Plunkett departed for England that year and his influence in Irish affairs waned. Although he remained IAOS President until his death in 1932, his direct involvement in Irish co-operation ended.[46]

The Civil War also reduced Æ's interest in co-operative matters. Æ appealed to *Irish Homestead* readers to support the government in 'the conflict between Builders and Destroyers'.[47] In September 1923, the *Irish Homestead* became incorporated into the *Irish Statesman*, a journal intended to mark the intellectual foundation to the Free State. Æ continued as editor of the *Statesman*. Reportage on co-operation remained a feature, but the remit of the journal concentrated more upon political issues and became a rallying point for those who championed liberal causes such as opposition to censorship.[48] Fr Finlay continued to serve on the IAOS executive and replaced Plunkett as the president. Robert Anderson provided continuity with the past and a source of leadership throughout this tumultuous period.[49] However, the foundation of the new state coincided with a new generation of leaders that began to populate the co-operative leadership. When Anderson moved to lead the Irish Agricultural Wholesale Society in 1926,

Dr Henry Kennedy replaced him as the IAOS Secretary and played a crucial role in the design of the DDC as a body to assist co-operative creameries.[50]

On a local level the Civil War disrupted business. Co-operative societies strived for normality after recent attacks by Crown forces, but recovery was frustrated by the resumption of violence in 1922.[51] Republicans destroyed trains and railway stations in an attempt to render government impossible.[52] In Kerry, the Civil War took on a particularly brutal hue and events in the final months of the conflict created a resentment that survived long after the end of the conflict.[53] Nicholas O'Brien's reports for the IAOS noted the negative effects of the Civil War as the region's societies struggled to ship butter from Tralee, owing to the closure of the town's ferry service. Rattoo Co-operative Society shipped via a smaller harbour in Fenit instead, where 'it is very difficult and costly to get the butter on board and it is only through very hard work that it can be done owing to broken roads etc.'.[54] Abbeydorney Co-operative Society also struggled to get butter to Fenit harbour due to broken roads.[55] Societies also experienced an alarming drop in milk supply. At Newtownsandes Co-operative Society, the daily milk volume fell by 300 gallons, a fifth of the normal supply, 'owing to the cutting of the roads locally'.[56] Nevertheless, the infrastructure created by the co-operative movement remained largely intact and offered the Irish Government a means to attend to the needs of farmers.

The movement of the National Army through Kerry in late 1922 and 1923 disrupted business. On 26 November 1922, National Army troops occupied the creamery at Rathmore and erected a machine gun there. In December no members attended the society's Annual General Meeting 'owing to military operations in the district that day'. Organiser Nicholas O'Brien wrote to Anderson that the 'Committee have done everything to oblige the troops since their advent to Rathmore'.[57] An attempt to hold the meeting on 19 December saw only seven out of 300 members attend. O'Brien concluded: 'it is quite possible that the poor attendance was due to a certain extent to the fact that sniping is an almost everyday occurrence in the village'.[58]

Personal antagonisms played out around co-operative societies as the Civil War continued. In January, the National Army held the manager of Rathmore Co-operative Society, Thomas de Lacy, prisoner on account of his son 'who is beyond my control being with the Irregulars'.[59] De Lacy confided to Anderson that he and his family were under 'grave suspicion of helping the irregulars due to stories on the part of the people I am most anxious to clear out of Rathmore family + all'.[60] Anderson responded without sympathy.

> I am very much afraid that the fact that your son appears to be actively engaged with the Irregulars practically deprives us in the IAOS of doing what we would very much like to do for you. I think if your son take it upon himself to adopt such a course as he appears to have adopted, you are no longer morally or in any other way, bound to shield him.[61]

Such a sentiment reflected the temper of the times when a father might be asked to abdicate responsibility over the actions and politics of his son. Anderson supported the new government enthusiastically and wanted no impression that linked the movement to subversive activities to circulate. While Civil War politics destabilised social relations in rural communities for years afterwards, the leadership of the IAOS remained resolute in its support for the new state.

Co-operativising the state: The Agricultural Commission and rural reform

In his assessment of the first five years of independence Denis Gwynn argued that to 'anyone who has visualised the organisation, whether economic or social, of the Free State, it must be apparent that no Ministry in the Government of the country is of equal importance, in the ordinary life of the people, with the Ministry of Agriculture'.[62] During its first two years the Irish Government appointed a plethora of commissions to investigate a variety of issues that encompassed tax, financial policy, policing, communications and agriculture.[63] The Agricultural Commission held the most significance for national development. The subsequent report was a sequel to a Commission of Inquiry into the dairy industry instigated by the revolutionary Dáil in 1920. That report, published in March 1922, established the 'cardinal principle that the first care of national production should be to supply and satisfy the Irish people at a remunerative price'. This belief proved to be 'especially true in regard to the production, or its manufacture into one or other of [the dairy industry's] various products'.[64]

The Agricultural Commission included politicians from the Cumann na nGaedheal, Labour and Farmers' Parties, Department of Agriculture officials, and economists such as George O'Brien and Joseph Johnston.[65] What remained of Sinn Féin still opposed the Treaty and therefore the party did not engage with the proceedings. The eventual report helped to establish the features of a new economic orthodoxy in Ireland. For George O'Brien, a professor of economics at University College Dublin, the Commission's proceedings revealed 'the general principles of agricultural policy in which I have continued to believe'.[66] The Agricultural Commission met for the first time in November 1922 to investigate agricultural conditions and provide 'an assured basis for future expansion and prosperity'. It sat fifty-six times in public and thirty-eight times in private over the next eighteen months, and cross-examined 121 expert witnesses that included Robert Anderson and Father Finlay along with other representatives from the IAOS.[67] Patrick Hogan received the Commission's Report in April 1924. The report provided the foundational text for agricultural policy going forwards and formed the basis for governmental thinking on rural matters for decades.

The Agricultural Commission and the policies it inspired show how a symbiotic relationship evolved between the co-operative movement and state throughout the 1920s. The *Irish Homestead* welcomed the decision to establish the Agricultural Commission, which Æ hoped would range further in its deliberations than mere reconstruction and consider the grandiose task of 'building up a rural civilisation'. Æ argued that the Commission should stimulate a conversation about what constituted the Irish mentality, which it described as 'virgin soil. Yet … like all virgin soil, once it was cultivated it would be immensely productive.' Through this process of 'cultivation' Æ believed the Agricultural Commission might provide a means by which 'we can begin to build up national life, trying to remedy defects and to burnish up our national virtues'.[68]

Co-operators embraced the opportunity to deliver evidence to the Commission and sometimes the process revealed the political partisanship that coloured the thinking of activists. Such slips revealed aspects of an Irish mentality, but not as Æ envisaged. For example, the IAOS organiser, W.P. Clifford, argued that the co-operative movement looked 'to assert itself' in the new nation-state. Questioned by George O'Brien, Clifford exhibited the strident belief that political independence provided the necessary conditions for the promotion of organised co-operation within governmental structures:

> O'Brien: What reason have you for assuming that the State will be favourable to the co-operative movement? … It seems to me that you are delivering yourself into the hands of a powerful agency?
> Clifford: The co-operative movement will be a popular agency. I am sure it will be able to assert itself.
> O'B: Do you think that the co-operative movement in Ireland would have received better facilities for the last twenty years if the whole question of financing had been in the hands of the Department of Agriculture?
> C: No, it was believed to be a Branch of the English Government in Ireland.
> O'B: You think the millennium has come, and that the future Irish Government will do everything right?
> C: I believe it is fair to infer that they will do a lot better than the British in the past. At least our experience so far has gone to prove that, disturbed as the state of the country has been.

Clifford expected political independence to instigate a change in the Department of Agriculture's attitude towards the IAOS. He equated the DATI with a 'Branch of English Government in Ireland', which reflected the attitude that developed towards that institution during the Great War. Clifford also betrayed a deep distrust of the civil service. When asked by O'Brien if he believed 'that the spots in the leopards in Merrion Street [where government buildings and civil service were based] will change?' Clifford responded, 'No, you will have to boil some of them.'[69] Clifford hoped political independence represented a millenarian moment whereby the sources of power in Ireland would be purged of British influence and lead to an attendant improvement to the co-operative movement's fortunes.

The Agricultural Commission's Report established a blueprint for Ireland's long-term economic direction that incorporated the influence of a co-operative political economy. The report's introduction stated that:

> Agriculture is the foundation on which the commercial and business life of the country is based, and the circumstances that affect agriculture react sensibly through the entire economic life of the nation.[70]

An agricultural depression combined with historical precedents to encourage a certain hard-headed approach to agricultural reform. 'Under such conditions,' the report continued, 'a bad season may precipitate a famine. Ireland has had a bitter experience of this. Any closer [land] settlement policy must, therefore, be handled with great care, or it may produce calamitous results.' This signalled the emergence of a pragmatic attitude in which the smallholder no longer held a privileged position within governmental discourse. Instead the report iterated that 'large holdings … afford a better standard of living to a smaller population'.[71]

Dissent from these conclusions was expressed. Thomas Johnson and Michael Duffy of the Labour Party submitted a Minority Report that differed from the central findings in important ways. Johnson and Duffy highlighted that population decline remained a problem and pointed out that Denmark and Holland, two countries with large agricultural sectors, did not experience similar demographic trends. While the Majority Report argued in favour of the need to deflate agricultural wages as a way to reduce farmers' costs, Johnson and Duffy condemned 'the error of treating every holder of agricultural land as an agriculturalist and the farming community as homogenous'. The main report overlooked small farmers and labourers in favour of 'the large farmer who depends wholly on wage labour and sells his produce for export'. The Minority Report recommended that the government should impose a limit to the maximum size of holding any farmer could own to increase the number of people who worked on the land.[72] The government ignored this advice.

Agricultural production and marketing deserved the main share of allocated funding, while improvement relied upon 'a better understanding both of the theory and practice of farming'. The Commission concluded that:

> *We firmly believe in the co-operative system*, as calculated to promote better business methods, and, we consider that the state may, with advantage spend substantial sums in the teaching of practical co-operation.[73] (Emphasis added)

The utilisation of co-operative principles to overcome economic challenges in agriculture established continuity with the Dáil's utilisation of co-operative principles to experiment with areas such as banking and land purchase during 1919–21. The report promised to synchronise the relationship between the government and co-operative movement. The Commission outlined a limited role for the state with co-operative societies envisaged as the agents through which the practical work of agricultural development would be carried out. While the government might achieve a certain amount through funding and provision of education, 'agricultural recuperation must rest with the individual farmer, whether working singly or organized in co-operation with his fellows'.[74]

The Agricultural Commission aimed to create an Ireland imbued with the principle of 'self-help through mutual help' and stressed the importance upon 'the immense advantages of unrestrained [v]oluntary effort'.[75] The state's role was to provide a context that allowed co-operation to flourish and enabled the population to instigate their own improvements to their industry. This held the benefit of economy in a time of austere financial planning as the government utilised a network of expertise already in operation. The Commission highlighted key areas for rural reform that occupied experts throughout the 1920s and the level of success achieved in each area carried long-term implications for economic development. The Agricultural Commission identified co-operation as the most effective tool to improve farmers, but believed that 'co-operation is imperfectly understood and practised in the country'.[76] The main proposals included the reorganisation of the co-operative movement, the standardisation of co-operative marketing and an attempt to re-stimulate co-operative credit provision.

Reorganisation of the co-operative movement

As the Agricultural Commission identified dairying as 'the foundation on which the whole structure of our agricultural economy depends',[77] an invigorated agricultural sector required a good working relationship between the government and IAOS. The failure to turn the general purpose societies into the flagship business of the movement meant that the IAOS concentrated once again on creameries. In evidence given to the Agricultural Commission in 1923, Robert Anderson highlighted that any gains in the distribution side of co-operation 'are always in connection with some other activity either a Creamery or a poultry co-operative effort. The co-operative stores [are] ... not a conspicuous success anywhere.'[78] Whatever progress co-operation made in new directions in previous years, by the 1920s any expansion of the movement remained associated with the creamery business. This suited the government's aims as dairying could play an important role in strengthening Irish agricultural productivity and directly contributed to Ireland's export trade in livestock.[79] Dairying encouraged a mixed-farm economy and led to greater diversity of agricultural outputs.[80] Dairy farmers used land more intensively than graziers who farmed to fatten cattle for sale as beef exports. Dairying incentivised a higher density of cattle per acre and these farmers tended to own pigs, calves and poultry.[81]

Working through the IAOS proved to be an attractive course of action for the Department of Agriculture. In 1922, the government approved a state grant for the IAOS to replace the Development Commissioner's funding which 'contributed in no small degree to the success of the co-operative movement in

Ireland'.[82] From the point of view of co-operators this decision vindicated the independence process and their support for the new administration. The funds guaranteed the long-term future of the IAOS and served as an endorsement of the movement by the Irish Government. However, the grant came with new conditions that paved way for greater government interference.

> The right co-operative spirit implies a new outlook in both business and social life and this change of mind can only be reached through slow and patient steps … It has not been our duty to inquire into the domestic arrangements and inner working of this society [IAOS], but we recommend the government to make such enquiry before it finally decides on the amount and conditions of any state grant.[83]

An annual renewal of the subsidy provided the government with an opportunity to re-make the IAOS and integrate it within the workings of the state. The reduction of the national debt remained the guiding financial principle of the 1920s. However, the Minister of Finance, Ernest Blythe, proved willing to deviate from this position to protect vital sections of the Irish economy. Blythe's budget statements earmarked special sums of capital for the co-operative movement under the categorisation of 'abnormal expenditure'. In 1927, Blythe spent £85,000 in special loans for co-operative creameries, which accounted for more than half of the abnormal expenditure granted to the Department of Agriculture.[84]

The IAOS worked to overhaul its creamery network and an expanding workload throughout the 1920s placed pressure upon its 'administrative, organising and inspectorial work'. This led to a temporary abandonment of publishing annual reports between 1924 and 1930.[85] During these years the government and IAOS collaborated to rationalise the creamery movement in Ireland. The Department of Agriculture surveyed the machinery of the IAOS in 1926 and proposed that:

> Meetings of the Committee of the IAOS should be attended by a representative of the Minister who will keep him informed of their proceedings and convey to them such information and advice as he may deem helpful for their guidance.[86]

The IAOS assented to these proposed changes, which included a restructured Executive Committee to incorporate six representatives of the Minister of Agriculture.[87] These representatives reported to Hogan on the subject matter discussed at IAOS meetings and provided detailed feedback on annual expenditure and the decisions taken by the Committee.[88] This provided the Department with significant influence over the IAOS and ensured the co-operative movement remained transparent for governmental purposes.

Government oversight of the co-operative movement went beyond IAOS reorganisation. In 1924 the Dairy Produce Act brought creameries under tighter regulation that policed hygiene, cleanliness, and inspected the quality of all butter produced. The legislation required all creameries and dairy produce exporters to register with the Department of Agriculture. The Act empowered inspectors to 'enter any premises upon which dairy produce is manufactured ... [to] inspect all plant, machinery, appliances, and utensils used in such manufacture'. While creamery inspections had previously occurred under the DATI, the Dairy Produce Act granted the state greater powers of intervention and laid greater responsibility with the individual society. Registered premises remained open to inspection with all produce subject to surprise tests and failure to comply led to prosecution and a revocation of their licence. The legislation also demanded that all premises maintained a high standard of cleanliness and hygiene, and policed the outward presentation of creamery employees. Meanwhile, creamery inspectors regulated butter quality and capped the acceptable level of moisture at 16 per cent.[89]

This new inspectorate performed similar functions to those carried out by IAOS organisers in previous years. Departmental inspectors visited certain premises more than once a month. These inspections focused upon issues such as ventilation, lighting of premises, cleanliness of staff and quality of butter.[90] The Department of Agriculture looked to standardise all creamery premises, which required the extensive reconstruction of some societies. However, the new inspectors created new workloads for IAOS around the maintenance and hygiene of their creameries. For example, following an inspection of the creamery at Rathmore, the Department ordered management to install modern machinery, which included vats for milk storage, refrigeration technology, hot water tanks, and arrange the erection of cold storage rooms. Creamery managers then passed these orders on to IAOS engineers whose expertise they remained reliant upon.[91] The manager of Rathmore Co-operative Society wrote to James Fant a month after the Department ordered the creamery to improve:

> the Dept are urging pretty hard the carrying out of their recommendations + I hope you will not take me as pressing unduly on you to kindly have specifications sent out at earliest convenient date.[92]

The Department of Agriculture placed pressure on co-operative societies to meet expected high standards through follow-up visits. The effect of these inspections raised the standard of milk supplied by farmers because the departmental inspector relieved 'the manager of the unpleasant duty of rejecting milk which is impure or stale'.[93] The Department of Agriculture built up a detailed understanding of dairying in this way.

In 1925, the new dairy inspectors gathered to discuss the application of the Dairy Produce Act. Assembled delegates debated where improvements on the Act should be targeted, but argued that any reform required the support of the IAOS to effect a serious change in this direction. Topics ranged from how to deal with suppliers of unhygienic milk to the possibility that dairy inspectors might co-opt the police force to monitor creameries. However, the most urgent topic that received their consideration related to the diffusion of creameries. Within a year, dairy inspectors concluded that 'in some districts there were far too many small creameries, several of which were running at a loss'. The inspectors proposed an amalgamation of many of these societies, but felt the Department of Agriculture 'could not usefully intervene'. Instead, they asserted that 'the Irish Agricultural Organisation Society would perhaps be in a better position to deal with matters of this kind'.[94]

The government instigated two important reforms to this end. These were the creation of the government-backed DDC in 1927, followed by the 1928 Creamery Act. Taken together these actions effectively granted the co-operative movement a state-sponsored monopoly over dairying, creating a policy intervention designed to deal with the problem of over-concentration of creameries in certain parts of the country. The IAOS and the Department of Agriculture agreed that more creameries were operating in the dairy heartlands than the available milk supply justified. A concentration of co-operative and private creameries in Ireland's south-western dairying districts created an inefficient system, with two types of firm competing for the same supplies. Furthermore, fierce competition to win the dairy pastures of the south-west provided no incentive to stimulate dairy farming in other regions.[95] In 1907, Father Finlay conceded that in the movement's formative years the number of creameries grew too rapidly. Finlay advocated a smaller number of creameries, rather than the large amount 'in whose members the spirit of co-operation was defective'.[96] However, overwhelming desire to oust private competitors meant the IAOS acquiesced in the unchecked growth and Finlay's advice on this issue remained unheeded.

The debate about a more streamlined co-operative movement emerged again during the Agricultural Commission. Denis Hegarty, secretary of the Irish Creamery Manager's Association (ICMA), argued that the quality of Irish butter had declined during the First World War – something he had witnessed as a wartime member of the Butter Export Committee. The resurgence of international competition after the war concerned Hegarty and he identified the major weakness of Irish dairying in the fact that 'the creameries in the best districts in Ireland are in very many cases too numerous, which means severe competition for milk, leading to many abuses'. Co-operative creamery managers accepted milk of dubious quality to secure the custom of suppliers away from local competitors. Hegarty highlighted that Danish creameries suffered from no such impediment, which meant 'the Danish Dairy Manager is only concerned with turning out butter of the highest quality'.[97] The legal precedent established by the *McEllistrim* v *Ballymacelligott* judgment proscribed co-operatives from compelling members to supply milk to one creamery. Furthermore, lower standards in Irish butter production stemmed from the presence of 'creameries at every cross roads'.[98] Two or three creameries operated in a district where one would have sufficed and the Agricultural Commission's final report found 'that steps should be taken to wind up all such non-effective societies'.[99]

The long-standing bitter rivalry that existed between co-operative and private creameries reached a fierce pitch during this period. In 1924, 580 creameries operated in the Free State, with 180 of these classified as proprietary concerns. Although co-operative creameries outnumbered private ones, in reality many struggled to compete with 'the financial resources of proprietary vested interests'.[100] County Kerry represented one of the regions where the dairy industry operated in a somewhat dysfunctional manner. The county housed 57 creameries and constituted a hotly contested battleground for milk supplies.[101] For example, the troubled Rathmore Co-operative Society tried to compete with a local creamery operated by Lakelands Dairying Company. Rathmore's manager complained to Robert Anderson that Lakelands sold low-quality, blended butter and marketed this product as high-quality creamery produce. He advised Anderson to 'have the matter investigated as Irish Creamery Butter has been tampered with too often + too long and it is now a national + not a local question'. Anderson informed the Department of Agriculture of these practices utilised by private creameries.[102] In July 1924, James Fant warned the IAOS, 'this Society [Rathmore] will need very careful watching otherwise the local prop. Creamery will wipe it out'.[103] However, the co-operative movement possessed one distinct advantage. The private sector lacked a coherent agency akin to the IAOS as each company pursued its own interests.

In 1926, the largest creamery proprietor, the Condensed Milk Company of Ireland (CMC), hovered on the brink of collapse as a result of competition with co-operatives. The CMC owned 113 creameries and the loss of these threatened to upset dairy production.[104] In November 1926, the CMC approached Henry Kennedy with a suggestion for the IAOS to purchase their creameries. The IAOS lacked the required funds to carry out such an ambitious transaction and Kennedy passed on the offer to Patrick Hogan to consider a state purchase of the private sector. In January 1927 the government agreed to the purchase of the largest proprietary concern as an important step in the reorganisation of the creamery sector.[105] Against a backdrop of falling agricultural prices this decision set an important industrial precedent as other creamery owners filed for bankruptcy and petitioned the government to buy out their premises.

Other proprietors attempted to offload creameries at as high a price as possible to their co-operative competitors but societies proved unable to pay the requested prices. Thomas de Lacy, the manager of Rathmore Co-operative Society, expressed disgust at the prices sought by private creamery owners in County Kerry. De Lacy equated these owners with the traditional enemy of farmers: 'Most undoubtedly', he wrote to Kennedy, 'Creamery Proprietors are a worse form of Landlordism than that of the Landlords.' A meeting of co-operative societies in Kerry passed a resolution that urged the county's politicians 'of all shades of politics' to persuade farmers who supplied private creameries to direct their milk to co-operatives.

According to de Lacy, 'I see no other way to get the Creameries under the control of the farmers & I believe no matter how long the business may hang fire Compulsion will have to come.'[106]

Compulsion grew out of necessity in the end. The government recognised the collapse of private dairying as an opportunity 'to arrange for the purchase of the interests controlling a considerable number of such [surplus] creameries'.[107] The first state-sponsored agency, the DDC, was established in 1927 to carry out such work. The DDC acted as a clearing house that administered the businesses until either a local co-operative took them over or absorbed the milk suppliers. Where a creamery proved unnecessary due to congestion, the DDC closed it down. Most of the creameries purchased by the DDC were located in Cork and Kerry, which led to the near extinction of the private creamery sector in those counties.[108] The government's actions consolidated the position of the IAOS and allowed their creameries to concentrate upon matters related to quality improvement and policing suppliers.

The government built upon the DDC's establishment with the introduction of the Creamery Act in 1928. This legislation tightened regulations around creamery operations and pursued reorganisation through restrictive regulations around the establishment of new creameries. The establishment of any new creamery required the permission of the Minister of Agriculture from this point onward.[109] The Act also locked in suppliers to their local co-operative creamery, and stated that if a society issued shares to a milk supplier 'it shall not be lawful without the consent of the Department signified in writing for any other society to take any supply of milk from such person'.[110] This tied Irish milk suppliers to a co-operative creamery in a similar fashion to the Danish model and effectively overturned the House of Lords' verdict on *McEllistrim* v *Ballymacelligott* to proscribe the locked-in relationship. The Act also prevented the establishment of co-operative societies in districts with little milk supply. The Creamery Act showed the willingness of the Irish Government to intervene in agricultural matters and shored up the position of the co-operative movement within the dairy industry.

Reorganisation expanded the frontiers for co-operative dairying as the process encouraged the spread of creameries into new regions. Creameries were introduced into the great midlands plain – a region long associated with grazier farming rather than dairying.[111] New creameries, such as Donaghmore Co-operative Society in County Laois, grew into long-standing fixtures of the local economy.[112] By 1929, forty-six new creameries had been established which included some 'built in districts where creameries did not exist before'. Experienced co-operators sometimes migrated to these areas and brought with them the expertise acquired over years. The *Irish Times* reported how some of these creameries were started by 'a colony of progressive emigrants' from County Kerry. 'These people brought with them the dairy farming tradition' and cattle which 'were already known as good milkers'. This diffusion of the creamery system into new territory represented 'the efforts of the Department of Agriculture and the Irish Agricultural Organisation Society in regard to the development of the Irish butter industry on a sound basis, so as to enable it to hold a foremost position on the markets of the world'.[113]

By 1931, the DDC had purchased 170 private creameries. This effectively ended private-sector involvement in Irish butter production. Of these, 44 creameries converted into co-operatives, 79 closed down permanently and 47 remained under the direct control of the DDC. The DDC absorbed 17 co-operative creameries during the same period. The IAOS organisers negotiated the transfer of former proprietary creamery suppliers to the nearest co-operative creamery, as well as the conversion of DDC-administered creameries into co-operative societies when required.[114] The state-sponsored body emerged as an ad hoc solution to the problem of reorganisation, but became a long-term one instead. The DDC ensured that the co-operative movement remained the dominant force in Irish dairying.

Reorganisation occurred at an opportune moment as the Wall Street Crash in 1929 presaged another period of great uncertainty within the industry. However, without government support throughout the previous decade, the consequences might have been more devastating. As it was, co-operative creameries survived the Great Depression and remained important sites around which developmental policies were conceived and carried out. The Agricultural Commission had emphasised the need for the reorganisation of the co-operative movement. While the impetus for this reform came from the government, the IAOS organising staff helped facilitate the successful application of these reforms. More importantly, the policies normalised the co-operative as the archetypal dairying business for much of the twentieth century. Independence brought about a new approach that saw a return to, and increased collaboration between, policymakers and co-operative experts.

Co-operative marketing and improvement of agricultural produce

Besides the root-and-branch reform of the dairy industry pursued by reorganisation, a drive to improve the reputation of Irish dairying also formed a key strand of the Agricultural Commission's deliberations. In the post-war period, Irish farmers proved slow to adopt new marketing techniques or respond to consumer feedback with the result that Irish butter carried a mixed reputation on the British market. Cormac Ó Gráda concludes that Irish farmers 'responded lackadaisically to the opportunities presented by the First World War'.[115] By the 1920s, any short-term gains won during the war dissipated. That decade saw a resumption of international competition between dairy producers as Irish farmers competed with new competitors. The introduction of refrigeration in the 1920s allowed New Zealand farmers to supply butter, meat and cheese to the British market.[116] A substantial problem for Irish butter producers related to the failure of creameries to co-ordinate their marketing. All creameries, including co-operatives, marketed their produce as individual concerns. Butter quality varied from one creamery to another, which harmed the reputation of all exports. At the same time, international competition grew ever more aggressive. In 1915, the Danes supplied over 102,000 tons of butter to Britain, but this dropped to 14,200 by 1918. By 1923, Danish farmers reasserted their dominance of the British market as they supplied 110,521 tons of butter.[117] Moreover, new competitors made the British marketplace a congested field for dairy farmers.[118]

The Agricultural Commission identified 'the present system of marketing farm produce ... [as] wasteful and uneconomic'.[119] A policy priority then existed around the need to raise the international profile of Irish dairy produce. Evidence from the continent showed that co-operative marketing raised the small farmer's productivity most effectively.[120] The co-operative movement emerged as the most likely instrument around which to build a new marketing approach. As such, the Agricultural Commission looked to the IAOS to organise marketing of creamery produce and argued that 'if farmers were to combine to sell their produce in larger quantities than at present, many of the economies inherent in large scale transactions could be effected'. Any effort towards this end 'must be the result of the farmer's co-operative and other organizations'. The Department of Agriculture envisaged its role as one that provided technical support and the report concluded, 'what is contemplated in this connection is a large scale development of co-operative marketing'.[121]

The IAOS long regarded the failure to unite co-operative farmers behind a single, recognisable brand as a major shortcoming to its work. Previous attempts to standardise co-operative creamery produce failed. In 1910, the IAOS launched its Co-operative Creamery Butter Control Scheme. The voluntary subscription of individual societies to the scheme enabled the IAOS to contract a dairy bacteriologist to monitor the butter made at each creamery. When the bacteriologist approved the quality of this butter, the society received the Control Mark which conveyed a standard of excellence to the consumer.[122] However, the majority of co-operative societies never embraced the scheme. Within four years, the IAOS Committee was lamenting the disappointing support and pronounced that 'with the exception of less than half a dozen creameries ... [the Control Scheme] has almost become a dead letter'.[123]

The Agricultural Commission received various recommendations about how to establish a national brand. The ICMA believed that Irish butter's improvement required a national grading system, but felt this should only be carried out on a voluntary basis.[124] W.P. Clifford argued that a degree of compulsion was necessary. Clifford believed that the creation of a national brand offered an important method to improve butter's quality and reputation, but for this to occur, 'every Irish creamery should be open to inspection and should be compelled to send samples regularly and frequently to surprise butter inspections ... linked up with bacteriological examination and research'.[125] The Dairy Produce Act partially resolved these concerns, but the precise mechanism of any marketing scheme required definition. A scheme co-ordinated by the IAOS offered a realistic possibility for success. Support for co-operative marketing transcended some political divisions as the Labour Party's Thomas Johnson and Michael Duffy stressed 'the necessity of [the marketing brand] being on a large scale'.[126] The co-operative movement represented the agent capable of rolling out an effective scheme, as it alone possessed the necessary reach and scale.

The IAOS launched its Butter Control Scheme in 1924 but to a largely indifferent movement. The manager of Rattoo Co-operative Society responded to an IAOS appeal with a pessimistic assessment of his committee's enthusiasm for the scheme. William O'Connell wrote to Robert Anderson informing him that the matter would be placed before the committee at the next meeting, but 'if participation in the scheme entails any expense in the way of further subscription this Society will not join'.[127] The pressure on societies' financial resources meant that the effort to ignite interest in the Butter Control Scheme failed.

The objective set out by the Dairy Produce Act to level up the quality of Irish produce remained unfulfilled. The next attempt to create a co-operative marketing scheme occurred in 1927 and coincided with the retreat of the private creamery sector. The decline of proprietary creameries meant farmers could no longer play two creameries off against each other and this promised to lead to a substantial improvement in creamery output. However, 'the long years' of creameries selling butter 'failed to secure anything more than spasmodic recognition for the general excellence of [Irish] butter'. The IAOS launched a new central marketing organisation in collaboration with the ICMA called the Irish Associated Creameries (IAC). Denis Hegarty served as the IAC's secretary alongside a board of directors drawn almost entirely from the co-operative creameries. As the creamery industry possessed a 'co-operative character and organization' it presented the first field of economic activity suitable for federated marketing. The IAC aimed to revolutionise the unsatisfactory position Irish dairy farmers found themselves in, 'by eliminating inter-competition in sale within our own fold, and by eliminating indifferent selling'.[128]

The IAC requested that co-operative societies subscribe and promise to distribute all produce through its auspices for a period of three years. The IAC employed marketing agents based in Britain who opened up new relations with buyers previously not contacted and ensured a wider distribution of Irish butter there. In return, the societies received a guaranteed fixed price for their produce. The IAC marketing scheme recorded impressive initial results. Throughout its first year, IAOS organisers tried to convince co-operative committees of the benefit attached to IAC membership. Societies who resisted previous efforts to federate in other organisations came in. Charles Riddall, promoted to the position of IAOS Assistant Secretary, wrote to Denis Hegarty to inform him that Rattoo Co-operative Society's decision to affiliate with the IAC 'would not have been made but for the attendance of our Organiser, Mr O'Brien'.[129] Rattoo Co-operative Society's affiliation to the IAC signalled a renewed enthusiasm for an active role in the national movement it had lacked in previous years. The relationships between IAOS employees and individual societies formed a key component to any success enjoyed by the IAC. In Rathmore, where the co-operative society still hoped to rebuild a creamery business in terminal decline, Thomas de Lacy informed Henry Kennedy that he 'had no difficulty in getting the [committee] meeting to consent to become members of the IAC'.[130]

Within one year 80 per cent of all co-operative creameries had subscribed to the IAC. The level of subscriptions suggested that individual societies viewed themselves as part of a national federation of co-operatives. The Department of Agriculture hoped that this uptake would lead to 'more economic marketing due to reduction in freight charges and cost of handling and the elimination of injurious competition between creamery and creamery on the British market'.[131] Although 80 per cent uptake represented a success of sorts, crucially one-fifth of all co-operatives did not subscribe to the IAC.[132] The IAC expressed dismay at the failure of sections of the creamery sector to affiliate. At the end of its first year, the IAC's board hoped that 'a juncture has been reached in the development of co-operative selling … when such an attitude towards the duties of citizenship … does not meet with the approval of the great majority of Dairy Farmers'.[133]

Co-operative creameries unaffiliated to the IAC traded without the restriction of a set maximum price. Enthusiasm for the scheme declined as a result. A year after joining the IAC, the manager of Rattoo Co-operative Society requested Henry Kennedy to send an organiser. Nicholas O'Brien arrived to find an unsettled committee who pointed out that 'creameries outside the Scheme were getting at least 8/- per cwt. nett more for their butters'.[134] O'Brien discovered ebbing support for the marketing scheme. The presence of only one nearby creamery operating outside the IAC's constraints undermined the commitment of those who already agreed to participate. Neighbouring Lixnaw Co-operative Society refused to affiliate, which created a source of local tension and encouraged hostility among Rattoo's milk suppliers towards the IAC. The committee at Rattoo directed the creamery manager to break the IAC contract and sell the society's produce elsewhere. Furthermore, the committee stated that if the IAC intervened, the 'Society will attack the IAC in the press with a view to bringing about its liquidation'.[135]

The breakdown in goodwill caused by a lack of support from all co-operative societies defeated efforts to make the IAC a success. Nicholas O'Brien observed wide disapproval towards the IAC among farmers in north Kerry. At Abbeydorney Co-operative Society, O'Brien noted that the attempt to frame co-operative marketing as a national issue backfired as committee members felt this undermined their local authority. Rather than strengthen the relationship between local and national organisations the IAC placed a strain on that relationship and alienated individual societies from the co-operative movement's national leadership. O'Brien filed his views on the subject in a report to Dublin:

> The most serious thing about our work at present is the wave of discontent of which you speak and, of course, it follows that discontent with the IAC means diminished confidence in the IAOS. However, I am an optimist and we will weather the present squall. The IAC will set itself right.[136]

O'Brien's optimism proved misplaced.

The rejection of the brand by a sizeable minority of co-operative societies revealed how local factors limited the extent to which the co-operative movement could implement the Agricultural Commission's recommendations on centralised marketing. The fact that 20 per cent of co-operative creameries refused to subscribe to the IAC undermined the effort to create a unified national brand and the purchaser of Irish butter remained 'well positioned to exploit the different creameries pricewise'.[137] The IAC did manage some successes on behalf of their members as it reduced the price differences between Irish butter and its competitors. IAC staff worked with potential customers on behalf of dairy farmers 'to re-establish confidence on the part of the buyers' and they managed to 'regain lost connections and consolidate existing ones'. Creameries played a greater role in the regulation of their own industry as the co-ordinated sales of butter that went through a quality-grading process, which strengthened their position to negotiate a fairer price. However, the fact that 'some of the outside creameries have done better than those inside' caused divisions within the co-operative movement.[138] The short-term perspective of those creameries that sat outside the scheme, and who indirectly benefited from the IAC's efforts, meant that a return to the system of individual marketing proved inevitable.

In 1930 and with the onset of global depression the IAC ceased trading as the attempt to create a national brand ended in failure. The collapse of the IAC highlighted the limitations of co-operative behaviour in practice. Its abandonment proved short-sighted as the Great Depression caused by the Wall Street Crash created unfavourable economic circumstances for agricultural producers. Although Irish farmers voluntarily associated around their local co-operative, the sense that they belonged to a national movement possessed limitations. In New Zealand, a similar marketing scheme saw complete uptake by dairy farmers. Every butter producer received 8–10 shillings more per cwt. even though the product was inferior to Irish butter.[139] Irish farmers proved more concerned with competition from several miles away than competitors from Denmark or New Zealand. The elimination of the threat from private creameries by the mid-1920s only amplified this tendency. In short, co-operatives struggled to co-operate with other co-operatives.

Co-operative credit

The 1920s saw a renewed impetus to create a vibrant co-operative credit sector. The IAOS's failure to build an effective co-operative credit movement in previous years proved imprudent as farmers experienced a squeeze on living standards. Although, in 1924, the farmer received on average '40 per cent more for his produce' compared to 1914, 'his cost of living has risen 80 per cent and the expenses and requirements of his trade have risen, in some cases, over 100 per cent'.[140] The Agricultural Commission presented policymakers with an opportunity to reintroduce the provision of co-operative credit as an important source of rural credit. The IAOS Annual Report for 1922 found that many of its existing credit societies maintained 'a moribund existence'. At the same time, the IAOS acknowledged that co-operative banks provided an invaluable service to a district by 'utilising the small deposits (which otherwise go out of the district if not out of the country) to irrigate and fertilise the parish through the local society'.[141] The neglect of agricultural credit by the IAOS represented a major failure to nurture a more co-operative economy.

H.F. Norman, Assistant Secretary of the IAOS, submitted evidence to the Agricultural Commission on the historical importance of co-operative credit to rural society. The emergence of local co-operative banks in the late 1890s sprang from the fact that 'joint stock banks did not lend as freely to the smaller type of farmer. I do not think that they still lend money to the very small farmer unless he has very sufficient security.' Norman argued that credit societies educated farmers to behave with greater financial responsibility. In considering loan applications, a credit society's committee paused to 'consider the economic character of the borrower. They must also consider if he is a good mark for the money, his general character for thrift as well as other matters, all these things have to be taken into account.' Farmers who used co-operative credit societies, 'began to be thrifty' as 'they began to add to their stock and laid the foundations of modest prosperity'. Thrifty farmers then 'from having been previously men that were pulling the devil by the tail [...] became fairly prosperous'.[142]

The primary purpose of co-operative credit societies was conceived as an educational one and rulebooks for these societies started: 'The objects of an Agricultural Bank are to assist its members with capital, to educate them in the true uses of credit, and to foster the spirit of mutual help or co-operation.'[143] Co-operative credit societies bound members together through a shared economic interest. They provided a forum in which local members drawn from one area influenced one another's financial position. Co-operative credit societies encouraged financial mutuality. Unlike loans offered by the joint-stock bank or shopkeepers, co-operative credit societies drew upon 'the expert knowledge of the community' and placed this 'at the service of the man who gets the loan'. The process of loan applications opened up the business of individual farmers to the scrutiny of their peers. Credit society committees granted loans 'for a purpose likely to effect economy'. Norman explained that he heard of 'many cases in which the borrower thinking he would take a loan for one particular purpose, has been induced to take it up for another purpose which in the studied opinion of the committee was more likely to pay him'.[144]

An ideal type of farmer for the post-independence era can be ascertained from Norman's evidence. Norman stressed that when one considered the position of 'the large farmer ... you are dealing with men with some education'. The role of the co-operative society held a different role for these subjects. Norman emphasised that the importance of co-operative credit societies lay in the aid they offered to 'the small farmer who live mainly in backward districts ... [where] the habit of having the purpose of the loan criticised leads to the development of a proper sense of credit amongst borrowers'.[145] Small farmers, long the target of improvement, remained defined by their backwardness. In contrast, the larger farmer, with access to greater agricultural resources, embodied the characteristics of an educated, modern rural subject. While Norman spoke about past efforts to provide assistance through co-operation for smaller farmers, he emphasised an idea that gained currency after independence. Larger farmers personified the desirable characteristics spoken about by agrarian experts.

The small farmer's position as an idealised subject within co-operative discourse declined after independence. In 1904 Plunkett praised the farmers' adoption of co-operative organisation as something that worked in the interests of all farmers, smallholders and large farmers alike. This mutual regard was central to the success of the movement in its earlier years and without this 'vein of altruism, the "strong" farmers would have held aloof and the small men would have been discouraged by the abstention of the better-off and presumably more enlightened of their class'.[146] By 1922, attitudes towards the small farmer among co-operative leaders shifted. Fr Finlay told the Agricultural Commission that the IAOS still aimed 'to raise the economical position of the small farmer and moderately sized farmer to a level of economic culture with the large farmer'.[147] W.P. Clifford provided a more hard-headed opinion when he stated, 'the small holding has not been a success. You don't find successful creameries there as a general rule. The most successful district from a dairying point of view is the medium farm.'[148] The views of leading co-operative activists contrasted with those found in the Minority Report, which lamented the lack of focus on the small farmer. As such, the IAOS provided an expert-backed justification for the government to prioritise larger farmers over their smaller counterparts and agricultural labourers.

Co-operative committees could act as important power-brokers in helping to dictate the dissemination of credit in a rural district. Robert Anderson illuminated the procedure by which someone became a member of a co-operative credit society. Committees decided upon eligibility for membership of a society based upon the condition that 'his character is all right ... where the application is rejected the Committee are not under any obligation to state their reasons for objection'.[149] This process gave the committees significant discretionary powers to direct a locality's social and economic make-up, which helped to bring about the idea of the larger, more financially reliable farmer as the ideal co-operative subject during a decade of economic challenges.

Still, a renewed co-operative credit sector appeared to provide one means to improve the social stature of small farmers. The parlous state of co-operative credit in the 1920s provided a cause for concern. H.F. Norman contrasted the development of Irish credit societies with the more successful German Raiffeisen credit movement. In Germany, local co-operative infrastructure started with the establishment of a credit society and other types of co-operatives followed. In Ireland, the opposite occurred. Creameries sprang up without reference to a local credit society and therefore bypassed the necessity for a society devoted to the provision of loan capital.[150] Instead, creamery societies often provided an informal, but unsound, credit function as they frequently paid advances to members in lieu of milk yet to be supplied. These loans often placed societies and their members in financial difficulty. For example, in April 1922 Ardfert Co-operative Society served a writ to the widow of a deceased member in order to retrieve over £175 due to the society in unpaid cash advances.[151] Rathmore Co-operative Society suffered as a result of its lax attitude to the supply of credit. An attempt to restart the retail business failed in June 1924. As Nicholas O'Brien reported, the 'Store Department has been closed for the past few weeks owing to the large amount of money outstanding for store goods ... too much credit was given'.[152]

Such occurrences led Fr Finlay to believe that farmers drew too heavily upon the financial resources of societies when they already possessed ample funds in the bank and he suggested 'we require a little tightening of the reins'.[153] Norman thought that the interest taken in the revitalisation of co-operative credit after independence offered an opportunity for the state to start again: 'I think that the State might do something ... to show its interest in these societies when they regard them as useful, and in general sound institutions'. Part of Norman's purpose in giving evidence to the Commission focused upon the need for the IAOS to perform a regulatory role in any effort to foster a new wave of credit societies. He recommended that he 'would make any encouragement by the State [in establishing credit societies] contingent on the affiliation of the Society to the ... IAOS, because I consider these societies require a good deal of supervision'.[154]

The Agricultural Commission criticised the existent financial position of credit societies, equating the practices of many as 'a negation of the true purpose of co-operation, whereby each member should bear his appropriate share of the responsibility'. Too many societies suffered from under-capitalisation and 'the character and training on the people engaged has been deplorable'. Over-reliance on informal credit provided at the creamery proved detrimental to the inculcation of self-reliance. Three major criticisms emerged from the report. First, members needed to subscribe a higher level of capital to their co-operative societies to end reliance upon bank loans. Second, 'a few "strong" men' bore financial responsibility for the society and by implication the community. Finally, societies proved too willing to give credit.[155] In order to remedy this, the Agricultural Commission decided that co-operative credit societies needed reintroduction. The report criticised the IAOS's long-term concentration upon creameries at the expense of other sectors and suggested promotional efforts needed to focus elsewhere than upon those societies that contributed 'more liberally than credit banks to the central funds'. The Agricultural Commission recommended that the Irish Government expand the co-operative credit sector with the argument that 'the existence of a number of active and solvent credit banks is evidence of mutual trust, which is the spirit of co-operation'.[156] Thus began a state co-ordinated attempt to achieve what Robert Anderson described as the 'capitalisation of honesty'.[157]

Efforts to revive the co-operative credit sector proved well timed. A memo prepared by the Department of Agriculture in 1925 emphasised the importance of co-operative credit societies to protect farmers from economic ruin. A potentially ruinous outbreak of fluke disease threatened to wipe out Ireland's dairy cattle stocks. The Department's support for the extension of co-operative credit targeted regions most affected.

> The Department's Agricultural Credit Scheme operates through the medium of approved Agricultural Credit Societies in districts where farmers have in recent months suffered losses of livestock, mainly as a result of Fluke disease.[158]

The outbreak of fluke, a parasitic worm that attacks cows' livers threatened the livelihoods of many dairy farmers. The need to avert an agricultural crisis confirmed the importance attached to reviving co-operative credit societies to the Department of Agriculture. IAOS organisers devoted themselves to the propagation of a new wave of credit societies.

County Kerry responded well to this drive. In 1922, only Newtownsandes Co-operative Credit Society existed in the county, but even there the society found that life in the early 1920s was incredibly difficult.[159] However, Newtown-sandes Secretary, Edmond Mulvihill, wrote to the Registrar of Friendly Societies in Dublin to explain their unsettled situation during the civil war years as they prepared to apply for the government capitalisation scheme.

> I enclose balance sheets for 1921–1922–1923–1924. I am sorry to have delayed them so long. The Society got mixed up in political matters, but things are normal again. The Society are trying to avail of the Government scheme and I will be obliged to you if you send me the 1924 balance sheet as the inspectors may require it.[160]

By 1928, the number of credit societies in County Kerry climbed to fourteen because thirteen fluke societies were organised. In Kerry where the cattle stocks were affected by the fluke outbreak co-operative societies took advantage of

interest-free loans offered by the Department of Agriculture. For example, Ballymacelligott Co-operative Society established a credit society in 1925. That June
the committee applied for an initial loan of £1,000 after guaranteeing initial
deposits of £1,000 from members who needed to replenish cattle stocks.[161] IAOS
support of Ballymacelligott Credit Society proved critical. Robert Anderson lobbied
the Department of Agriculture on the society's behalf putting forward a case for
a government advance. The Department responded by sending Anderson a cheque
for £826, which he forwarded to the secretary of Ballymacelligott Society.[162] The
government matched deposits lodged by members at a ratio of 2:1 to incentivise
farmers to place deposits in the new society.[163] Further loans from the government
resulted – £840 on 23 December 1925; £931 on 1 March 1926; £1,032 on 24
March 1926; and £1,140 on 30 March 1926.[164]

Credit societies sparked a recovery from the fluke epidemic as farmers replenished
their herds. Charles Riddall's report for 4 February 1926 showed that Ballymacelligott Co-operative Credit Society counted 111 members, who drew modest
amounts from the new bank. The average loan granted was about £40, while
the largest single loan was £50 pounds. Early enthusiasm was high. By 4 February
1926 local members had deposited a combined total of £1,814 and received
£1,666 from the Department of Agriculture. An important feature of the government loans related to the fact that no interest was charged for the first three
years. The credit society primarily issued loans for the purchase of milk cows to
replenish cattle stocks. Riddall visited again a fortnight later and noted that the
membership climbed to 153. He described Ballymacelligott as an area that revolved
around the creamery business and observed that 'the people in the locality generally
are thrifty and, potentially at least, well off'. Riddall detailed with satisfaction
that traditional opponents to co-operation derived no benefit from the new
society's existence:

> No case of a shopkeeper having been admitted to membership or having been
> granted a loan or of any deposit having been received from a shopkeeper has come
> under my personal notice in this or any other credit societies in the County Kerry
> which I have recently visited.[165]

The establishment of the fluke co-operative credit societies shored up the position
of local dairy farmers and cemented the successful embedding of a local co-operative
infrastructure in north Kerry.

The new co-operative credit societies highlight how committee members accrued
local power. Committees used informal discretionary powers to exclude certain
local inhabitants from the benefits of membership to the local co-operative.
When asked by one committee member about the criteria to be met when
admitting members to one of these new societies, Robert Anderson responded:
'The chief consideration to which they should give attention would be the character
of the applicant rather than upon the security the society should rely for

repayment.' The quality of an applicant's character emerged as an important principle when it came to working out who qualified for a loan: 'Every loan must be secured by two persons besides the borrower, but the known good character of the borrower is of far more importance than anything else from the Society's point of view.'[166]

What constituted good character remained open to interpretation, but complaints from smaller farmers suggested a connection to social status. One member of the Tralee Co-operative Credit Society complained to the Department of Agriculture that the society's committee rejected his loan application without satisfactory justification. Michael O'Sullivan described himself as 'a small farmer holding over twenty-one acres of good land on which I have only two cows presently … the farm is capable of carrying eight'. He requested a loan of £50 to replenish his small herd and described conditions in the rural hinterland around Tralee as one of 'dire distress … amongst small farmers here'. Despite O'Sullivan's membership of the society the loan application was refused and he accused 'large farmers and cattle dealers [of] drawing the money which I'm sure was intended for the small farmers'.[167] Co-operative committees exerted control over the direction of societies by policing the distribution of vital credit resources. Larger farmers with greater potential for development benefited while smaller farmers became marginalised. Committees interpreted what constituted character in terms of an individual's economic position and processed loan applications duly. The emigration of small farmers and labourers remained an important feature of land development in Ireland throughout the twentieth century, with smallholdings consolidated under the ownership of larger farmers.[168] While in the past Horace Plunkett had promoted co-operatives as one way to stem emigration, by the 1920s the way in which the co-operative credit market operated suggested that financial support that might otherwise keep people on the land proved elusive.

Co-operative credit societies provided the government with an effective instrument to placate an unsettled and vulnerable rural population. Combined efforts between the IAOS and Department of Agriculture resulted in the establishment of 52 new credit societies, while many moribund societies started up once again. By 1931, 114 credit societies worked with only one of the new wave of societies winding up in that time. Most of these new societies were those established during the fluke epidemic. Throughout the 1930s and 1940s the fluke credit societies made no new loans and largely existed to service outstanding debts made to farmers during the outbreak. The second wave of credit societies remained a part of the IAOS movement but maintained a nominal existence only. Like the co-operative credit movement before 1914, new societies remained reliant upon state funding for capitalisation. The government earmarked a sum of £100,000 to provide initial capital to new credit societies, which received this money in proportion to deposits invested by prospective members.[169]

In a period where the legitimacy of the state remained contested, the government gained the support of farmers by directing funding through this revived co-operative credit network. In 1927, the government created a state-sponsored agency, the Agricultural Credit Corporation (ACC) to improve credit provisions for farmers.[170] The ACC collaborated with the IAOS to co-ordinate the release of loan capital via the national network of co-operative societies. These societies lent to farmers in order to purchase more dairy cows and stimulate levels of butter production.[171] The ACC had distributed about £1,000,000 to farmers through the co-operative credit network by 1932.[172] This body issued loans to undercapitalised co-operative creameries to purchase new equipment and also helped finance the new midlands creameries.[173] The creation of the ACC confirmed the enmeshed role of the state and co-operative movement in driving Irish development. Through the instrument of the co-operative society, the government recapitalised depressed rural communities, and demonstrated a commitment to the improvement of Irish agricultural produce – although not all people shared equally in this independence dividend.

Co-operation in the 1930s

In 1932, the Irish Government published *Saorstát Éireann: Official Handbook* to commemorate the tenth anniversary of the foundation of the Irish Free State. The publication's timing coincided with the handover of power from Cumann na nGaedheal to Fianna Fáil. This represented a significant, but tense, political moment for the young state, as it meant the transfer of power from the political party that supported the Treaty to a party made up of Republicans opposed to it. The book offered a defence of the Cumann na nGaedheal administration, arguing that the political, social and economic institutions which underpinned the Free State provided satisfactory evidence that the previous decades of struggle represented a worthwhile price. The main source of the Free State's claim to political success related to its work towards the modernisation of Irish society born out of free political institutions. Bulmer Hobson, a veteran nationalist, edited the book, which offered an opportunity to survey the progress made 'at the end of the first decade of national freedom'. Hobson stated that centuries of conflict between English government and Irish people meant that Cumann na nGaedheal, 'assumed control of a country reduced by war and misgovernment to a state bordering on chaos' and its record needed to be understood in this context. Ireland required 'an immense work of political, legal, social and economic reconstruction'. In the end, Hobson concluded:

> Constructive work and development in every direction which, under the old regime, could never have been attempted are now possible, and the energies which for generations were absorbed in the struggle for political autonomy set free for the work of social and economic reconstruction.[174]

The book celebrated different aspects of society in the Free State and codified a range of discourses about the character and ideals of Irish life repeated by nationalists and agrarian experts over the course of previous decades. Topics ranged from literature and history to banking and agriculture. Joseph Hanly, an inspector of agricultural science, authored an essay arguing that agriculture formed the historic basis of Ireland's economy and that 'Gaelic Civilization Ireland was entirely rural'. Hanly encapsulated an official view of national development that prevailed by the early 1930s. He cited the abundance of evidence found in Gaelic literature, both 'direct and implied', to show that Ireland possessed a long and successful tradition as an agricultural nation.[175] Hanly reminded readers that the IAOS pre-dated the Free State and referred to the important role played by the co-operative movement when it 'undertook the work of advising farmers on agricultural matters as well as co-operation [and] … carried out a great amount of pioneer work'. The Free State reaped the benefit of this work and the government continued to utilise co-operative societies to improve the quality of agricultural output. In the end, 'agriculture is not only the most important industry of the Irish Free State, but that in view of the valuable resources of the country, each aspect is capable of very great development'.[176]

In an uncompromising book published a year earlier, Hanly went into more detail about his ideal form of the Irish nation-state. In *The National Ideal*, Hanly envisaged a Gaelic, Catholic state that used co-operative institutions to realise a superior national archetype. On the front cover was an etching by the artist Sean Keating. Keating's illustration echoed a soviet realist style that portrayed an idealised, rural family looking towards a source of light upon which is emblazoned the image of a crucifix, sickle and anvil. Under the image is stated, '*Dia, Tír is Teanga*', which translates as 'God, Country and Language' (see figure 6.1). One contemporary reviewer for a Jesuit journal described this frontispiece as 'at once severely spiritual and pointedly practical in its lesson'.[177]

The idea of co-operation as a desirable and normative basis for national behaviour showed how deeply embedded elements of its ideology became within contemporary political discourse. In economic terms, Hanly argued that all forms of activity needed to work in subservience to an idealised form of an Irish nationality, which he equated to 'a supreme form of co-operation'. The Irish past showed how strong English influences promoted an individualistic and selfish conception of development. To counter this effect 'co-operation must be made a gigantic implement for national economic cultivation in Ireland'.[178] Hanly's conception of an ideal co-operative organisation moved away from Plunkett's professed non-political and non-sectarian version towards one that accentuated the intersections between economics, religion and nationalism. Hanly anticipated a corporatist tendency that emerged in Ireland during the 1930s, which advocated the organisation of socio-economic structures compatible with Catholic social teaching.[179] As Ireland continued to define its position as an independent nation-state in the 1930s,

Figure 6.1 Sean Keating's frontispiece to Joseph Hanly's *The National Ideal*

co-operation remained a recognisable and familiar paradigm along which future success might derive – albeit one with potential to be incorporated into a Catholicisation of Irish life.

The Irish Free State projected itself as an agricultural country. Nationalists believed that agricultural improvement provided the best means to achieve successful economic development and national prosperity. Intellectuals, policymakers and civil servants made the case for agricultural development as the natural economic policy and the co-operative movement featured in this process. The IAOS used its influence to affect the trajectory of Irish agricultural policy after 1922. Even as the Irish Government adopted a policy of economic protectionism after 1932, the improvement of agricultural production remained a major concern. The economist and co-operative advocate, Joseph Johnston, was no supporter of the new Fianna Fáil Government's chosen trade policy, but conceded that 'the main problem of the Irish economy now is, not the creation of new industries, but the expansion of the home market for the products of our agriculture and of existing industries'.[180] While a debate about whether to adhere to free trade or to embrace protectionism occurred on an international level, in Ireland the commitment to the intensification of agricultural production remained entrenched as the economic orthodoxy until the 1950s.[181]

The economic record for Irish agriculture until 1932 was mixed. A global fall in prices at the end of the 1920s affected all Irish farm produce. Disappointing price movements during the 1920s and 1930s meant dairying experienced no spectacular economic return and butter exports dropped from a value of £4.6 million in 1929 to £3.3 million in 1930.[182] Nevertheless, the Irish share of the British market in butter, eggs and cattle remained stable throughout the 1920s.[183] The Irish Government passed measures that ensured Irish farmers remained competitive and without the targeted legislation and utilisation of the co-operative infrastructure, the experience could have been more fraught. George O'Brien argued that the Department of Agriculture utilised the maximum potential of agricultural resources and developed pre-existent branches of production within the Free State. The stimulation of food production allayed fears of food scarcity and Patrick Hogan's policies 'ensured that any public money spent on agriculture would be employed productively by being devoted to the building up of the efficiency of the industry'.[184]

Patrick Hogan remained Minister for Agriculture until the fall of the Cumann na nGaedheal Government and has been assessed as 'a talented and hard-working minister' who instigated much-needed improvement in the quality of agricultural inputs and outputs. His decision to establish state agencies such as the ACC proved influential interventions.[185] Yet the effectiveness of these policies required the pre-existence of co-operative societies to facilitate this work. The IAOS and the co-operative movement remained the most dynamic network in Irish agriculture. Co-operative societies utilised the available state assistance to ensure they outlived the private creamery sector, but there was a price to pay. After the Wall Street crash the movement relied more heavily on this state support – a far cry from the voluntary movement envisaged by Plunkett, Æ and Finlay.[186] Co-operative societies embodied the state for much of the rural population. For many rural people, the state revealed itself at the site of the local co-operative. Whether through financial support from credit societies or the everyday business of working through the creamery, a popular understanding of the state and its effect upon the population was understood through the co-operative movement's network.

The 1930s marked the end of an era for the Irish co-operative movement. Horace Plunkett died in Surrey in March 1932, but lived to see the movement he created leave an extraordinary impact upon his home country. Throughout his final years, he remained in touch with the movement he founded as President of the IAOS but his interest shifted to mainstreaming agricultural co-operation across the globe. He organised a conference in July 1924 that gathered delegates from across the British Empire to discuss how agricultural co-operation might be promoted as a solution to problems of underdevelopment elsewhere. He founded the Horace Plunkett Foundation in Oxford to continue the study and promotion of agriculture in rural settings. The uptake of co-operation in other rural countries allowed Plunkett to point to the influence of the policy maxim of 'Better Farming, Better Business, Better Living' as evidence of his 'Irish formula accepted'.[187]

Æ continued as the editor of *Irish Statesman* until its demise in 1930. Throughout his final years he remained a popular character in Dublin as he nurtured the next generation of literary and artistic talent. When he died in July 1935 his funeral cortège in Dublin extended for over a mile as his remains made their final journey from Plunkett House, where so much of his life was spent, to Mount Jerome cemetery. The funeral revealed the extent of Æ's diverse and popular appeal as the *Irish Times* reported: 'At his coffinside were bankers, journalists, labour men, leaders of State, poets and artists of international distinction, unknown workers, university professors – mostly representatives of social and economic opposition – all in sympathy by the side of Æ's bier.'[188] All came to pay their respects to a man who at some stage offered inspiration, intellectual guidance and support.

By the time the two most famous and committed of Irish co-operators passed, the original idealism that once animated the movement had settled down into the mundane business of rural life. The co-operative societies framed everyday working practices, provided a social space, and showed that an alternative and radical economic model could become an accepted social norm. The co-operative creameries that once proved to be such a point of contention in the structure of rural society graduated into business institutions familiar to families across the countryside.

Notes

1 A subsequent Act passed on 6 December 1922 confirmed the Irish Free State's legal status as an autonomous Dominion of the British Empire. D.W. Harkness, *The Restless Dominion: The Irish Free State and the British Commonwealth of Nations, 1921–1931* (Dublin: Gill & Macmillan, 1969), 21–29.

2 'The New Era', *Irish Homestead*, 17 December 1921, 841–844.

3 'Its Future Work', *Irish Homestead*, 11 February 1922, 83.

4 IAOS, *Annual Report, 1921*, 44–48.

5 Basil Chubb, *The Government and Politics of Ireland*, 3rd edn (London: Longman, 1992), 3–5.

6 Garret Fitzgerald, *Reflections on the Irish State* (Dublin: Irish Academic Press, 2003), 20–21.

7 Chubb, *The Government*, 1–21.

8 Francis MacManus (ed.), *The Years of the Great Test, 1926–1939* (Cork: Mercier Press, 1967).

9 Alvin Jackson, *Ireland, 1798–1998: Politics and War* (Oxford: Blackwell Publishers Ltd, 1999), 258–262; John M. Regan and Mike Cronin, 'Introduction: Ireland and the Politics of Independence, 1922–49: New Perspectives and Re-considerations', in *Ireland: The Politics of Independence, 1922–49*, ed. by Mike Cronin and John M. Regan (Basingstoke: Macmillan, 2000), 1–12 (p. 2).

10 Clifford Geertz, *The Interpretation of Cultures: Selected Essays* (New York: Basic Books, 1973), 234–5.

11 Akhil Gupta, 'Blurred Boundaries: The Discourse of Corruption, the Culture of Politics and the Imagined State', *American Ethnologist*, 22.2 (1995), 375–402 (pp. 376–378).

12 Mícheál Ó Fathartaigh, *Irish Agriculture Nationalised: the Dairy Disposal Company and the Making of the Modern Irish Dairy Industry* (Dublin: Institute of Public Administration).

13 IAOS, *Annual Report, 1923*, 14.

14 Ciara Meehan, *The Cosgrave Party A History of Cumann na nGaedheal, 1923–33* (Dublin: Royal Irish Academy, 2010).

15 John M. Regan, *The Irish Counter-Revolution, 1921–1936: Treatyite Politics and Settlement in Independent Ireland* (Dublin: Gill & Macmillan, 1999).

16 On these efforts see Michael Kennedy and Joseph Skelly (eds), *Irish Foreign Policy, 1919–1966: From Independence to Internationalism* (Dublin: Four Courts, 2000).

17 Paul Murray, *The Irish Boundary Commission and its Origins, 1886–1925* (Dublin: University College Dublin Press, 2011).

18 Donal Corcoran, 'Public Policy in an Emerging State: The Irish Free State, 1922–25', *Irish Journal of Public Policy*, 1 (2009), http://publish.ucc.ie/ijpp/2009/01/corcoran/05/en [accessed 19 August 2013].

19 J.J. Lee, *Ireland, 1912–1985: Politics and Society* (Cambridge: Cambridge University Press, 1989), 69–71.

20 IAOS, *Annual Report, 1923*, 7.

21 Mary E. Daly, *Industrial Development and Irish National Identity, 1922–39* (Dublin: Gill & Macmillan, 1992), 16.

22 Saorstát Éireann, *Agricultural Statistics, 1847–1926: Reports and Tables* (Dublin: Stationery Office, 1928), lxv.

23 Daly, *Industrial Development*, 15.

24 Evidence of T.P. Gill to Commission on Agriculture, 16, 17 and 18 January 1923, NAI AGF/2005/68/80.

25 Kieran A. Kennedy, Thomas Giblin and Deirdre McHugh, *The Economic Development of Ireland in the Twentieth Century* (London: Routledge, 1988), 37.

26 Donal Corcoran, *Freedom to Achieve Freedom: The Irish Free State, 1922–1932* (Dublin: Gill & Macmillan, 2013), 153.

27 Eunan O'Halpin, 'Politics and the State, 1922–1932', *A New History of Ireland, Volume VII: Ireland 1921–1984*, ed. by J.R. Hill (Oxford: Oxford University Press, 2003), 86–126 (p. 113).

28 George O'Brien, 'Patrick Hogan: Minister for Agriculture, 1922–1932', *Studies*, 25.99 (1936), 353–368 (p. 360).

29 Cormac Ó Gráda, *A Rocky Road: The Irish Economy Since the 1920s* (Manchester: Manchester University Press, 1997), 145.

30 Cormac Ó Gráda, *Ireland Before and After the Famine: Explorations in Economic History, 1800–1925* (Manchester: Manchester University Press, 1988), 172. This contrasts with James Meenan who argued that voluntary organisations were irretrievably weakened by independence. Meenan, *The Irish Economy Since 1922* (Liverpool: Liverpool University Press, 1970), 34–35.

31 O'Halpin, 'Politics and the State', 115.

32 Joseph Johnston, 'Free Trade or Protection for Irish Industries?' *Irish Economist*, 8.1 (1923), 54–65 (pp. 64–65).

33 Ronan Fanning, *The Irish Department of Finance, 1922–1958* (Dublin: Institute of Public Administration, 1978), 202–206; Lee, *Ireland*, 118–120.

34 Ó Gráda, *A Rocky Road*, 46; Lee, *Ireland, 1912–1985*, 108.

35 Patrick Hogan to the Post-Master General, 22 May 1922, NAI FIN/1/3086.

36 James Gordon to Captain Petherick, 8 March 1922, PRONI, FIN/18/2/332.

37 IAOS, *Annual Report, 1923*, 6.

38 IAOS, *Annual Report, 1922*, 9; IAOS, *Annual Report, 1924*, 6.

39 Desmond A Gillmor, 'Land and People, c.1926', in *A New History of Ireland, Volume VII: Ireland, 1921–84*, ed. by J.R. Hill (Oxford: Oxford University Press, 2003), 62–85 (p. 70).

40 Michael Hopkinson, *Green Against Green: The Irish Civil War* (Dublin: Gill & Macmillan, 1988), 115–122.

41 Bill Kissane, *The Politics of the Irish Civil War* (Oxford: Oxford University Press, 2005), 1.

42 Kissane, *Politics of the Irish Civil War*, 4; Peter Hart, *The IRA at War, 1916–1923* (Oxford: Oxford University Press, 2003), 41.

43 Anne Dolan, *Commemorating the Irish Civil War: History and Memory, 1923–2000* (Cambridge: Cambridge University Press, 2003).

44 Hopkinson, *Green Against Green*, 273.

45 Michael Hopkinson, 'Civil War and Aftermath, 1922–4', *A New History of Ireland: 1921–1984*, ed. by J.R. Hill (Oxford: Oxford University Press, 2003), 31–61 (p. 54).

46 Trevor West, *Horace Plunkett, Co-operation and Politics* (Gerrards Cross, Bucks.: Colin Smythe, 1986), 197–216.
47 'Fate of the Irish Laodiceans', *Irish Homestead*, 3 February 1923, 61–62.
48 Henry Summerfield, *That Myriad-Minded Man: A Biography of George William Russell 'AE' 1867–1935* (Gerrards Cross, Bucks.: Colin Smythe, 1975), 218–227; Nicholas Allen, *Modernism, Ireland and Civil War* (Cambridge: Cambridge University Press, 2009), 36.
49 James J. Kennelly, 'Normal Courage: R.A. Anderson and the Irish Co-operative Movement', *Studies*, 100 (2011), 319–330.
50 Ó Fathartaigh, *Irish Agriculture Nationalised*, 16.
51 Meenan, *The Irish Economy*, 35.
52 Donal O'Sullivan, *The Irish Free State and its Senate: A Study in Contemporary Politics* (London: Faber & Faber, 1940), 99.
53 Gavin Foster, 'In the Shadow of the Split: Writing the Irish Civil War', *Field Day Review*, 2 (2006), 294–303 (pp. 295–296). For more on the Civil War in Kerry see Tom Doyle, *The Civil War in Kerry* (Cork: Mercier Press, 2008).
54 N.W. O'Brien to R.A. Anderson, 1 October 1922, NAI 1088/800/3.
55 N.W. O'Brien's Report, 6 October 1922, NAI 1088/2/4.
56 N.W. O'Brien to R.A. Anderson, 17 October 1922, NAI 1088/751/8.
57 N.W. O'Brien's Report on Rathmore, 2 December 1922, NAI 1088/798/4.
58 N.W. O'Brien's Report on Rathmore, 20 December 1922, NAI 1088/798/4.
59 'Irregular' was the pejorative term used for Republicans opposed to the Treaty.
60 Thomas de Lacy to R.A. Anderson, 15 and 16 January 1923, NAI 1088/798/4.
61 R.A. Anderson to Thomas de Lacy, 19 January 1923, NAI 1088/798/4.
62 Denis Gwynn, *The Irish Free State, 1922–1927* (London: Macmillan and Co., 1928), 285.
63 Corcoran, 'Public Policy'.
64 Commission of Inquiry into the Resources and Industries of Ireland, *Report on Dairying and the Dairy Industry, March, 1922* (Dublin: Commission of Inquiry into the Resources and Industries of Ireland, 1922), 1.
65 Roy H.W. Johnston, *Century of Endeavour: A Biographical and Autobiographical View of the Twentieth Century in Ireland* (Dublin: The Lilliput Press, 2006), 40.
66 James Meenan, *George O'Brien: A Biographical Memoir* (Dublin: Gill & Macmillan, 1980), 127.
67 Preface to the Report of the Agricultural Commission, NAI AGF/2005/68/401.
68 'The Agricultural Commission', *Irish Homestead*, 28 October 1922, 629–630.
69 Evidence of W.P. Clifford to Agricultural Commission, 9 March 1923, NAI AGF/2005/68/35. Also see Martin Maguire, *The Civil Service and the Revolution in Ireland: 'Shaking the Blood-Stained Hand of Mr Collins'* (Manchester: Manchester University Press, 2008).
70 Report of the Agricultural Commission, 2, NAI AGF/2005/68/401.
71 Report of the Agricultural Commission, 11, NAI AGF/2005/68/401.
72 Report of the Agricultural Commission, 89–102, NAI AGF/2005/68/401.
73 Report of the Agricultural Commission, 9, NAI AGF/2005/68/401.
74 Report of the Agricultural Commission, 66, NAI AGF/2005/68/401.

75 Report of the Agricultural Commission, 41, NAI AGF/2005/68/401.

76 Report of the Agricultural Commission, 46, NAI AGF/2005/68/401.

77 Report of the Agricultural Commission, 46, NAI AGF/2005/68/401.

78 R.A. Anderson's evidence to Agricultural Commission, 13 December 1923, NAI AGF/2005/68/6.

79 Commission of Inquiry, *Report on Dairying*, 14–15.

80 T.W. Freeman, *Ireland: Its Physical, Historical, Social and Economic Geography* (London: Methuen and Co., Ltd, 1950), 202–204.

81 Saorstát Éireann, *Agricultural Statistics*, xxii.

82 IAOS, *Annual Report, 1921*, 39.

83 Report of the Agricultural Commission, 46, NAI AGF/2005/68/401.

84 Gwynn, *The Irish Free State*, 260–261.

85 IAOS, *Annual Report, 1931*, 5.

86 Confidential Report, Reorganisation of the IAOS, Internal Minute, Department of Agriculture, undated [1926], NAI AGF/2005/82/1497.

87 IAOS, *Annual Report, 1924*, 31–32.

88 Proposed Re-organisation Scheme of IAOS, 1924–1928, 31 October 1927; B. McAuliffe's Report of Meeting to Dr Smith, Department of Agriculture, 31 October 1927, NAI AGF/2005/82/1495.

89 Saorstát Éireann, *Dairy Produce Act, 1924*, www.irishstatutebook.ie/eli/1924/act/58/enacted/en/print.html [accessed 2 October 2017].

90 Dairy Disposal Company Ltd; Re Inspection and Registration of Tubrid Creamery, Ardfert, County Kerry, under Dairy Produce Act 1924, 30 October 1925–5 March 1930, NAI AGF/92/3/655.

91 Thomas de Lacy, Rathmore, to James Fant, 23 February 1928, NAI 1088/798/6.

92 Thomas de Lacy, Rathmore, to James Fant, 21 March 1928, NAI 1088/798/6.

93 R.A. Anderson, *With Horace Plunkett in Ireland* (London: Macmillan and Co., 1935), 236–237.

94 Conference with Dairy Produce Inspectors, 29 September–2 October 1925, NAI AGF/92/3/570.

95 Ó Fathartaigh, *Irish Agriculture Nationalised*, 3.

96 IAOS, *Annual Report, 1907*, 55–56.

97 Evidence of Denis Hegarty, Secretary of the Irish Creamery Manager's Association to the Agricultural Commission, 8 March 1923, NAI AGF/2005/68/95.

98 Evidence of Denis Hegarty, 19 April 1923, NAI AGF/2005/68/95.

99 Report of the Agricultural Commission, 43–44, NAI AGF/2005/68/401.

100 Report of the Agricultural Commission, 42, NAI AGF/2005/68/401.

101 Saorstát Éireann, *Agricultural Statistics*, xx–xxi.

102 Thomas de Lacy, Rathmore, to R.A. Anderson, Dublin, 29 September 1923; Anderson to Secretary, Department of Agriculture, 2 October 1923, NAI 1088/798/5.

103 James Fant's handwritten note on N.W. O'Brien's Report, 8 July 1924, NAI 1088/798/5.

104 John O'Donovan, 'State Enterprises', *Journal of the Statistical and Social Inquiry Society of Ireland*, 8.3 (1950), 327–348 (p. 330).

105 Ó Fathartaigh, *Irish Agriculture Nationalised*, 16–17.

106 Thomas de Lacy, Rathmore, to Henry Kennedy, IAOS, 15 December 1927, NAI 1088/798/6.
107 Department of Agriculture of Saorstát Éireann, *Saorstát Éireann, Agriculture: A Note on Some Outstanding Features of the Irish Free State's Agricultural Resources* (Dublin: Department of Agriculture, Saorstát Éireann, 1928), 23–24.
108 Mary E. Daly, *The First Department: A History of the Department of Agriculture* (Dublin: Institute of Public Administration, 2002), 128–133.
109 Saorstát Éireann, *Creamery Act, 1928*, www.irishstatutebook.ie/1928/en/act/pub/0026/print.html (Section 13) [accessed 13 September 2012].
110 Saorstát Éireann, *Creamery Act, 1928* (Section 10).
111 R.F. Foster, *Modern Ireland, 1600–1972* (London: Penguin, 1989), 426.
112 Teddy Fennelly, *A Triumph Over Adversity: The History of Donaghmore Co-operative Creamery Ltd, Founded in 1927* (Portlaoise: Arderin Publishing Company, 2003).
113 'New Creameries in Free State', *Weekly Irish Times*, 25 May 1929, 19.
114 IAOS, *Annual Report, 1931*, 14–15.
115 Cormac Ó Gráda, *Ireland: A New Economic History, 1780–1939* (Oxford: Clarendon Press, 1995), 389–390.
116 G.A. Fleming, 'Agricultural Support Policies in a Small Open Economy: New Zealand in the 1920s', *Economic History Review*, 52.2 (1999), 334–354.
117 Report of the Agricultural Commission, 26, NAI AGF/2005/68/401.
118 Meenan, *The Irish Economy*, 35.
119 Report of the Agricultural Commission, 20, NAI AGF/2005/68/401.
120 Ó Gráda, *Ireland*, 261.
121 Report of the Agricultural Commission, 20, NAI AGF/2005/68/401.
122 IAOS, *Annual Report, 1910*, 89–90.
123 IAOS, *Annual Report, 1914*, 10.
124 Evidence of Denis Hegarty, NAI AGF/2005/68/95.
125 Evidence of W.P. Clifford, NAI AGF/2005/68/35.
126 Report of the Agricultural Commission, 104, NAI AGF/2005/68/401.
127 William O'Connell, Rattoo, to R.A. Anderson, 19 May 1924, NAI 1088/800/3.
128 Irish Associated Creameries Limited, *Report of the Committee to the Members for the Year ended December 31st, 1928* (Dublin: Browne and Nolan, n.d.), 2–4.
129 C.C. Riddall, IAOS, Dublin to Denis Hegarty, Irish Associated Creameries, Dublin, 22 July 1927, NAI 1088/800/3.
130 Thomas de Lacy to Henry Kennedy, 22 March 1927, NAI 1088/798/5.
131 Department of Agriculture, *Saorstát Éireann*, 24.
132 Ó Fathartaigh, *Irish Agriculture Nationalised*, 84.
133 IAC, *Report … 1928*, 2.
134 Jerry O'Connor, Rattoo to Henry Kennedy, Dublin 7 September 1928, NAI 1088/800/3.
135 N.W. O'Brien to Henry Kennedy, 15 September 1928, NAI 1088/800/3.
136 N.W. O'Brien to Henry Kennedy, 22 September 1928, NAI 1088/800/3.
137 Daly, *The First Department*, 140.
138 'The Future of the IAC', *IAC Bulletin*, 1.12 (September 1930), 1–3 (p. 2).
139 Ó Fathartaigh, *Irish Agriculture Nationalised*, 84.

140 Report of the Agricultural Commission, 3, NAI AGF/2005/68/401.

141 IAOS, *Annual Report, 1922*, 17.

142 Evidence of H.F. Norman to Agricultural Commission, 23 May 1923, NAI AGF/2005/68/164.

143 *Rules of the Valentia Island Agricultural Bank* (Dublin: Irish Agricultural Wholesale Society, n.d.), 3, NAI RFS/SA/374/A, Valentia Island Agricultural Bank, Kerry.

144 Evidence of H.F. Norman, 23 May 1923, NAI AGF/2005/68/164.

145 Evidence of H.F. Norman, NAI AGF/2005/68/164.

146 Horace Plunkett, *Ireland in the New Century: with an Epilogue in Answer to Some Critics* (London: John Murray, 1905), 210.

147 Evidence of Rev T.A. Finlay, NAI AGF/2005/68/58.

148 Evidence of W.P. Clifford, NAI AGF/2005/68/35.

149 Evidence of R.A. Anderson, NAI AGF/2005/68/6.

150 Evidence of H.F. Norman, NAI AGF/2005/68/164.

151 *Ardfert Society* v *Jane Dowling*, 11 April 1922, KLHA, O'Connell Papers.

152 N.W. O'Brien, Report of Visit, 14 June 1924, NAI 1088/798/5.

153 Evidence of Rev. T.A. Finlay, NAI/AGF/2005/68/58.

154 Evidence of H.F. Norman, NAI/AGF/2005/68/164.

155 Report of the Agricultural Commission, 42–43, NAI/AGF/2005/68/401.

156 Report of the Agricultural Commission, 44, NAI AGF/2005/86/401.

157 Anderson, *With Horace Plunkett*, 251.

158 C.C. Riddall and H.F. Norman Correspondence to Department of Agriculture, re Memo, 'Agricultural Credit', 5 August 1925, NAI AGF/92/3/879.

159 Newtownsandes Co-operative Credit Society Correspondence File, NAI/1088/751/3.

160 Edmond Mulivihill to O'Connor Miley, 1 July 1925, NAI RFS/SA/403/B.

161 John Byrne, Ballymacelligott to Dr Smith, Secretary, Department of Agriculture, June 1925, NAI 1088/70/2.

162 R.A. Anderson to Dr Smith, 9 December 1925; Smith to Anderson, 12 December 1925, NAI 1088/70/2.

163 Department of Agriculture Memo, 'Agricultural Credit', 5 August 1925, NAI 92/3/879.

164 Dr Smith to R.A. Anderson, 23 December 1925, 1, 24 and 30 March, 1926, NAI 1088/70/2.

165 C.C. Riddall, Reports on Ballymacelligott Co-operative Credit Society, 4, 17 and 18 February 1926, NAI 1088/70/2.

166 R.A. Anderson to John Byrne, 7 September 1925, NAI 1088/70/2.

167 Dr Smith to H.F. Norman, 7 December 1925, NAI 1088/70/2.

168 Robert E. Kennedy, *The Irish: Emigration, Marriage and Fertility* (London: University of California Press, 1973), 207–208.

169 IAOS, *Annual Report, 1931*, 16.

170 Ó Gráda, *A Rocky Road*, 145.

171 Anderson, *With Horace Plunkett*, 260–261.

172 J.P. Colbert, 'The Banking and Currency System', in Bulmer Hobson (ed.), *Saorstát Éireann: Official Handbook* (Dublin: Talbot Press, 1932), 97–108 (p. 103); Daly, *The First Department*, 137.

173 IAOS, *Annual Report, 1931*, 16; Patrick Bolger, *The Irish Co-operative Movement: Its History and Development* (Dublin: Institute of Public Administration, 1877), 179.

174 Bulmer Hobson, 'Introduction', *Saorstat Eireann: Official Handbook* (Dublin: Talbot Press, 1932), 15–16.

175 Joseph Hanly, 'Agriculture', *Saorstat Eireann: Official Handbook* (Dublin: Talbot Press, 1932), 115–127 (p. 115).

176 Hanly, 'Agriculture', 125–127.

177 T.C., 'Review of "The National Ideal"', *Studies*, 21.83 (1932) 499–500 (p. 500).

178 Joseph Hanly, *The National Ideal: A Practical Exposition of True Nationality Appertaining to Ireland* (Dublin: Dollard Printinghouse, 1931), 270–271.

179 Brian Girvin, 'The Republicanisation of Irish Society, 1932–48', *A New History of Ireland, Volume VII: Ireland 1921–1984*, ed. by J.R. Hill (Oxford: Oxford University Press, 2003), 127–160 (p. 153); Michel Peillon, 'Interest Groups and the State in the Republic of Ireland', *Irish Society: Sociological Perspectives*, ed. by Patrick Clancy, Sheelagh Drudy, Kathleen Lynch and Liam O'Dowd (Dublin: Institute of Public Administration, 1995), 358–378 (pp. 368–370).

180 Joseph Johnston, *The Nemesis of Economic Nationalism and Other Lectures in Applied Economics* (London: P.S. King and Son Ltd, 1934), 94.

181 Tom Garvin, *Preventing the Future: Why Was Ireland So Poor For So Long?* (Dublin: Gill & Macmillan, 2004), 145.

182 Lee, *Ireland*, 113–115.

183 Daly, *The First Department*, 141.

184 O'Brien, 'Patrick Hogan', 360–361.

185 Ó Gráda, *A Rocky Road*, 144–145.

186 IAOS, *Annual Report, 1934*, 7.

187 Horace Plunkett Foundation, *Agricultural Co-operation: in its Application to the Industry, the Business, and the Life of the Farmer in the British Empire* (London: George Routledge and Sons, 1925), 4.

188 A Friend, 'The Home-coming of Æ', *Irish Times*, 22 July 1935, 6.

Conclusion

When he collected the Nobel Prize for literature in 1922, the poet W.B. Yeats recalled a 'moment of supernatural insight' in the late nineteenth century when he became certain that 'Ireland was to be like soft wax for years to come'.[1] The arrival of many cultural, political and social movements at this time highlighted how different people and groups expended significant energy as they devised various projects to modernise Ireland. As a primary participant in the Irish cultural revival, Yeats saw that an opportunity to wield cultural and intellectual influence over an emerging Irish nation had presented itself. He approached this work from the perspective of one who believed the creation of a distinct national literature nurtured Irish character and culture. In doing so, he placed himself amid the social and cultural experimentation that took place in the decades that preceded independence, and which helped define the institutions that made up the Irish Free State. What Yeats attempted through his literary work, Plunkett and his supporters attempted through their promotion of a new form of economics. The Irish co-operative movement represented one of the most important movements in this national process as it aimed to revitalise Irish character with its economic interventions. In this way the Irish Agricultural Organisation Society (IAOS) exercised a crucial influence over the form taken by the Irish nation-state as its leaders, organisers and members came together to mould the 'soft wax' of Irish society.

Historians have long argued over how the political conflict between nationalists and unionists formed the dominant feature of the 'Irish Question'.[2] A focus upon the co-operative movement repositions social and economic anxieties at the heart of early twentieth century Irish political discourse, thus emphasising a central, yet overlooked, component of the 'Irish Question'. The Irish nation-state did not emerge fully formed out of the tense political negotiations that led to the acceptance, and collapse, of a Home Rule settlement for the country nor did it owe its character and institutions mainly to the violent experiences of war and revolution. Instead, critical ideas about the nation emanated from the sphere of economics and social organisation.

The mundane rhythms and experiences of everyday life also played a crucial part in this process. The practice of co-operation between citizens mattered as much as the effects of conflict. Through the gradual assimilation of its network of co-operative businesses built around creameries, credit societies and other forms of association, the IAOS helped to create a modern agrarian state. Many rivals contested the extension of co-operative businesses, but by the outbreak of the First World War, these societies played a central role in the organisation of rural work even if this occurred outside the official circuits of power. The ability of the movement to exert influence within the governmental structures of the Irish Free State reveals the significance attached to tracking the development of interstitial movements and ideologies in a larger process of nation-state building.

The co-operative movement's evolution in Ireland demonstrated long social and cultural continuities. The establishment of the IAOS in the late nineteenth century led to a considered response by social reformers to long-term and tumultuous social adjustments instigated by the Great Famine. Throughout the second half of the nineteenth century, the rural economy was characterised by emigration, which complemented a move from subsistence farming to more commercialised agricultural practices.[3] As Irish farmers were integrated into a global capitalist economy, the rise of international competition left them vulnerable. Informed by economic developments in Britain and Denmark, figures like Horace Plunkett concluded that co-operative societies offered farmers one way of mediating the significant transitions experienced throughout the nineteenth and twentieth centuries.

Co-operative leaders such as Plunkett, Æ, Robert Anderson, Fr Finlay and Ellice Pilkington conceived of Ireland as a primarily rural nation. Through the proliferation of a wealth of social and economic knowledge in the form of lectures, pamphlets, reports, articles, correspondence and books, these people helped to perpetuate the image of Ireland as a rural civilisation that became firmly embedded within a popular imagination inside the country and abroad.[4] This vision captured the imaginations of Irish policymakers, citizens and artists, and established the long-term blueprint for Irish economic development over the course of the early twentieth century. Co-operation shaped a state system that survived the political transition from British to Irish rule and even more, foreign observers paid attention to the rural economic experiment that took place in Ireland. What happened in Kerry, Limerick, Donegal and Sligo mattered to farmers in the United States, Finland and England and helped to chart a course for similar efforts to stimulate rural development elsewhere.

The work of state building in Ireland occurred gradually and in a variety of settings. The relationship between the population and the co-operative movement represented an important component in this process. Viewing economic development at the level of individual societies illustrates a complex sequence of interactions between managers, IAOS officials and organisers around the co-operative society.

These interactions manifested a type of modernised rural district desired by the co-operative movement's leaders, a goal which led to a continuous self-disciplining of farmers. At a local level, the impetus behind state formation in Ireland can be located in the interactions between expert and farmer that took place in farms and creameries. On the level of national politics, the co-operative movement was relevant to the state-building process through the IAOS. This body contributed to parliamentary inquiries and commissions, and helped to frame debates between agricultural policymakers and experts. Co-operative ideas were located in a range of important texts. IAOS annual reports and Sinn Féin-penned treatises shaped a discourse of Irish identity and development. In these ways, the co-operative movement shaped the *mentalités* of Irish administrators and helped to embed the idea that economic progress came from the pursuit of agrarian economic strategy, and one in which co-operative societies were utilised in pursuit of that objective.

By pursuing its own conception of modernisation, the co-operative movement attempted to bring about a new type of Irish population, economy and society. Led by the IAOS, activists sought to embed a co-operative form of organisation in the countryside that shaped economic arrangements and gave farmers mutualised and democratic control over their own industry. Indeed, co-operative organisers and engineers played a critical role as they literally transformed the landscape of rural Ireland when they worked to convert the IAOS's vision of an ideal countryside into reality. Ultimately, the Co-operative Commonwealth remained an unrealised utopian ideal. The co-operative movement in Ireland stayed confined to the countryside and failed to make significant advances into urban centres. In the IAOS's rhetoric, the interests of Irish consumers remained subordinated to that of producers. The refusal of co-operative societies to co-ordinate their activities with other local co-operatives was a great limitation to the co-operative project. Instead, inter-co-operative rivalry persisted as an entrenched feature of economic activity in Ireland.

This picture suggests that the attempts by the IAOS to embed its blueprint for the organisation of Irish society proved ineffective, or at best, highly limited. Despite its limitations, and perhaps even because of them, the co-operative movement's interventions proved significant for the long-term development of Ireland, a finding that contradicts prevailing analyses of the movement in this period.[5] The rural community provided the crucible within which co-operative reformers tried to engineer their project of improvement. Co-operative societies helped spread new technologies throughout the rural economy. The spread of creamery separators transformed Irish dairy production and provided the means for dairy farmers to remain competitive with their international counterparts. The technology reorganised the pattern of work with milk delivered to the creamery on a daily basis. Dairying moved outside of the home with an attendant conse-quence in terms of the gendered nature of work as butter making shifted from a feminine occupation to a masculine one. The creamery represented a new social and economic hub around which modern rural communities coalesced and relied for their sustainability. It was no accident that Crown forces targeted co-operative creameries when they attempted to punish a local community for their support of Republican activity.

Much of the co-operative movement's work occurred at a grass-roots level. Co-operative societies redrew local fields of relations wherever their influence extended. This allowed the IAOS to occupy a unique position, whereby the cumulative experience of local organisation informed its role on the national level. This material of local politics informed the terms of national debate. Consequently, the IAOS succeeded in converting its support in the countryside into substantial influence on the national stage. While the political landscape in Ireland underwent a considerable change across the period reviewed, the co-operative movement managed to retain a position of strategic importance between the state and communities. Although this position remained fragile, the vision of a rural civilisation propagated by the co-operative movement contributed to a 'rural fundamentalism' that persisted within the political culture throughout the twentieth century. This Irish rural fundamentalism emphasised the necessity of agriculture to provide the basis of national prosperity.[6] The established foundations of rural communities and the prioritisation of agricultural development allowed the co-operative movement to attain a prominent platform to impact upon the direction of socio-economic policy beyond 1922.

The outbreak of the First World War and the subsequent War of Independence that culminated in the establishment of the Irish Free State in 1922, cemented political change in Ireland. The events of these years represented a significant rupture in terms of the demands made upon farmers. These events also marked a definite change in the role played by co-operative societies in the countryside. These societies and their organisers helped to manage the new burdens placed upon agriculturalists during the First World War as they equipped farmers with the tools needed to adapt to new production methods and mitigate the rising cost of living. Violent events prevented many creameries from functioning during the revolutionary situation that prevailed during 1919–21. However, the network of societies proved resilient enough to endure such challenges and remained a significant fixture in the rural economy.

It has been argued that by coming through challenging circumstances, the co-operative movement became 'nationalised' in the sense that supporters of Irish political autonomy accepted the presence of co-operative societies in the Irish economy. This study has examined Ireland at a specific point where ideas with international antecedents became 'greened' and part of a distinctive Irish critique of British rule. These revolutionary years represent the moment wherein the leaders of the co-operative movement became political insiders after 1922. The character of rural society that prevailed in the Irish Free State during the 1920s and 1930s owed a great deal to the distinct features promoted by the IAOS ever since 1894.

Similarly, the co-operative movement demonstrated the limiting influence of governmental factors upon its own development. Although the movement shaped the generation of nationalists that ascended to office in the 1920s, this process proved to be a dialectical one. In order to curry favour, co-operative experts and activists acquiesced to the shifting demands and expectations made by those who wielded political influence. The IAOS's desire to retain funding meant that a loss of autonomy was necessary. Sinn Féin's increased power after December 1918 saw members of Dáil Éireann become involved in the workings of the IAOS committee. However, a willingness to mould its developmental template in the 1920s, to wield influence with the Department of Agriculture, was best illustrated by its abandoning a commitment to promote the interests of small farmers. Instead, a tacit agreement between the IAOS and the government to ensure that larger farmers remained productive and competitive was the most urgent priority of an economic policy constructed in the midst of an economic slump and civil war. In return, the IAOS received preferential treatment and the network of co-operative creameries and credit societies formed an important, though not a formal statutory element of the fabric of Irish government.

Co-operative ideas were versatile. The intellectual legacy of co-operation is discernible in its influence over Irish nationalist thought. Just as adherents argued that co-operative solutions might be applied to a wide array of economic problems, co-operative ideas also proved rather promiscuous. As a movement led by an Anglo-Irish landlord whose initial political credentials were impeccably unionist, the adoption of co-operative ideas by separatist nationalists appears initially surprising. Yet these ideas held a great deal of intellectual purchase with Sinn Féin ideologues. That influence carried through to those who had attained official administrative power in Ireland by the 1920s. By exploring the intellectual development of the co-operative movement, it has been shown that the political economy of co-operation affected the development of Irish nationalism in the early twentieth century.

One way in which Sinn Féin nationalists differentiated themselves from their constitutionalist rivals who dominated Irish politics was in the attitude towards co-operative societies. Sinn Féin's appropriation of a pro-co-operative position positioned the party as sympathetic to the socio-economic concerns of the farming population. Before the First World War, Sinn Féin had been the preserve of an urban bourgeois intelligentsia. By the end of the war, Sinn Féin was reflecting the interests of the rural population. By displaying a more sympathetic attitude to co-operative organisation, and later implementing policies that relied upon a vibrant co-operative sector, the Irish nationalists who ascended to administrative power after 1922 reserved a special status for co-operative societies within their economic planning. A pragmatic approach to government in the 1920s encouraged reliance by the Cumann na nGaedheal administration upon co-operative societies. However, a growing consensus among Sinn Féin intellectuals who viewed co-operatives as *national* economic instruments suggests a degree of sincerity in their support among some nationalists. Nevertheless, whether ideological or pragmatic, co-operative societies were utilised as important governmental instruments.

Throughout the twentieth century, the IAOS continued to direct the dairying industry in Ireland. Henry Kennedy remained at the IAOS from 1926 until he retired in 1963. An organisational conservatism characterised Kennedy's tenure as he prioritised IAOS support for creameries, but he also received criticism for his preference to support stronger societies over smaller, less established ones.[7] A lack of dynamism led the Minister of Agriculture to appoint Joseph Knapp, the Administrator of the American Farmer Co-operative Service based at the US Department of Agriculture, to conduct an independent review of the IAOS to find out what 'might be done to strengthen it [the co-operative movement] and to increase its influence in the agricultural sphere generally'.[8] The main problem that faced the movement was one of education. For Knapp the 'lack of emphasis on cooperative business education since World War I partially explains why the movement has not achieved greater success'.[9]

The shift away from the IAOS's educational mission came from the change in leadership after independence, but also reflected that from the First World War onwards, co-operators moved from one crisis to another as violence, economic depression and global warfare hamstrung efforts to explore new avenues of potential. Knapp believed that great work was needed to 'reinvigorate the IAOS' and restore it to the dynamic leadership role it displayed in its first three decades in order to ensure the movement remained in a position to meet the challenges offered by technological change and international competition. His main recommendations included more state funding for the IAOS, more responsibility granted to the IAOS in order to reorganise creameries once more, a replacement of the Dairy Disposal Company (DDC) with a co-operative body, and the need for the movement to diversify its agricultural business beyond dairying into crops and livestock farming.[10]

While the IAOS voted to accept the Knapp recommendations, no major reorganisation of the movement took place until Ireland's entry into the European Economic Community (EEC) in 1973. The effect on Irish agriculture was transformative as membership opened up a new European marketplace, but also meant greater competition for the UK market. Furthermore, the continued existence of the DDC as a player in the Irish dairy industry stood in contravention of European regulations that prohibited state participation in agriculture. In County Kerry, some of the co-operative creameries and the DDC-operated creameries made the decision to amalgamate into a larger regional organisation called Kerry Co-operative Limited. However, this process of amalgamation led to the public flotation of the organisation on the stock market and the ejection

of the co-operative ownership of the business. The establishment of Kerry Group
Plc in 1986 saw the emergence of a global food brand, but also saw an erosion
of the co-operative structures in a region that once underpinned the dairying
industry. After Kerry, other reorganised creamery businesses also diluted the
co-operative principles. Today, the Irish Co-operative Organisation Society (following the decision to re-name the IAOS in 1979) oversees the activities of the
different types of co-operatives at work in Ireland. The majority of these still
revolve around dairying and other agricultural businesses, but also include co-
operative water schemes, cattle breeding societies and other societies organised
for farm-oriented purposes.[11]

If traditional agricultural co-operation appeared to decline in more recent
years, other forms of co-operation have started to grow. The second half of the
twentieth century also witnessed a renaissance in the co-operative credit movement
as the end of the 1950s saw the establishment, followed by a rapid growth, of
the credit union movement. Nora Herlihy, a teacher from Ballydesmond; Séamus
MacEoin, a civil servant from Kilkenny; and Sean Forde, an employee of Peter
Kennedy Bakers, sought to counter the effects of poverty, unemployment and
moneylending on families which they witnessed in Dublin city. They opened a
small credit union and from there societies soon spread. The Irish League of
Credit Unions (ILCU) was formed in 1960 to co-ordinate the growth of these
societies across the island of Ireland. As of 2017, 389 active branches serve a
membership that totals about 2.9 million members.[12] In recent years, the regulation
of the credit union sector has become a contested issue between the ILCU and
the Central Bank of Ireland, with the latter attempting to reform the movement
into few much larger branches.[13] However, the success of the credit union movement in some small way represents a vindication of the aims of an earlier generation
of co-operators who attempted to institutionalise a form of credit supply that
sat outside the ordinary banking sector.

By tracing the influence of the co-operative movement upon the nationalist
project in Ireland, this book has argued that the political economy of nationalism
contained important co-operative ideas that carried a long-term influence upon
Irish development. The type of institutions that emerged in Ireland during the
late nineteenth and early twentieth centuries came out of acute political crises
and conflict; but equally, other long-term factors also informed this process of
state development. The co-operative movement maintained a complex and shifting
relationship with Ireland's state institutions and exerted significant influence over
the character of the rural population. By tracking the development of organisations,
regions and practices that receive less attention than the overtly political conflicts
and personalities, a more nuanced understanding about the nature of the Irish
state can be uncovered. As Ireland moved into the twenty-first century, the effects
of economic liberalisation from the late 1950s saw the co-operative presence in
the agrarian economy roll back. However, the popularity of the credit union

movement, the rise of consumer co-operatives such as the Dublin Food Co-operative and Quay Co-op in Cork, and brewing co-operatives such as Boundary Brewing in Belfast and the Dublin Brewing Co-operative suggest that the model still has an important part to play in imagining how the Irish economy might develop once again, following an extended period of economic austerity.

At the start of the twentieth century, the existence of a robust co-operative movement in Ireland that articulated a distinct vision for national development mattered. The IAOS saw its primary role 'to render self-help effective through organisation, in the working lives of the agricultural population'.[14] The co-operative model became embedded in Ireland despite a wide range of challenges and shaped the conduct of agricultural business. A political economy of co-operation formed an important strand of a wider political culture by the time Ireland achieved independence. However, this political economy emerged as a product of its particular historical experiences. The experience of the Irish co-operative movement shows how social and economic debates, which looked beyond the moment when some form of political independence might be achieved, proved to be an important dynamic within the wider 'Irish Question'. This study has shown the importance of an integrated local and national analysis, highlighting how the modernisation project that the co-operative movement drove could articulate a version of an ideal national identity alongside a programme of long-term socio-economic development. By attempting to make Irish farmers into the co-operative subject, the IAOS left a long-lasting legacy inscribed into the institutions of the modern Irish state.

Notes

1 W.B. Yeats, *Autobiographies* (New York: Scribner, 1999), 169.
2 Paul Bew, *Ideology and the Irish Question: Ulster Unionism and Irish Nationalism, 1912–1916* (Oxford: Clarendon Press, 1994); Michael Laffan, *The Resurrection of Ireland: The Sinn Féin Party, 1916–1923* (Cambridge: Cambridge University Press, 1999).
3 Timothy W. Guinnane, *The Vanishing Irish: Households, Migration, and the Rural Economy in Ireland, 1850–1914* (Princeton, NJ: Princeton University Press, 1997).
4 Tara Stubbs, *American Literature and Irish Culture, 1910–55* (Manchester: Manchester University Press, 2013).
5 Giovanni Federico, *Feeding the World: An Economic History of Agriculture, 1800–2000* (Princeton: Princeton University Press, 2005), 136; Timothy W. Guinnane, 'A Failed Institutional Transplant: Raiffeisen's Credit Cooperatives in Ireland, 1894–1914', *Explorations in Economic History*, 31 (1994), 38–61; Cormac Ó Gráda, 'The Beginnings of the Irish Creamery System, 1880–1914', *Economic Review of History*, 30.2 (1977), 284–305.
6 Damian F. Hannan and Patrick Commins, 'The Significance of Small-Scale Landholders in Ireland's Socio-Economic Transformation', in *The Development of Industrial Society*

in Ireland, ed. by J.H. Goldthorpe and C.T. Whelan (Oxford: Oxford University Press, 1992), 79–104 (pp. 101–102).

7 Patrick Bolger, *The Irish Co-operative Movement: Its History and Development* (Dublin: Institute of Public Administration, 1877), 131–132.

8 Joseph Knapp, *An Appraisement of Agricultural Co-operation in Ireland* (Dublin: Stationery Office, 1964), 7.

9 Knapp, *Agricultural Co-operation in Ireland*, 49–50.

10 Knapp, *Agricultural Co-operation in Ireland*, 108–109.

11 James J. Kennelly, *The Kerry Way: The History of Kerry Group, 1972–2000* (Dublin: Oak Tree Press, 2001); Maurice Henry, Pat Bolger and Trevor West (eds), *Irish Co-operative Organisation Society: Fruits of a Century: An Illustrated Centenary History, 1894–1999* (Dublin: Irish Co-operative Organisation Society, 1994); Irish Co-operative Organisation Society, *122nd Annual Report and Accounts 2016* (Dublin: Irish Co-operative Organisation Society, 2016).

12 www.creditunion.ie/whoweare/aboutus/abouttheirishleagueofcreditunions/ [accessed 23 March 2018].

13 Conor Pope, 'Credit Unions Call for Credit Bank Showdown to be Held in Public', *Irish Times*, 14 October 2013, www.irishtimes.com/business/credit-unions-call-for-central-bank-showdown-to-be-held-in-public-1.1558098 [accessed 23 March 2013].

14 IAOS, *Annual Report, 1915*, 25.

Bibliography

Primary sources

Co-operative College, Manchester
Co-operative News
Co-operative Wholesale Society Limited, *Annuals*

Dáil Debates
Blythe, Ernest, 'National Land Bank', *Dáil Eireann Debates*, Volume 16.21, 20 July 1926, http://oireachtasdebates.oireachtas.ie/debates%20authoring/debateswebpack.nsf/takes/dail1926072000039?opendocument
Dáil Éireann, 'Democratic Programme of Dáil Éireann', *Parliamentary Debates*, Volume 1, 21 January 1919, http://oireachtasdebates.oireachtas.ie/debates%20authoring/debateswebpack.nsf/takes/dail191901210001l

Dublin Diocesan Archive
Archbishop William Walsh Papers

Galway Diocesan Archive
Bishop MacCormack Papers, Notebook

Hansard Debates
House of Commons Debates 28 November 1906 vol. 166 cc65–67, http://hansard.millbanksystems.com/commons/1906/nov/28/subsidies-to-the-irish-agricultural

House of Commons Parliamentary Papers
HCPP [Cd. 1749], *Committee on Butter Regulations, Final Report* (1903).
HCPP [Cd. 3572], *DATI Report of the Departmental Committee of Inquiry* (1907).
HCPP [Cd. 3574], *DATI Minutes of Evidence Taken Before the Departmental Committee of Inquiry* (1907).
HCPP [Cd. 5092], *Department of Agriculture and Technical Instruction for Ireland. Report of the Departmental Committee on the Irish Butter Industry* (1910).
HCPP [Cd. 5093], *Departmental Committee on the Irish Butter Industry. Minutes of Evidence, Appendices and Index* (1910).

HCPP [Cd. 6735], *Copy of Treasury Letter, dated 1st April 1913, respecting the conditions on which a Grant will be made to the Society, from the Development Fund, Vice-Regal Commission on the Irish Milk Supply* (1913).

HCPP [Cd. 7375], Department of Agriculture and Technical Instruction for Ireland. *Report of the Departmental Committee on Agricultural Credit in Ireland* (1914).

HCPP [Cd. 8016], Department of Agriculture and Technical Instruction for Ireland. Report of the Departmental Committee on Food Production in Ireland (1914–16).

HCPP [Cmd. 808], *Department of Agriculture and Technical Instruction for Ireland, Report of the Departmental Committee on the Decline of Dairying in Ireland* (1920).

Irish Military Archives

Bessie Cahill Witness Statement, 1143
Thomas McEllistrim Witness Statement, 0882

Kerry Local History Archive, Kerry County Library, Tralee

Dr John O'Connell Legal Papers
Listowel Rural District Council Minute Book

Lexis Library

'*McEllistrim v Ballymacelligott* Co-operative Agricultural and Dairy Society Limited [1918–19] All E R Rep Ext 1294', in *Lexis Library*, www.lexisnexis.com/uk/legal/results/enhdocview.do?docLinkInd=true&ersKey=23_T18046105861&format=GNBFULL&startDocNo=0&resultsUrlKey=0_T18046105862&backKey=20_T18046105863&csi=279847&docNo=1&scrollToPosition=0

Limerick Diocesan Archive

BI/ET/K, Bishop Edward O'Dwyer Papers

National Archives of Ireland

1088/2, Abbeydorney Co-operative Dairy Society Ltd., General Correspondence Files
1088/70, Ballymacelligott Co-operative A&D Society, General Correspondence Files
1088/751, Newtownsandes Co-operative Society, General Correspondence Files
1088/752, Newtownsandes Co-operative Credit Society, General Correspondence Files
1088/798, Rathmore Co-operative Society, General Correspondence Files
1088/800, Rattoo Co-operative Society, General Correspondence Files
AGF/92/2/1573, Creamery Managers
AGF/92/3/570, Conference with Dairy Produce Inspectors, 29 September–2 October 1925
AGF/92/3/655, Dairy Disposal Company Ltd; Re Inspection and Registration of Tubrid Creamery, Ardfert, County Kerry, under Dairy Produce Act 1924
AGF/92/3/879, Riddall and Norman Correspondence to Department of Agriculture, re. Agricultural Credit
AGF/2005/68, Agricultural Commission, 1922–24, Report and Evidence
AGF/2005/68/6, Evidence of R.A. Anderson to the Agricultural Commission
AGF/2005/68/35, Evidence of W.P. Clifford to the Agricultural Commission
AGF/2005/68/80, Evidence of T.P. Gill to the Commission on Agriculture

AGF/2005/68/95, Evidence of D. Hegarty, Secretary of the Irish Creamery Managers' Association, to the Agricultural Commission

AGF/2005/68/164, Evidence of H.F. Norman to the Agricultural Commission

AGF/2005/68/401, Report of the Agricultural Commission (Majority and Minority Reports)

AGF/2005/82/1495, Proposed re-organisation scheme of IAOS, 1924–28

AGF/2005/82/1497, Confidential Report, Reorganisation of the IAOS

BR/ROS/12, Ballaghderreen Co-operative Agricultural and Dairy Society Papers

FIN/1/3086, Development Fund: as to payment of instalment of grants due to the Irish Agricultural Organisation Society, March 1922–April 1924

RFS/SA/374/A, Valentia Island Agricultural Bank, Kerry

RFS/SA/403/B, Newtownsandes Credit Society

National Library of Ireland

DATI, Second Annual General Report of the Department, 1901–02 (Dublin: His Majesty's Stationery Office, 1902).

DATI, Seventh Annual Report of the Department, 1906–07 (Dublin: His Majesty's Stationery Office, 1908).

DATI, Eighth Annual Report of the Department, 1907–08 (Dublin: His Majesty's Stationery Office, 1908).

DATI, Eighteenth Annual General Report of the Department, 1917–18 (Dublin: His Majesty's Stationery Office 1919).

Horace Plunkett Papers, Correspondence.

Horace Plunkett Papers, Diaries.

IAC, *Report of the Committee to the Members for the Year ended December 31st, 1928* (Dublin: Browne and Nolan, n.d.).

IAOS, *Annual Reports.*

ITGWU, Return to Registrar of Friendly Societies 1917–25, Ms. 27,034.

The National Land Bank: Its Constitution and its Aims (*c.* 1921).

The Society of the United Irishwomen, Annual Report, 1912 (Wexford: The People, 1913).

Newspapers

Anglo-Celt
Evening Independent [St Petersburg, Florida]
Freeman's Journal
IAC Bulletin
Irish Economist
Irish Homestead
Irish Times
Kerry Sentinel
The Kerryman
Manchester Guardian
New York Times
The Observer
Skibbereen Eagle
Sligo Independent

Southern Star
The Times
Weekly Irish Times
Workers' Republic

Public Record Office of Northern Ireland
D4131/M/11A, Josslyn Gore-Booth Papers, Drumcliffe Co-operative Dairy Society and Related Papers.
D4131/M/11B, Josslyn Gore-Booth Collection, Drumcliffe Co-operative Dairy Society and Related Papers.
D/4131/M/14, Josslyn Gore-Booth Collection, IAOS Papers.
D/4131/M/15, Josslyn Gore-Booth Collection, IAOS Papers.
FIN/18/2/332, Ministry of Agriculture Grant to the Ulster Agricultural Organisation Society.

Published primary material
Æ, *A Plea for Justice: Being a Demand for a Public Enquiry into the Attacks Upon the Co-operative Societies in Ireland* (Dublin: Irish Homestead, 1920).
Æ [George William Russell], *The National Being: Some Thoughts on an Irish Polity* (Dublin: Maunsel and Co., 1916).
American Commission to Investigate Agricultural Credit and Cooperation, *Agricultural Cooperation and Rural Credit in Europe* (Washington: Government Printing Office, 1913).
Anderson, R.A., 'Agricultural Co-operation in Ireland', in *Department of Agriculture and Technical Instruction*, ed., *Ireland: Industrial and Agricultural* (Dublin: Brown and Nolan, Limited, 1902), 218–234.
Anderson, R.A., 'The IAOS and the Food Problem', *Studies*, 6.21 (1917), 8–14.
Anderson, R.A., *With Horace Plunkett in Ireland* (London: Macmillan and Co., 1935).
Birmingham, George A, 'Politics in the Nude', *Irish Review*, 1.10 (1911), 469–476.
Campbell, J.R., 'The War and Irish Agriculture', *Department of Agriculture and Technical Instruction Journal*, 15.1 (1914), 10–19.
Commission of Inquiry into the Resources and Industries of Ireland, *Report on Dairying and the Dairy Industry, March, 1922* (Dublin: Commission of Inquiry into the Resources and Industries of Ireland, 1922).
Coyne, William P., 'Preface', in *Department of Agriculture and Technical Instruction*, ed., *Ireland: Industrial and Agricultural* (Dublin: Brown and Nolan, Limited, 1902).
DATI, *Conference on the Poultry Industry, Dublin, May, 1911: Report of Proceedings* (London: HMSO, 1911).
de Blacam, Aodh, *Towards the Republic: A Study of New Ireland's Social and Political Aims* (Dublin: T. Kiersey, 1918).
de Blacam, Aodh, *What Sinn Féin Stands For: The Irish Republican Movement: Its History, Aims and Ideals Examined as the Their Significance to the World* (Dublin: Mellifont Press Limited, 1921).
Department of Agriculture of Saorstát Éireann, *Saorstát Éireann, Agriculture: A Note on Some Outstanding Features of the Irish Free State's Agricultural Resources* (Dublin: Department of Agriculture, Saorstát Éireann, 1928).

Editor, '[Untitled Introduction]', *The Irish Review*, 1.1 (1911), 1–6.

Figgis, Darrell, *The Economic Case for Independence* (Dublin: Maunsel and Co., 1920).

Figgis, Darrell, *The Gaelic State in the Past and Future or 'The Crown of the Nation'* (Dublin: Maunsel & Co. Ltd, 1917).

Figgis, Darrell, *George W. Russell: A Study of a Man and a Nation* (New York: Dodd, Mead and Company, 1916).

Finlay, T.A., 'Agricultural Co-operation in Ireland', *Economic Journal*, 6.22 (1896), 204–211.

Gallagher, Patrick (Paddy the Cope), *My Story*, revised edn (Dungloe: Templecrone Co-operative Society, n.d.).

Gebhard, Hannes, *Co-operation in Finland* (London: Williams and Norgate, 1916).

Gill, T.P., 'Address to the Council of Agriculture', *Department of Agriculture and Technical Instruction Journal*, 20.1 (1919), 12–19.

Houston, D., *The Milk Supply of Dublin: Report of a Bacteriological Investigation of the City of Dublin Milk Supply* (Dublin: The Co-operative Reference Library, 1918).

IAOS, *Home Rule in the Dairy* (Dublin: Irish Agricultural Organisation Society, 1903).

Labour Party [Great Britain], *Report of the Labour Commission to Ireland* (London: Caledonian Press, 1921).

Lloyd, Henry Demarest, *Labor Copartnership: Notes of a Visit to Co-operative Workshops, Factories and Farms in Great Britain and Ireland, in which Employer, Employé, and Consumer Share in Ownership, Management, and Results* (London: Harper & Brothers Publishers, 1898).

Moore, George, *Hail and Farewell! Ave, Salve, Vale* (Gerrards Cross, Bucks.: Colin Smythe Limited, 1985 [1911]).

O'Brien, Cruise, *Co-operative Mills and Bakeries*, Series: Miscellaneous Publications No. 2 (Dublin: Co-operative Reference Library, 1918).

O'Flanagan, Rev. M., *Co-operation* (Dublin: Cumann Léigheacht an Phobail, 1922).

Paul-Dubois, L, *Contemporary Ireland* (Dublin: Maunsel and Co., 1908).

Pilkington, Ellice, 'United Irishwomen – Their Work', in Horace Plunkett, Ellice Pilkington and George Russell (eds), *The United Irishwomen: Their Place, Work and Ideals* (Dublin: Maunsel and Co., 1911), 19–35.

Plunkett, Horace, 'The Aims of the Co-operative Movement (1894)', in Declan Kiberd and P.J. Mathews (eds), *Handbook of the Irish Revival: An Anthology of Irish Cultural and Political Writings 1891–1922* (Dublin: Abbey Theatre Press, 2015), 90.

Plunkett, Horace Curzon, *Co-operative Dairying: an Address to the Farmers of the Dairy Districts of Ireland* (Manchester: Co-operative Union Limited, 1890).

Plunkett, Horace Curzon, 'Co-operative Stores for Ireland', *Nineteenth Century*, 24.139 (1888), 410–418.

Plunkett, Horace, *A Country Life Institute: A Suggested Irish-American Contribution to Rural Progress* (Dublin: Plunkett House, 1909).

Plunkett, Horace, *The Crisis in Irish Rural Progress: Being Three Letters Reprinted from* The Times (London: John Parkinson Bland, 1912).

Plunkett, Horace, *Ireland in the New Century: with an Epilogue in Answer to Some Critics* (London: John Murray, 1905).

Plunkett, Horace, *Noblesse Oblige: An Irish Rendering* (Dublin: Maunsel and Co., 1908).

Plunkett, Horace, 'The Recess Committee and Remedial Legislation for Ireland', *The Economic Journal,* 7.25 (1897), 131–136.

Plunkett, Horace, 'The Relations between Organized Self Help and State Aid in Ireland', *The North American Review,* 67.503 (1898), 497–498.

Plunkett, Horace, 'Rural Regeneration', *North American Review,* 214.791 (1921), 470–476.

Plunkett, Horace, *The Trend of Co-operation in Great Britain and Ireland* (Dublin; n.p., 1902).

Rashad, Ibrahim, *An Egyptian in Ireland* (n.a.: privately printed by the author, 1920).

Russell, George (Æ), 'The Self-Supporting Community', *Studies,* 7.26 (1918), 301–306.

Russell, George William, *The National Being: Some Thoughts on an Irish Polity* (Dublin: Maunsel and Co., 1916).

Russell, George W., 'The Problem of Rural Life', *Irish Review* 1.8 (1911), 365–372.

Russell, Ruth, *What's the Matter with Ireland?* (New York: Devin-Adair Co., 1920).

Shemus, 'Tales of a Kerry Creamery', in H.F. Norman (ed.), *A Celtic Christmas: The Irish Homestead Christmas Number* (Dublin: Irish Agricultural Organisation Society, 1898), 17–18.

Sinn Féin, [*Letter to Various Cumanns on Prospects of Co-operative Societies in Ireland*] (Dublin: Sinn Féin, 1919).

Smith-Gordon, Lionel, 'Agricultural Organisation in Ireland', *The Economic Journal,* 27.107 (1917), 355–363.

Smith-Gordon, Lionel, *The Irish Milk Supply* (Dublin: Co-operative Reference Library, 1919).

Smith-Gordon, Lionel, *The Place of Banking in the National Programme* (Dublin: Cumann Léigheacht an Phobail, 1921).

Smith-Gordon, Lionel, and Cruise O'Brien, *Co-operation in Denmark,* Series: International Co-operative Series, vol. 4 (Manchester: Co-operative Union Limited, 1919).

Smith-Gordon, Lionel, and Cruise O'Brien, *Co-operation in Ireland* (Manchester: Co-operative Union Limited, 1921).

Smith-Gordon, Lionel, and Cruise O'Brien, *Ireland's Food in War Time,* Series: Miscellaneous Publications No. 1 (Dublin: Co-operative Reference Library, 1914).

Smith-Gordon, Lionel, and Laurence S. Staples, *Rural Reconstruction in Ireland: A Record of Co-operative Organization* (London: P.S. King and Son, 1917).

Ulster Imperialist, 'An Appreciation of the Situation', *Irish Review,* 2.13 (1912), 1–11.

Wolff, Henry W., *People's Banks: A Record of Social and Economic Success* (London: P.S. King and Son, 1910, 3rd edn [originally published 1893]).

Published online

Rerum Novarum: Encyclical of Pope Leo XIII on Capital and Labour, http://w2.vatican.va/content/leo-xiii/en/encyclicals/documents/hf_l-xiii_enc_15051891_rerum-novarum.html

Saorstát Éireann, 'Creamery Act, 1928', *Irish Statute Book,* 26 (1928), www.irishstatutebook.ie/1928/en/act/pub/0026/print.html.

Saorstát Éireann, 'Dairy Produce Act, 1924', *Irish Statute Book,* 58 (1924), www.irishstatutebook.ie/1924/en/act/pub/0058/print.html.

Secondary sources

Allen, Nicholas, *George Russell (AE) and the New Ireland, 1905–1930* (Dublin: Four Courts Press, 2003).

Allen, Nicholas, *Modernism, Ireland and Civil War* (Cambridge: Cambridge University Press, 2009).

Arensberg, Conrad M, *The Irish Countryman*, 2nd edn (Garden City, New York: The Natural History Press, 1968).

Arensberg, Conrad M., and Solon T Kimball, *Family and Community in Ireland* (Gloucester Massachusetts: Peter Smith, 1961).

Augusteijn, Joost (ed.), *The Irish Revolution, 1913–1923* (Houndmills, Basingstoke: Palgrave, 2002).

Barnet, Margaret L., *British Food Policy during the First World War* (London: George Allen & Unwin, 1985).

Bell, Jonathan and Mervyn Watson, *A History of Irish Farming, 1750–1950* (Dublin: Four Courts Press, 2009).

Bew, Paul, *Enigma: A New Life of Charles Stewart Parnell* (Dublin: Gill & Macmillan, 2012).

Bew, Paul, *Ideology and the Irish Question: Ulster Unionism and Irish Nationalism, 1912–1916* (Oxford: Clarendon Press, 1994).

Birchall, Johnston, *The International Co-operative Movement* (Manchester: Manchester University Press, 1997).

Black, Lawrence, and Nicole Robertson (eds), *Consumerism and the Co-operative Movement in Modern British History: Taking Stock* (Manchester: Manchester University Press, 2009).

Bolger, Patrick, *The Irish Co-operative Movement: Its History and Development* (Dublin: Institute of Public Administration, 1977).

Bourke, Joanna, *Husbandry to Housewifery: Women, Economic Change and Housework in Ireland, 1890–1914* (Oxford: Clarendon Press, 1993).

Bradley, Dan, *Farm Labourers: Irish Struggle, 1900–1976* (Belfast: Athol Books, 1988).

Brearton, Fran, *The Great War in Irish Poetry: W.B. Yeats to Michael Longley* (Oxford: Oxford University Press, 2000).

Breathnach, Ciara, *The Congested Districts Board of Ireland, 1891–1923: Poverty and Development in the West of Ireland* (Dublin: Four Courts Press, 2005).

Bull, Philip, *Land, Politics and Nationalism: A Study of the Irish Land Question* (Dublin: Gill and Macmillan, 1996).

Byrne, L.P., *Twenty-One Years of the IAWS, 1897–1918* (Dublin: IAWS, 1919).

Campbell, Colm, *Emergency Law in Ireland, 1918–1925* (Oxford: Clarendon Press, 1994).

Campbell, Fergus, *The Irish Establishment, 1879–1914* (Oxford: Oxford University Press, 2009).

Campbell, Fergus, *Land and Revolution: Nationalist Politics in the West of Ireland, 1891–1921* (Oxford: Oxford University Press, 2005).

Campbell, Fergus, and Kevin O'Shiel, 'The Last Land War? Kevin O'Shiel's Memoir of the Irish Revolution (1916–1921)', *Archivium Hibernicum*, 57 (2003), 155–200.

Chubb, Basil, *The Government and Politics of Ireland*, 3rd edn (London: Longman, 1992).

Clavin, Patricia, *Securing the World's Economy: The Reinvention of the League of Nations, 1920–1946* (Oxford: Oxford University Press, 2013).

Clune, Michael, 'The Work and the Report of the Recess Committee, 1895–6', *Studies,* 71.281 (1982), 72–84.

Colbert, J.P., 'The Banking and Currency System', in Bulmer Hobson (ed.), *Saorstát Éireann: Official Handbook* (Dublin: The Talbot Press, 1932), 97–108.

Collins, Michael, *The Path to Freedom* (Dublin: Talbot Press, 1922).

Connolly, James, *Labour in Ireland: Labour in Irish History; The Re-conquest of Ireland* (Dublin: Maunsel & Roberts Ltd, 1922).

Coolahan, John, *Irish Education: Its History and Structure* (Dublin: Institute of Public Administration, 1981).

Corcoran, Donal, *Freedom to Achieve Freedom: The Irish Free State, 1922–1932* (Dublin: Gill & Macmillan, 2013).

Corcoran, Donal, 'Public Policy in an Emerging State: The Irish Free State, 1922–25', *Irish Journal of Public Policy,* 1 (2009), http://publish.ucc.ie/ijpp/2009/01/corcoran/05/en.

Craig, E.T., *An Irish Commune: The History of Ralahine* (Dublin: M. Lester, 1920).

Crossman, Virginia, *Politics, Pauperism and Power in Late Nineteenth-Century Ireland* (Manchester: Manchester University Press, 2006).

Daly, Mary E., *The Famine in Ireland* (Dundalk: Dundalgen Press, 1986).

Daly, Mary E., *The First Department: A History of the Department of Agriculture* (Dublin: Institute of Public Administration, 2002).

Daly, Mary E., *Industrial Development and Irish National Identity, 1922–39* (Dublin: Gill & Macmillan, 1992).

de Blacam, Aodh, 'Æ as I Knew Him', *Irish Monthly,* 63.747 (1935), 606–613.

Delaney, Enda, 'Our Island Story? Towards a Transnational History of Late Modern Ireland', *Irish Historical Studies,* 37 (2011), 599–621.

Digby, Margaret, *Horace Plunkett: An Anglo-American Irishman* (Oxford: Basil Blackwell, 1949).

Dewey, P.E., *British Agriculture in the First World War* (London: Routledge, 1989).

Dolan, Anne, *Commemorating the Irish Civil War: History and Memory, 1923–2000* (Cambridge: Cambridge University Press, 2003).

Donnelly, James S. Jr, *The Great Irish Potato Famine* (Stroud: Sutton, 2001).

Dooley, Terence, 'Land and Politics in Independent Ireland, 1923–1948: The Case for Reappraisal', *Irish Historical Studies,* 34.134 (2004), 175–197.

Dooley, Terence, *'The Land for the People': The Land Question in Independent Ireland* (Dublin: University College Dublin Press, 2004).

Douglas, James G, *Memoirs of Senator James G. Douglas: Concerned Citizen,* ed. by J. Anthony Gaughan (Dublin: University College Dublin Press, 1998).

Doyle, Patrick Mary, 'Reframing the "Irish Question": the Role of the Co-operative Movement in the Formation of Irish Nationalism, 1900–1922', *Irish Studies Review,* 22.3 (2014), 267–284.

Doyle, Tom, *The Civil War in Kerry* (Cork: Mercier Press, 2008).

Eichenberg, Julia, 'The Dark Side of Independence: Paramilitary Violence in Ireland and Poland After the First World War', *Contemporary European History,* 19.3 (2010), 231–248.

Elliott, Marianne, *When God Took Sides: Religion and Identity in Ireland – Unfinished History* (Oxford: Oxford University Press, 2009).

Fanning, Bryan, *Irish Adventures in Nation-Building* (Manchester: Manchester University Press, 2016).

Fanning, Ronan, *Fatal Path: British Government and Irish Revolution 1910–1922* (London: Faber & Faber, 2013).

Fanning, Ronan, *The Irish Department of Finance, 1922–1958* (Dublin: Institute of Public Administration, 1978).

Fanon, Frantz, *The Wretched of the Earth* (London: Penguin, 2001 [1965]).

Farrell, Brian, *The Founding of Dáil Éireann: Parliament and Nation Building* (Dublin: Gill & Macmillan, 1971).

Federico, Giovanni, *Feeding the World: An Economic History of Agriculture, 1800–2000* (Princeton: Princeton University Press, 2005).

Fennelly, Teddy, *A Triumph Over Adversity: The History of Donaghmore Co-operative Creamery Ltd, Founded in 1927* (Portlaoise: Arderin Publishing Company, 2003).

Ferriter, Diarmaid, *The Transformation of Ireland, 1900–2000* (London: Profile Books, 2004).

Fitzgerald, Garret, *Reflections on the Irish State* (Dublin: Irish Academic Press, 2003).

Fitzpatrick, David, *Politics and Irish Life, 1913–1921: Provincial Experience of War and Revolution* (Dublin: Gill & Macmillan, 1977).

Fitzpatrick, David, *The Two Irelands, 1912–1939* (Oxford: Oxford University Press, 1998).

Fitzpatrick, Edward A., *McCarthy of Wisconsin* (New York: Columbia University Press, 1944).

Fleming, G.A., 'Agricultural Support Policies in a Small Open Economy: New Zealand in the 1920s', *Economic History Review*, 52.2 (1999), 334–354.

Foster, Gavin, 'In the Shadow of the Split: Writing the Irish Civil War' *Field Day Review*, 2 (2006), 294–303.

Foster, R.F., *Modern Ireland, 1600–1972* (London: Penguin: 1988).

Foster, R.F., *W.B. Yeats: A Life, I: The Apprentice Mage, 1865–1914* (Oxford: Oxford University Press, 1997).

Foucault, Michel, *The Birth of Biopolitics: Lectures at the Collège de France, 1978–1979* (Houndmills, Basingstoke: Palgrave Macmillan, 2010).

Freeman, T.W., *Ireland: Its Physical, Historical, Social and Economic Geography* (London: Methuen and Co., Ltd, 1950).

Gailey, Andrew, *Ireland and the Death of Kindness: The Experience of Constructive Unionism 1890–1905* (Cork: Cork University Press, 1987).

Garvin, Tom, *The Evolution of Irish Nationalist Politics* (Dublin: Gill & Macmillan, 1981).

Garvin, Tom, *Nationalist Revolutionaries in Ireland, 1858–1928* (Oxford: Oxford University Press, 1987).

Garvin, Tom, *News from a New Republic: Ireland in the 1950s* (Dublin: Gill & Macmillan, 2011).

Garvin, Tom, *Preventing the Future: Why Was Ireland So Poor For So Long?* (Dublin: Gill & Macmillan, 2004).

Gatrell, Peter, *Russia's First World War: A Social and Economic History* (Harlow: Pearson Longman, 2005).

Geertz, Clifford, *The Interpretation of Cultures: Selected Essays* (New York: Basic Books, 1973).

Geoghegan, Vincent, 'Robert Owen, Co-operation and Ulster in the 1830s', in *Politics and the Irish Working Class, 1830–1945* (Houndsmills, Basingstoke: Palgrave Macmillan, 2005), 6–26.

Gibbon, Peter, and MD Higgins, 'Patronage, Tradition and Modernisation: The Case of the Irish "Gombeenman"', *Economic and Social Review*, 6.1 (1974), 27–44.

Gide, Charles, with preface by Diarmid Coffey, *Consumers' Co-operative Societies* (Manchester: The Co-operative Union Limited, 1921).

Gillmor, D.A., 'Agriculture', in D.A. Gillmor (ed.), *Irish Resources and Land Use* (Dublin: Institute of Public Administration, 1979), 109–136.

Gillmor, Desmond A., 'Land and People, c.1926', in J.R. Hill (ed.), *A New History of Ireland, Volume VII: Ireland, 1921–84* (Oxford: Oxford University Press, 2003), 62–85.

Girvin, Brian, 'The Republicanisation of Irish Society, 1932–48', in J.R. Hill (ed.), *A New History of Ireland, Volume VII: Ireland 1921–1984* (Oxford: Oxford University Press, 2003), 127–160.

Goswami, Manu, *Producing India: From Colonial Economy to National Space* (London: University of Chicago Press, 2004).

Gregory, Augusta, 'Ireland, Real and Ideal', *Nineteenth Century* 44.261 (1898), 769–782.

Griffith, Arthur, *The Resurrection of Hungary: A Parallel for Ireland with Appendices on Pitt's Policy and Sinn Féin*, 3rd edn (Dublin: Whelan and Son, 1918).

Guinnane, Timothy W, 'A Failed Institutional Transplant: Raiffeisen's Credit Cooperatives in Ireland, 1894–1914', *Explorations in Economic History*, 31 (1994), 38–61.

Guinnane, Timothy W, *The Vanishing Irish: Households, Migration, and the Rural Economy in Ireland, 1850–1914* (Princeton, NJ: Princeton University Press, 1997).

Gupta, Akhil, 'Blurred Boundaries: The Discourse of Corruption, the Culture of Politics and the Imagined State', *American Ethnologist*, 22.2 (1995), 375–402.

Gupta, Akhil, *Postcolonial Developments: Agriculture in the Making of Modern India* (London: Duke University Press, 1998).

Gurney, Peter, *Co-operative Culture and the Politics of Consumption in England, 1870–1930* (Manchester: Manchester University Press, 1996).

Gwynn, Denis, *The Irish Free State, 1922–1927* (London: Macmillan and Co., 1928).

Gwynn, Stephen, *The History of Ireland* (New York: The Macmillan Company, 1923).

Gwynn, Stephen, *Ireland* (London: Ernest Benn, 1924).

Hall, F., and W.P. Watkins, *Co-operation: A Survey of the History, Principles, and Organisation of the Co-operative Movement in Great Britain and Ireland* (Manchester: Co-operative Union, 1937).

Hanly, Joseph, 'Agriculture', in Bulmer Hobson (ed.), *Saorstat Eireann: Official Handbook* (Dublin: The Talbot Press, 1932), 115–127.

Hanly, Joseph, *The National Ideal: A Practical Exposition of True Nationality Appertaining to Ireland* (Dublin: Dollard Printinghouse, 1931).

Hannan, Damian F., and Patrick Commins, 'The Significance of Small-Scale Landholders in Ireland's Socio-Economic Transformation', in *The Development of Industrial Society in Ireland*, ed. by J.H. Goldthorpe and C.T. Whelan (Oxford: Oxford University Press, 1992)), 79–104.

Harding, Keith, 'The "Co-operative Commonwealth": Ireland, Larkin and the *Daily Herald*', in Stephen Yeo (ed.), *New Views of Co-operation* (London: Routledge, 1988), 88–107.

Harkness, D.W., *The Restless Dominion: The Irish Free State and the British Commonwealth of Nations, 1921–1931* (Dublin: Gill & Macmillan, 1969).

Hart, Peter, *The IRA and its Enemies: Violence and Community in Cork, 1916–1923* (Oxford: Oxford University Press, 1998).

Hart, Peter, *The IRA at War, 1916–1923* (Oxford: Oxford University Press, 2003).

Henriksen, Ingrid, 'Avoiding Lock-In: Cooperative Creameries in Denmark, 1882–1903', *European Review of Economic History,* 3 (1999), 57–78.

Henriksen, Ingrid, and Kevin H. O'Rourke, 'Incentives, Technology and the Shift to Year-Round Dairying in Late Nineteenth Century Denmark', *Economic History Review,* 58.3 (2005), 520–554.

Henriksen, Ingrid, Eoin McLaughlin and Paul Sharp, 'Contracts and Co-operation: the Relative Failure of the Irish Dairy Industry in the Late Nineteenth Century Reconsidered', *European Review of Economic History,* 19.4 (2015), 412–431.

Henriksen, Ingrid, Morten Hviid and Paul R. Sharp, 'Law and Peace: Contracts and the Success of the Danish Dairy Cooperatives', *Journal of Economic History,* 72.1 (2012), 197–224.

Henry, Maurice, Pat Bolger and Trevor West (eds), *Irish Co-operative Organisation Society: Fruits of a Century: An Illustrated Centenary History, 1894–1999* (Dublin: Irish Co-operative Organisation Society, 1994).

Hilson, Mary, Pirjo Markkola and Ann-Catrin Ostman (eds), *Co-operatives and the Social Question: The Co-operative Movement in Northern and Eastern Europe (1880–1950)* (Cardiff: Welsh Academic Press, 2012).

Hobson. Bulmer, 'Introduction', in Hobson Bulmer (ed.), *Saorstat Eireann: Official Handbook* (Dublin: The Talbot Press, 1932), 15–16.

Hobson, Bulmer, ed., *Saorstat Eireann: Official Handbook* (Dublin: The Talbot Press, 1932).

Hopkinson, Michael, 'Civil War and Aftermath, 1922–4', in J.R. Hill (ed.), *A New History of Ireland: 1921–1984* (Oxford: Oxford University Press, 2003), 31–61.

Hopkinson, Michael, *Green Against Green: The Irish Civil War* (Dublin: Gill & Macmillan, 1988).

Hoppen, K. Theodore, *Governing Hibernia: British Politicians and Ireland 1800–1921* (Oxford: Oxford University Press, 2016).

Horace Plunkett Foundation, *Agricultural Co-operation: in its Application to the Industry, the Business, and the Life of the Farmer in the British Empire* (London: George Routledge and Sons, 1925).

Hutchinson, John, *The Dynamics of Cultural Nationalism: The Gaelic Revival and the Creation of the Irish Nation State* (London: Allen & Unwin, 1987).

Jackson, Alvin, *Home Rule: An Irish History, 1800–2000* (Oxford: Oxford University Press, 2003).

Jackson, Alvin, *Ireland, 1798–1998: Politics and War* (Oxford: Blackwell Publishers, 1999).

Jenkins, William, 'Capitalists and Co-operators: Agricultural Transformation, Contested Space, and Identity Politics in South Tipperary, Ireland, 1890–1914', *Journal of Historical Geography,* 30 (2004), 87–111.

Johnston, Joseph, 'Free Trade or Protection for Irish Industries?' *The Irish Economist,* 8.1 (1923), 54–65.

Johnston, Joseph, *The Nemesis of Economic Nationalism and Other Lectures in Applied Economics* (London: P.S. King and Son, Ltd, 1934).

Johnston, Roy H.W., *Century of Endeavour: A Biographical and Autobiographical View of the Twentieth Century in Ireland* (Dublin: The Lilliput Press, 2006).

Kane, Robert, *The Industrial Resources of Ireland* (Dublin: Hodges and Smith, 1845).

Kavanagh, Patrick, *The Green Fool* (London: Penguin, 2001).

Kennedy, Michael, and Joseph Skelly (eds), *Irish Foreign Policy, 1919–1966: From Independence to Internationalism* (Dublin: Four Courts, 2000).

Kennedy, Kieran A., Thomas Giblin and Deirdre McHugh, *The Economic Development of Ireland in the Twentieth Century* (London: Routledge, 1988).

Kennedy, Liam, 'The Early Response of the Irish Catholic Clergy to the Co-operative Movement', *Irish Historical Studies*, 21.81 (1978), 55–74.

Kennedy, Liam, 'Farmers, Traders and Agricultural Politics in Pre-Independence Ireland', in Samuel Clark and James S. Donnelly, Jr (eds), *Irish Peasants: Violence and Political Unrest, 1780–1914* (Manchester: Manchester University Press, 1983), 339–373.

Kennedy, Robert E., *The Irish: Emigration, Marriage and Fertility* (London: University of California Press, 1973).

Kennelly, James J., *The Kerry Way: The History of Kerry Group, 1972–2000* (Dublin: Oak Tree Press, 2001).

Kennelly, James J., 'Normal Courage: R.A. Anderson and the Irish Co-operative Movement', *Studies*, 100 (2011), 319–330.

King, Carla, 'The Early Development of Agricultural Cooperation: Some French and Irish Comparisons', *Proceedings of the Royal Irish Academy: Archaeology, Culture, History, Literature*, 96C.3 (1996), 67–86.

King, Carla, 'The Recess Committee, 1895–6', *Studia Hibernica*, 30 (1998/1999), 21–46.

Kissane, Bill, *The Politics of the Irish Civil War* (Oxford: Oxford University Press, 2005).

Knapp, Joseph, *An Appraisement of Agricultural Co-operation in Ireland* (Dublin: Stationery Office, 1964).

Kohn, Leo, *The Constitution of the Irish Free State* (London: George Allen & Unwin, 1932).

Kotsonis, Yannis, *Making Peasants Backward: Agricultural Cooperatives and the Agrarian Question in Russia, 1861–1914* (Houndmills: Macmillan Press Ltd, 1999).

Laffan Michael, *The Resurrection of Ireland: The Sinn Féin Party, 1916–1923* (Cambridge: Cambridge University Press, 1999).

Lane, Leeann, '"It is in the Cottages and Farmers' Houses that the Nation is Born": Æ's "Irish Homestead" and the Cultural Revival', *Irish University Review*, 33.1 (2003), 165–181.

Lee, J.J., *Ireland 1912–1985: Politics and Society* (Cambridge: Cambridge University Press, 1989).

Lee, Joseph, *The Modernisation of Irish Society, 1848 – 1918*, revised edn (Dublin: Gill & Macmillan, 2008).

Logan, James, *Ulster in the X-Rays: A Short Review of the Real Ulster, its People, Pursuits, Principles, Poetry, Dialect and Humour* (London: Arthur H. Stockwell, n.d.).

Loughlin, James, 'TW Russell, the Tenant Farmer Interest and Progressive Unionism in Ulster, 1886–1900', *Eire-Ireland*, 25.1 (1990), 44–63.

Lucey, Donnacha Seán, *Land, Popular Politics and Agrarian Violence in Ireland: The Case of County Kerry, 1872–1886* (Dublin: University College Dublin Press, 2011).

Lyons, F.S.L., *Ireland Since the Famine* (London: Fontana Press, 1975).

Lyons, F.S.L., *The Irish Parliamentary Party, 1890–1910* (London: Faber, 1951).

Lysaght, Edward E., *Sir Horace Plunkett and his Place in the Irish Nation* (Dublin: Maunsel & Co., 1916).

Mac Suibhne, Breandán, *The End of Outrage: Post-Famine Adjustment in Rural Ireland* (Oxford: Oxford University Press, 2017).

MacDonagh, Oliver, *States of Mind: Two Centuries of Anglo-Irish Conflict, 1780–1980* (London: Pimlico, 1992).

MacManus, Francis (ed.), *The Years of the Great Test, 1926–1939* (Cork: Mercier Press, 1967).

Maguire, Martin, *The Civil Service and the Revolution in Ireland: 'Shaking the Blood-Stained Hand of Mr Collins* (Manchester: Manchester University Press, 2008).

Mann, Michael, The Sources of Social Power, *Volume I: A History of Power from the Beginning to A.D. 1760* (Cambridge: Cambridge University Press, 1986).

Mathews, P.J., *Revival: The Abbey Theatre, Sinn Féin, The Gaelic League and the Co-operative Movement* (Cork: Cork University Press, 2003).

Maume, Patrick, 'Hannay, James Owen ("George A Birmingham")', in *Dictionary of Irish Biography: From Earliest Times to the Year 2002, Volume 4,* ed. by James McGuire and James Quinn (Cambridge: Cambridge University Press, 2009).

McCabe, David A., 'The Recent Growth of Co-operation in Ireland', *Quarterly Journal of Economics,* 20.4 (1906), 547–574.

McCormack, W.J., *Dublin 1916: The French Connection* (Dublin: Gill & Macmillan, 2012).

McDowell, R.B., *The Irish Convention, 1917–18* (London: Routledge & Kegan Paul, 1970).

McLaughlin, Eoin, 'Competing Forms of Co-operation?: Land League, Land War and Co-operation in Ireland, 1879 to 1914', *Agricultural History Review,* 63.1 (2015), 81–112

Meehan, Ciara, *The Cosgrave Party: A History of Cumann na nGaedheal, 1923–1933* (Dublin: Royal Irish Academy, 2010).

Meenan, James, *The Irish Economy Since 1922* (Liverpool: Liverpool University Press).

Meenan, James, *George O'Brien: A Biographical Memoir* (Dublin: Gill & Macmillan, 1980).

Meleady, Dermot, *John Redmond: The National Leader* (Dublin: Merrion, 2014).

Meleady, Dermot, *Redmond: The Parnellite* (Cork: Cork University Press, 2008).

Micks, William L., *An Account of the Constitution, Administration and Dissolution of the Congested Districts Board for Ireland from 1891 to 1923* (Dublin: Eason & Son, Limited, 1925).

Miller, Ian, *Reforming Food in Post-Famine Ireland: Medicine, Science and Improvement, 1845–1922* (Manchester: Manchester University Press, 2014).

Milward, Alan S., *The Economic Effects of the Two World Wars on Britain* (London: The Macmillan Press Ltd., 1972).

Mitchell, Arthur, *Revolutionary Government in Ireland: Dáil Éireann, 1919–1922* (Dublin: Gill & Macmillan, 1995).

Morley, John, *British Agricultural Cooperatives* (London: Hutchinson Bentham, 1975).

Morrissey, Thomas J., *Thomas A. Finlay, SJ, 1848–1940: Educationalist, Editor, Social Reformer* (Dublin: Four Courts Press, 2004).

Murphy, Jeremiah, *When Youth was Mine: A Memoir of Kerry, 1902–1925* (Dublin: Mentor Press, 1998).

Murphy, William, 'Figgis, Darrell', in *Dictionary of Irish Biography: From Earliest Times to the Year 2002, Volume 3*, ed. by James McGuire and James Quinn (Cambridge: Cambridge University Press, 2009)), 775–777.

Murray, Bruce K., *The People's Budget 1909/1910: Lloyd George and Liberal Politics* (Oxford: Oxford University Press, 1980).

Murray, Paul, *The Irish Boundary Commission and its Origins, 1886–1925* (Dublin: University College Dublin Press, 2011).

Ó Fathartaigh, Mícheál, *Irish Agriculture Nationalised: the Dairy Disposal Company and the Making of the Modern Irish Dairy Industry* (Dublin: Institute of Public Administration).

Ó Gráda, Cormac, 'The Beginnings of the Irish Creamery System, 1880–1914', *Economic Review of History*, 30.2 (1977), 284–305.

Ó Gráda, Cormac, *Black '47 and Beyond: The Great Irish Famine in History, Economy, and Memory* (Princeton: Princeton University Press, 1999).

Ó Gráda, Cormac, *Ireland: A New Economic History, 1780–1939* (Oxford: Clarendon Press, 1994).

Ó Gráda, Cormac, *Ireland Before and After the Famine: Explorations in Economic History, 1800–1925* (Manchester: Manchester University Press, 1993).

Ó Gráda, Cormac, *A Rocky Road: The Irish Economy Since the 1920s* (Manchester: Manchester University Press, 1997).

Ó Riain, Seán, 'The Flexible Developmental State: Globalisation, Information Technology and the "Celtic Tiger"', *Politics and Society*, 28.2 (2000), 157–193.

O'Brien, George, 'Patrick Hogan: Minister for Agriculture, 1922–1932', *Studies*, 25.99 (1936), 353–368.

O'Callaghan, Margaret, *British High Politics and a Nationalist Ireland: Criminality, Land and the Law under Forester and Balfour* (Cork: Cork University Press, 1994).

O'Connor, Emmet, *A Labour History of Ireland, 1824–2000* (Dublin: University College Dublin Press, 2011).

O'Connor, Emmet, *Syndicalism in Ireland, 1917–1923* (Cork: Cork University Press, 1988).

O'Donnell, Thomas, *A Trip to Denmark* (Dublin: Gill & Macmillan, 1908).

O'Donovan, John, 'State Enterprises', *Journal of the Statistical and Social Inquiry Society of Ireland*, 8.3 (1950), 327–348.

O'Dowd, Anne, *Meitheal: A Study of Co-operative Rural Labour* (Dublin: Comhairle Bhéaloideas Éireann, 1981).

O'Halpin, Eunan, 'Politics and the State, 1922–1932', in J.R. Hill (ed.), *A New History of Ireland, Volume VII: Ireland 1921–1984* (Oxford: Oxford University Press, 2003), 86–126.

O'Halpin, Eunan, *The Decline of the Union: British Government in Ireland, 1892–1920* (Dublin: Gill & Macmillan, 1987).

O'Rourke, Kevin H., 'Culture, Conflict and Co-operation: Irish Dairying Before the Great War', *Economic Journal*, 117.10 (2007), 1357–1379.

O'Rourke, Kevin, 'Property Rights, Politics and Innovation: Creamery Diffusion in pre-1914 Ireland', *European Review of Economic History*, 11 (2007), 395–417.

O'Sullivan, Donal, *The Irish Free State and its Senate: A Study in Contemporary Politics* (London: Faber & Faber, 1940).

Olby, Robert, 'Social Imperialism and State Support for Agricultural Research in Edwardian Britain', *Annals of Science*, 48.6 (1991), 509–526.

Paseta, Senia, *Before The Revolution: Nationalism, Social Change and Ireland's Catholic Elite, 1879–1922* (Cork: Cork University Press, 1999).

Peillon, Michel, 'Interest Groups and the State in the Republic of Ireland', *Irish Society: Sociological Perspectives*, ed. by Patrick Clancy, Sheelagh Drudy, Kathleen Lynch and Liam O'Dowd (Dublin: Institute of Public Administration, 1995), 358–378.

Pope, Conor, 'Credit Unions Call for Credit Bank Showdown to be Held in Public', *Irish Times*, 14 October 2013, www.irishtimes.com/business/credit-unions-call-for-central-bank-showdown-to-be-held-in-public-1.1558098.

Quinn, Anthony P., *Credit Unions in Ireland* (Dublin: Oak Tree Press, 1994).

Quinn, Peggy, Des Aylmer, Donal Cantwell and Louis O'Connell, *An Irish Banking Revolution* (Dublin: Bank of Ireland, 1995).

Redfern, Percy, *The Story of the CWS: The Jubilee History of the Co-operative Wholesale Society Limited. 1863–1913* (Manchester: The Co-operative Wholesale Society Limited, 1913).

Regan, John M., *The Irish Counter-Revolution, 1921–1936: Treatyite Politics and Settlement in Independent Ireland* (Dublin: Gill & Macmillan, 1999).

Regan, John M., and Mike Cronin, 'Introduction: Ireland and the Politics of Independence, 1922–49: New Perspectives and Re-considerations', in *Ireland: The Politics of Independence, 1922–49*, ed. by Mike Cronin and John M. Regan (Basingstoke: Macmillan, 2000), 1–12.

Rhodes, Rita, *Empire and Co-operation: How the British Empire used Co-operatives in its Development Strategies, 1900–1970* (Edinburgh: John Donald, 2012).

Riordan, E.J., *Modern Irish Trade and Industry* (New York: E.P. Dutton and Company, 1920).

Robertson, Nicole, *The Co-operative Movement and Communities in Britain, 1914–1960: Minding their Own Business* (Farnham: Ashgate, 2010).

Roddy, Sarah, *Population, Providence and Empire: The Churches and Emigration from Nineteenth-Century Ireland* (Manchester: Manchester University Press, 2014).

Saddlemyer, Ann (ed.), *The Collected Letters of John Millington Synge: Volume One, 1871–1907* (Oxford: Oxford University Press, 1983).

Saorstát Éireann, *Agricultural Statistics, 1847–1926: Reports and Tables* (Dublin: Stationery Office, 1928).

Scheper-Hughes, Nancy, *Saints, Scholars and Schizophrenics: Mental Illness in Rural Ireland*, 2nd edn (Berkeley: University of California Press, 2001).

Scott, James C., *Seeing Like a State: How Certain Schemes to Improve the Human Condition Have Failed* (London: Yale University Press, 1998).

Sen, Amartya, *Development as Freedom* (Oxford: Oxford University Press, 1999).

Sennett, Richard, *Together: The Rituals, Pleasures and Politics of Cooperation* (London: Allen Lane, 2012).

Sewell, William H., Jr, *Logics of History: Social Theory and Social Transformation* (Chicago: The University of Chicago Press, 2005).

Smith, Louis P.F., *The Evolution of Agricultural Co-operation* (Oxford: Blackwell, 1961).

Solow, Barbara Lewis, *The Land Question and the Irish Economy* (Cambridge Mass.: Harvard University Press, 1971).

Stubbs, Tara, *American Literature and Irish Culture, 1910–55* (Manchester: Manchester University Press, 2013).

Summerfield, Henry, *That Myriad-Minded Man: A Biography of George William Russell, 'Æ', 1867–1935* (Gerrards Cross, Bucks.: Colin Smythe, 1975).

Townshend, Charles, *Easter 1916: The Irish Rebellion* (London: Penguin, 2006).

UN Secretary-General, *Co-operatives in Social Development* (2015), http://undocs.org/A/70/161

Webster, Anthony, 'Building the Wholesale: The Development of the English CWS and British Co-operative Business 1863–90', *Business History,* 54.6 (2012), 883–904.

Webster, Anthony, 'Co-operatives and the State in Burma/Myanmar, 1900–2012: A Case-Study of Failed Top-Down Co-operative Development Models?' in Rajeswary Ampalavanar Brown and Justin Pierce (eds), *Charities in the Non-Western World: The Development and Regulation of Indigenous and Islamic Charities* (New York: Routledge, 2013), 65–87.

Webster, Anthony, Alyson Brown, David Stewart, John K. Walton and Linda Shaw (eds), *The Hidden Alternative: Co-operative Values, Past, Present and Future* (Manchester: Manchester University Press, 2011).

West, Trevor, 'Gallagher, Patrick', in *Oxford Dictionary of National Biography* www.oxforddnb.com/view/article/65846?docPos=2.

West, Trevor, *Horace Plunkett, Co-operation and Politics: An Irish Biography* (Gerrards Cross, Bucks.: Colin Smythe, 1986).

Wheatley, Michael, *Nationalism and the Irish Party: Provincial Ireland, 1910–1916* (Oxford: Oxford University Press, 2004).

Whyte, Nicholas, *Science, Colonialism and Ireland* (Cork: Cork University Press, 1999).

Wilson, John F., Anthony Webster and Rachel Vorberg-Rugh, *Building Co-operation: A Business History of the Co-operative Group, 1863–2013* (Oxford: Oxford University Press, 2013).

Woods, Lawrence M., *Horace Plunkett in America: An Irish Aristocrat on the Wyoming Range* (Norman, Oklahoma: Arthur H. Clarke Co., 2010).

Yeats, W.B., *Autobiographies* (New York: Scribner, 1999).

Index

Lightning Source UK Ltd.
Milton Keynes UK
UKHW051545240920
370395UK00007B/187

9 781526 150561